Scottish Ancestry
Research Methods
for Family Historians

Sherry Irvine, CGRS, FSA Scot

ancestry publishing

Library of Congress Cataloging-in-Publication Data

Irvine, Sherry.
  Scottish ancestry : research methods for family historians / by Sherry
Irvine.—Rev. 2nd ed.
    p. cm.
  Rev. ed. of: Your Scottish ancestry. c1997.
  Includes bibliographical references (p.) and index.
    ISBN 10: 1-59331-027-7 (alk. paper)
    ISBN 13: 978-1-59331-027-1
    1. Scotland—Genealogy—Handbooks, manuals, etc. 2. North
America—Genealogy—Handbooks, manuals, etc. I. Irvine, Sherry. Your
Scottish ancestry. II. Title.
  CS463.I78 2003
  929'.1'0720411—dc21

                                                                    2003006560

In memory of my mother,
Mary Joan Patricia (Nuttall) Howland,
who passed away 17 November 1994
while I was in Edinburgh.

Sherry Irvine

24 Oct '09

Contents

Introduction

he world of genealogical research has undergone significant change in the five years since this book first appeared as *Your Scottish Ancestry: A Guide for North Americans*. At that time it seemed to make sense to write a guide for those living in Canada and the USA— all the guides I was using in my classes at the time were written by people in Scotland for people researching in Scotland. Now, thanks to the Internet, this distinction is largely irrelevant; so, this edition has been updated to help genealogists wherever they may be.

Scotland is leading the way in making major national resources available over the Internet. The census returns 1841 to 1901, civil registration records since 1855, testamentary records, and the registers of the Church of Scotland from earliest times to 1854 are now available totally or in part on the Web. For access to the major genealogical sources, a reseacher's location simply does not matter as much. Other agencies and private enterprise also contribute to the mass of electronic data.

Most of us come face to face with the impact of change in our day-to-day research. Records are definitely more accessible and the perception is that genealogical research is therefore much easier. It is true that a lot of routine things can be done faster and some unwieldy searches formerly considered foolish to attempt are now possible. Secure online ordering and digital images bring copies of documents to the genealogist. Nevertheless, new problems arise, the sheer mass of data and information must be sorted through and understood, technical problems need to be overcome, and, the necessity for sound strategy and organization never goes away.

Back in 1997 I summarized the elements that lie behind successful research. There are four and they do not change. In fact, being fully aware of your search choices, with respect to access, location, and cost is probably now a little more difficult to achieve. Not everyone is online and not every problem can be resolved with a computer database; so, it remains essential to understand the full picture.

1. Be aware of what you know at the start and its significance.

2. Identify what you next need to find out.

3. Identify the records that fit the problem, and learn about their origins, arrangement, and any potential difficulties.

4. Find out about finding aids, their format, location, and access.

Methodology books appear in various forms; for example, some seek to be simple, step-by-step explanations; others hope to cover every record known to be useful to genealogists; others focus on time periods. It is impossible to be all things to all students of Scottish family history. What I hope to achieve here is a readable tour of the records with enough background and enough about technique to eradicate the feelings of frustration and of being overwhelmed that we all know so well. I also steer you to more detailed information when you need it or when your curiosity is aroused. The greatest satisfaction that I received with respect to the first edition of this book was being told it could be read right through—people did this, and kept it handy afterwards.

My acknowledgments have to begin with my Scottish ancestors. You come across some of them in a few of the examples; the Fords and Aitkens of Montrose and the Island of St. Croix are leading me on a wonderful journey into Scottish records and history. Help has come from the living as well. I am grateful to David W. Webster of Edinburgh for chasing down a few facts and for some fascinating discussions. To the Institute of Genealogy and Historical Research at Samford University, a very special thank you for the opportunity to teach there and to take study tours to London and Edinburgh – it is as much a learning experience for me as for the participants.

My association with editors at Ancestry goes back many years. Anne Lemmon was there for the English book and the first edition of this one; this time I have worked with Matthew Wright. I have nothing but praise and thanks for their contributions, knowledge, and friendship. In addition, Jennifer Utley and Lou Szucs have been with Ancestry for many years and have everything to do with my long-standing relationship with the publisher.

Finally and most importantly is a word of appreciation for the support of my husband, Russell. Books would be impossible without him.

Sherry Irvine
Victoria, British Columbia
March 2003

1 • Prudent Preliminaries

A young Scotsman of your ability let loose upon the world with £300, what could he not do? It's almost appalling to think of; especially if he went among the English. (J.M. Barrie, *What Every Woman Knows*)

 scan through the volumes of national biography for the United States, Canada, and many other nations reveals a high proportion of entries for men and women whose origins were in Scotland. Many of them started with a good deal less than £300. If some measure of determination, thrift, and ambition is lurking in the character of all of you of Scottish descent, then you have the essential qualifications for genealogical research. Add a thirst for knowledge and a dose of common sense, and you will do even better.

About Scotland

Scottish genealogical research has some unique characteristics. Until the Act of Union in 1707, Scotland had its own parliament and its own legal system. The latter remains distinctly different to this day, and, over the centuries, has produced many records which have no counterpart in England or Wales. It is particularly important that researchers of Scottish family history give some time and attention to identifying and understanding these differences. Equally important is some knowledge of Scottish history, taking note of patterns of migration, within the British Isles and overseas.

Scotland is located on the northern edge of Europe. Geography has placed the country in a harsher climate and away from the economic pulse, factors which have contributed to its status as a nation of emigrants. For centuries, the adventurous, the talented, the risk-takers, and the impoverished have sought new opportunities in the centers of activity and commerce in England, Europe, and all other parts of the world.

Scottish Emigration

North America has been a favorite destination. Before 1770, the Thirteen Colonies were the destination of choice. Some settlers found their way to the Canadian eastern colonies in what is now Nova Scotia, New Brunswick, and Prince Edward Island, but the largest numbers went to the colonies further south. The five regions with the highest Scottish population in the 1790 census were Virginia and West Virginia, Kentucky and Tennessee, North Carolina, South Carolina, and Georgia.

The Scots left their homeland for religious, political, and economic reasons. Covenanters were transported or left the turbulent religious situation of the seventeenth century. The Jacobite uprisings of 1715 and 1745 contributed both refugees and those sentenced to servitude in America, and the Highland Clearances fit into the economic category as a cause of emigration. Another fairly significant number of Scottish settlers came from the disbanded soldiers left behind at the end of the French and Indian War (the Seven Years' War), 1756-1763. Before 1815 the migrants were more likely to be Highlanders, but after 1815 the pattern changed and the majority were from the Lowlands.

Other conclusions can be drawn by looking at some numbers. Between 1820 and 1900, roughly 365,000 Scots emigrated to the United States and 250,000 to Canada. When considered in the context of the populations of the two countries, the post 1815 Scottish element in Canada is huge relative to the total population. Not so in the United States. In other words, proportionately, Canadians are more likely to be engaged in nineteenth century Scottish research.

If the origins of your Scottish ancestors are unclear, no matter where they went, you can draw useful insights from accounts of migration to the area where first they settled. It is extremely important that you identify the ancestor or ancestors who made the trip, but almost as important is an understanding of the context of their migration. Knowing the place of first settlement is particularly important because its history may offer clues about the region, perhaps even the parish, of birth. In other words, when beginning your research, do everything possible at the destination end first.

There is another very good reason for building extensive knowledge of the family in its new home. The best way to describe this reason is family reconstruction. Many of you will face the problem of very few different surnames in the area of origin in Scotland. It will help to sort out all the MacKinnons or MacDonalds if you carry a batch of given names into your Scottish research. If you are fortunate, you may also have a wife's or mother's maiden name. In Scotland, a woman retained her maiden name throughout her lifetime. Although she may have used a husband's surname while married, she was recorded in parish registers and many other records by her maiden name, and she might have reverted to this name if predeceased by her husband. Knowing a woman's maiden name may be the key to beginning successful research in Scotland. On the other hand, there may be confusion if you have not correctly identified a woman's name as her maiden or her married name.

At this early stage, it will do no harm to question the validity of any assumptions about Scottish origins; for example, when so many were going to North America in the 1700s, there was also a great outflow of Scots-Irish from Ulster. They left Ireland because of high rent, famine, and the decline in the linen industry. The Scottish-sounding name in your background may not be a direct import from Scotland. The family may have spent many generations in Ulster.

More than a simple lack of knowledge may hide the truth. My maternal grandmother's maiden name was Blackhall. The family sprang from Aberdeenshire and was very proud of it. In fact, this was the only beginning I, or my mother, ever heard about (her mother died when she was six). It was not until I researched the family that I discovered it had been transplanted from Aberdeenshire to County Down in Northern Ireland nearly two hundred years before emigrating to New York State, and from thence two generations later to Canada. In nineteenth-century Toronto, it was more acceptable to be Scottish; thus, the Irish interlude faded from the family tradition.

A further caution is warranted for those of you who find a name in a list of the so-called septs of a particular clan. *Sept*, from the Irish language, has a connotation similar to *clan* and is a subject of some debate. The lists have been the creations of the manufacturers and sellers of mementos and tartan-traps created by nineteenth- and twentieth-century romantics and opportunists more interested, then and now, in a sale than the truth. Some families and clans have recognized the connections, but the better term is *associated families*. There are other lists that link names with suggested tartans to be worn, but they are nothing more than that; they should never be taken as indicating a connection to a clan. To find out more about surnames—in particular, their origin and use in the Highlands—and about clans, their history, tartans, and associated families, refer to the books listed in the bibliography.

Pitfalls

Even after you are past the issues of being certain about origins and whether or not a clan association is meaningful, names can still hold traps for the unwary. The most frequently mentioned difficulty among my students stems from too many individuals of the same surname. This can occur at any geographical level—the country as a whole, the county, or the parish. If there are too many individuals of one surname, checking for naming patterns among the families in the parish might help. This pattern was not followed rigidly but was common enough to warrant consideration. The eldest son was named after his paternal grandfather, the next boy after the maternal grandfather, and third after the father. A parallel pattern was followed for girls, who were named after their grandmothers.

Sometimes you will continue to be stymied because several families of the same surname were remarkably unimaginative when selecting given names. In this case, you can only hope that the parish registers and other records may slip in additional identifiers such as address or location or occupation.

If common names are not enough, interchangeable names are another trap. Jean might be Janet or Jane, Daniel might be Donald, and James, Hamish. More interesting naming problems, especially associated with the north and remote areas of Scotland, are found in the introduction to *Surnames of Scotland* (Black, 1999).

There are several other possible name problems to watch for. First, remind yourself that outright errors by officials, transcribers, and indexers are not unknown. These errors come in many forms because something was written as it sounded, copied in haste, or missed completely. The use of patronymics may also cause confusion (the surname changes in each genera-tion based upon the given name of the father, i.e., Duncan MacDonald, the son of Donal Robertson). Spelling variations are another problem, sometimes several in one person's lifetime. Variations in surnames can be surprisingly dif-ferent, to the extent that the connection isn't obvious. The variation may be in a completely different part of an index, perhaps outside the list of stan-dardized spellings used in some finding aids. Some variations come readily to mind, such as those arising from the addition or deletion of a silent letter, the doubling of a vowel or consonant, or confusion between two letters resem-bling each other. *Surnames of Scotland* (Black, 1999) lists many variations, especially the less obvious. Two examples illustrate the difficulties. Without looking it up, you might not know that MacMurchie is a form of Murdoch, nor would you think of checking for Slater under Sclater. Other themes to watch for are changes between M', Mc, and Mac (which, in some records, are indexed separately), a change in the order of names, and differences due to a phonetic representation of what was heard. Scan lists carefully if you must look for several variations, and be prepared to search more than one part of an alphabetical index.

Place names also create possible pitfalls. The same place name is often found in more than one location. Is your ancestor from Craigton? There were four, two of them in Forfarshire (Angus). Not only that, but Craigton estate in Dumbartonshire sits in the parish of New Kilpatrick, which happens to strad-dle the county line and is also partly in Stirlingshire. Seven Newtons are list-ed in the *Ordnance Gazetteer of Scotland* (Groome, 1883-85), and twenty-two other places have Newton as the first part of their names. Another possible problem is altered spellings and complete name changes. Far from home, an ancestor may not have used the name of his actual place of origin, but instead used that of a nearby town. Villages have been swallowed up by the spread of cities and may no longer be shown on maps. The name you are dealing with may be an estate name rather than an actual place name. Resolving place name problems is discussed in chapter 2.

Coping with old handwriting is usually a matter of practice. If you are tracing one or more families back through several generations in one register, you will probably be able to follow and interpret the various styles of hand-writing. Difficulties are more likely to arise with documents and registers which predate 1750. Some useful guides are listed in the bibliography. If you come across what appears to be an unfamiliar combination of letters, consult glossaries of Scottish terms. The Scottish Association of Family History Societies publishes *A Scottish Historian's Glossary* (Burness, 1997), and a helpful list of words can be found in *Tracing Scottish Ancestors* (Bigwood, 1999). The Scottish Archives Network (SCAN) includes an extensive glossary within the research tools area at its website.

Problems with dates arise more often from misinformation or incorrect estimates than from the calendar itself. Scotland adopted 1 January as New Year's Day at the beginning of 1600. This eliminates the problem, present in English research, of what year to date events that occurred between 1 January and 25 March (Lady Day, which was considered the first day of the new year in England until 1752). There is less certainty about what happened to the eleven days that disappeared from the calendar south of the border in 1752. Evidence provided in an article in the *Scottish Genealogist* ("Gregorian Calendar," Gillespie, 1988), and generally accepted, suggests that Scotland realigned its days at the same time. The necessity for change arose from a slight miscalculation in the Julian Calendar, instituted by Julius Caesar in 45 B.C. By the late sixteenth century, an eleven-minute error per year had created a ten-day discrepancy between the lunar and calendar years. The church had terrible problems calculating feast days. Pope Gregory removed ten days from the month of March and at the same time decreed that the year 1582 would begin on 1 January. The Gregorian Calendar was adopted at the same time by Catholic Europe, but it was not accepted by Protestant countries until much later.

The Internet

The Internet has become an increasingly important tool for genealogical research, but almost every advantage is counterbalanced by a hazard. The indexes to civil registration and to the Old Parochial Records are online. Indexes to testaments can be searched through the SCAN site, which is also constantly adding to the images of testaments that can be viewed or ordered. Thousands of researchers have contributed their data to online databases or created their own websites that include family trees and biographical details. Quick, electronic access to indexes and images of documents is very convenient but carries the dangers of accepting a connection as true before proof is found and of becoming lazy about the value of browsing through the original documents. Sharing data has long been an attractive aspect of genealogy but information is now so accessible that the linking together of unrelated lines is a common occurrence.

Use the Internet wherever possible because it can save time and money, as well as open up avenues of research that previously were impossible or too tedious to try. Reference is made to the major computer tools for Scottish genealogy throughout this book. They are presented as part of a research process, which helps ensure that contents are understood and results are useful.

Conclusion

The chapters of this book are arranged by record type, beginning with the most recent. For many it may be tempting to skip some sections. Census returns and civil registration may not seem to fit the search; the emigrant Scot left before 1841 or 1855. Some other records, such as sasines and services of heirs, may appear irrelevant because the family was poor. This is a good place for a word of caution; family history can go awry the moment assumptions are made.

Read the book through once in its entirety. You will see that all sorts of records include all sorts of people and that it is just as important to research siblings, cousins, and other collaterals. It may also prove useful to chase after a distant branch that never left Scotland or to study an entire parish. Records can be used in different ways and direct assault on a fact doesn't always work.

A prudent genealogist carrying research into Scotland starts from a solid base of evidence then blends it with knowledge and curiosity. The odds for success improve and the pursuit is bound to be interesting.

2 • Well Begun Is Half Done

ou will learn as you go. This chapter outlines the skills you should develop and the background knowledge you should acquire, all of which will go a long way toward making the research more interesting and less frustrating. Don't worry about asking silly questions—once—and never mind your mistakes; each and every one contains a lesson that will contribute to your expertise. This chapter is divided into two sections, one about the skills you should develop and the other about the knowledge and experience you should acquire.

Develop Skills

Library Skills

When did you last really explore a library? Computers and the Internet have probably cut back on your visits, but they shouldn't. Libraries continue to offer wonderful opportunities, and computers and the Internet make them more useful than ever before. Catalogs can be searched online in advance of a visit, and many libraries offer public access to other databases.

The catalog is the search tool, so first develop a familiarity with public and university library classification systems. Public libraries use the

Dewey Decimal system; university libraries use the Library of Congress system. Areas of particular interest to genealogists under each of these arrangements are highlighted in tables 2-1 and 2-2. The Family History Library Catalog (FHLC) is unique in its organization. The FHLC is the guide to the contents of the Family History Library (FHL) in Salt Lake City, where the collection of the Family History Department of The Church of Jesus Christ of Latter-day Saints (LDS or Mormons) is housed. There is little doubt that most of you will use the resources of one of the LDS Family History Centers around the world; so, a good understanding of this catalog is essential. Appendix B describes the FHLC in detail.

Genealogy is not confined neatly to a single classification in one particular area of a library. Three or four generations of one family might turn up a dozen or more occupations, several religious denominations, more than one country of residence, wealthy individuals, poor ones, the famous, or the criminal. Finding facts or background material on these individuals and the related subjects will take a researcher into many different areas of the library, far beyond the confines of the 929s or the CSs. Some rudimentary knowledge of catalog structure will transform random wanderings through the stacks into strategic browsing sessions.

Dewey is a number-based system. It suffers from a lack of main divisions, which results in some very long, complex decimal numbers. The 929.** classification for genealogy, names, heraldry and related subjects gets particularly complicated. Browsing would be difficult if the titles did not appear on the spines! The Library of Congress system is a combination of letters and numbers; hence, it allows for many more headings and subheadings. In both systems, general categories are listed at the beginning of each section. For example, the start of the 900s in Dewey is dictionaries of dates; the start of D within Library of Congress organization is general world history.

Equally as useful as knowledge of the classification systems is an understanding of subject headings. Many are obvious, such as a country name or a topic like immigration. However, some of these subject headings may be so general that hundreds or even thousands of entries might fit, and a qualifying subheading must be found to reduce the catalog search to manageable proportions. There are huge tomes describing headings and their subcategories. If you have trouble deciding which subject to look under, or if all your efforts have failed to produce an entry, there are two options. The obvious one is to seek the assistance of a librarian. On your own, you can try working backward from a known title in the subject area to its catalog entry where the heading and subheading would appear. Then use these categories to continue the catalog search.

Most libraries now have their catalogs online, accessible from computer terminals and the Internet. Help with mastering search skills usually

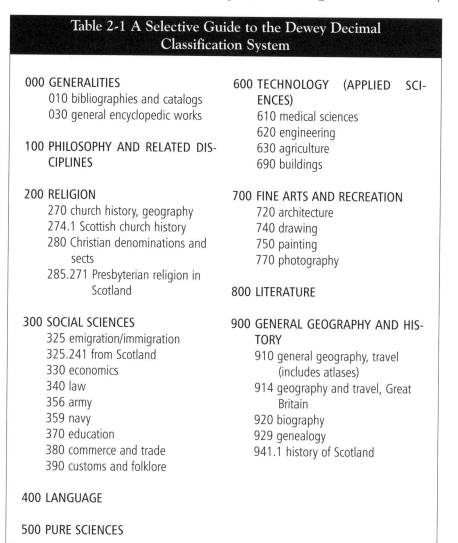

Table 2-1 A Selective Guide to the Dewey Decimal Classification System

000 GENERALITIES
010 bibliographies and catalogs
030 general encyclopedic works

100 PHILOSOPHY AND RELATED DISCIPLINES

200 RELIGION
270 church history, geography
274.1 Scottish church history
280 Christian denominations and sects
285.271 Presbyterian religion in Scotland

300 SOCIAL SCIENCES
325 emigration/immigration
325.241 from Scotland
330 economics
340 law
356 army
359 navy
370 education
380 commerce and trade
390 customs and folklore

400 LANGUAGE

500 PURE SCIENCES

600 TECHNOLOGY (APPLIED SCIENCES)
610 medical sciences
620 engineering
630 agriculture
690 buildings

700 FINE ARTS AND RECREATION
720 architecture
740 drawing
750 painting
770 photography

800 LITERATURE

900 GENERAL GEOGRAPHY AND HISTORY
910 general geography, travel (includes atlases)
914 geography and travel, Great Britain
920 biography
929 genealogy
941.1 history of Scotland

	Table 2-2 Selective Guide to the Library of Congress Classification System
A	GENERAL WORKS
B	PHILOSOPHY-RELIGION
	BL-BX Religion
C	AUXILIARY SCIENCES OF HISTORY
	CD Holdings of Archives and Libraries
	CS genealogy, names, peerage
D	HISTORY-GENERAL AND OLD WORLD
	DA Great Britain
E-F	HISTORY OF AMERICA
G	GEOGRAPHY, ANTHROPOLOGY, FOLKLORE
H	SOCIAL SCIENCES
	HC production and economic conditions
	HD agriculture
	HE transportation and communication
	HN social history and conditions
J	POLITICAL SCIENCE
K	LAW
L	EDUCATION
M	MUSIC
N	FINE ARTS
	NA architecture
P	LANGUAGE AND LITERATURE
Q	SCIENCE
R	MEDICINE
S	AGRICULTURE
T	TECHNOLOGY
U	MILITARY SCIENCE
V	NAVAL SCIENCE
Z	BIBLIOGRAPHY AND LIBRARY SCIENCE

is found in the library and at the website. Older versions of a catalog, on microfiche or index cards, may still be available, and while panning across a fiche or flipping cards may seem simpler, there are advantages to mastering the computer version. Old ways are not lost; it is possible to search computer catalogs as before, according to title and author, and to browse backwards and forwards from any entry. The keyword search overcomes problems such as not knowing a title or a subject heading. Perhaps the greatest advantage of online catalogs is the opportunity to plan ahead. Details of potentially helpful books can be collected before going to the library, and items can be placed on hold for later collection.

Archives Skills

Archives are different from libraries. Libraries seek to distribute books and information; archives are primarily in the business of preservation, and dissemination of information is of secondary importance. Library books are located on open shelves. Browsing in archives is restricted or even not allowed. Books, manuscripts, and artifacts are located in closed shelves, classified by record type rather than by name. Items must be requested on an order slip. Whereas books given to a library are spread about according to subject or author, a box of family papers donated to the local archives, although it covers many subjects, is kept together. This retention of original order is the reason materials must be classified by type in manuscript and record groups with finding aids to describe their contents. It is therefore much more important to have a clear sense of research objectives before visiting archives. If you cannot identify the record you want to view, at least be able to state clearly the facts you are seeking. Some advance knowledge of a repository's holdings will also contribute to the success of a visit or a written enquiry.

Fortunately this is becoming much easier to do. The Scottish Archives Network (SCAN) expects to make available through its website by the end of 2003 archive catalogs or collections summaries from repositories throughout the country. A typical description includes title, reference code, notes on scope and content, and available finding aids. In some cases requests for records can be placed in advance; for any in remote storage, it may be a necessity. Planning ahead should also include checking whether seats and/or readers must be reserved.

Objectives and Strategy

Some of you will have thought out what you are trying to achieve and may even have written specific objectives. Objectives facilitate the search and are reasonably easy to determine. Make sure that your pedigree charts are filled out as completely as possible. Where the information on the charts ends is where the objectives begin. This concept is shown clearly in figure 2-1. At the simplest level, one objective is to select a line to work on first. Next, identify an individual and the new facts that are required. Finally, consider the documents to be consulted. Thinking things through in this manner takes you from the general (which family?) to the particular (what records?).

The pedigree chart is an excellent guide for planning your strategy. It clearly shows where you run out of fact on the direct line, and this point can be highlighted by marking the details which have been proven. The chart, by its structure, also encourages the formulation of research plans, which should always take you from known information to the unknown. As obvious as this may sound, many people are tempted to begin research on some colorful figure reputed to exist in the family's history, and move forward toward the present. The surest way to prove any line of ancestry is to begin with recent family and work back. The search is focused, the easy part comes first, and a logical chronology is followed.

Each research plan is based on stipulating who is being researched, over what time period, over what geographical area, and in what records. Where little is known, estimate. The information known about Mary Rennie (see figure 2-1) is approximate, so allowances must be made for searching outside the years of death and birth shown on the chart. The information on James and William Russell is specific and has come from statutory records and church registers. This provides more surely defined boundaries for the research into the next generation. The records selected for the plan should meet several criteria:

- The record exists for all or part of the time span covered by the search.
- The record exists for all or part of the geographic area covered by the search.
- The record has been indexed, grouped, or summarized in some way to facilitate research.
- The facts required for access to the record are straightforward.
- Information gained from the record should be useful.
- Access is neither a serious problem nor a great expense.

As your knowledge and experience grow, these thought processes will become almost automatic. One additional piece of advice—whenever something fails to turn up, carefully review your file on the family, the sources for the time and place, and the points in your research plan. It may surprise you how a different approach or a forgotten fact may suddenly become apparent.

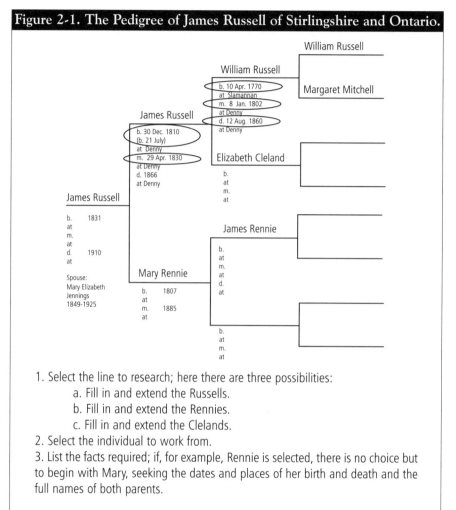

Figure 2-1. The Pedigree of James Russell of Stirlingshire and Ontario.

1. Select the line to research; here there are three possibilities:
    a. Fill in and extend the Russells.
    b. Fill in and extend the Rennies.
    c. Fill in and extend the Clelands.
2. Select the individual to work from.
3. List the facts required; if, for example, Rennie is selected, there is no choice but to begin with Mary, seeking the dates and places of her birth and death and the full names of both parents.

Note: Items circled have been located in statutory or parish records.

Research Skills

The more familiar you are with a library, the sooner you can find materials. The better you understand the organization of the record groups in the archives, the more efficiently you can work. Other good habits are also worth practicing. Always check for finding aids, online and in print. Purchase those you use most often; consider donating an index to your local genealogical society. All indexes and collections summaries save time and effort. The selection of research aids is extensive, and they are accessible through gateway websites such as Genuki and from the shops of societies, archives, and libraries. There are also lists of lists (i.e., bibliographies of finding aids) to help you discover the finding aids that relate to different classes of records. These lists and the resources they outline are referenced throughout the book.

Develop note-taking patterns that suit you and that speed up your work. If you use abbreviations and point form notations, be consistent so you are not baffled by what you wrote weeks before. Do not expand abbreviations seen in old records unless you are absolutely sure of what they stand for, and note that the document used the abbreviation. An inaccurate expansion could lead you in the wrong direction. Note any gaps in a record to prevent erroneous conclusions. If you cannot read what you are trying to note, copy it as closely as possible, or make a photocopy, and record your uncertainty.

Record the bibliographic details for the sources you consult, including those that produce no result; otherwise, the search may have to be repeated if you forget. Teachers, librarians, archivists, and professional genealogists continually ask the question, "Where did you get this?" You should always have the answer. Advice is easier to provide when the provenance of the information is known. Just as important as the origin of a fact is the degree of authority that should be ascribed to the source. Probate records, military records, and statutory records are good examples of primary sources. The information is contemporary and probably accurate. Secondary sources cannot be regarded with the same assurance. They may be based on memory, on point of view, or on documentary evidence, all subject to selectivity and personal interpretation. Autobiographies, biographies, history books, and newspaper accounts are examples of secondary sources.

Computers have changed the way we perform research, so much so that computers skills are a necessity. Some genealogists adapt easily right from the start; they enter all research data, as well as narrative and pictures into a genealogy program, and they prefer to use computer-based resources. Others find the transition more difficult, perhaps daunting, if family data presently resides in numerous binders or card files. Either way, effective research should incorporate computer resources, otherwise opportunities are missed. Different strategies are possible, such as wide-ranging searches never imagined in the days of building indexes with slips of paper. The Internet, resources on CD-ROM, e-mail, and software bring new people to genealogy and old records out in the open.

Organization

Organization is a personal thing, whether it is a supremely logical filing system or creative chaos understandable only by the perpetrator. A pedigree chart, like the one shown in figure 2-1, neatly separates ancestors into families and families into generations. This is a good basis for any system, whether built around index cards, or three-ring binders or computers. Regardless of your chosen instrument of storage, be sure your system accomplishes the following:

- Incorporates a system of ready reference. It must be easy to determine quickly what facts are known and what sources have been consulted. This is the basis for further planning. One way to do this is to keep a short summary of known facts and a log of all sources consulted for each ancestor.

- Contains a record of all work done. Make a full bibliographic notation for all sources consulted, whether or not they revealed any helpful information. Note when and where the work was done and the thoroughness of the search. A missing fact may be due to your rushed efforts, rather than because it wasn't there. You will also avoid duplication of effort. Maintain a separate record of useful general sources (local histories, gazetteers, etc.) to consult as you research new family lines. A computer database is an ideal way to do this as you can search it by keyword.

- Has room for expansion. The system must be able to accommodate the insertion of new material in the right place.

- Is standardized. Standardization applies to paper size and abbreviations. Try to avoid having to recopy notes from odd chits of paper, envelopes, etc., by carrying a stock of standard paper with you. Some of you carry your notebook computer along, or your data manager (if it has good notepad space and can be uploaded into your home computer). Consistency in abbreviations ensures that you or someone else will know what was intended.

- Is followed consistently. Adding material on a regular basis is not a time-consuming chore, but catching up a long time after can be a daunting task, not only because of the backlog, but because the work is no longer fresh in your mind.

Seeking Assistance

Begin by recognizing your own style and preferences, and your own strengths and limitations. If you are a joiner, attend classes and get involved in a local society. Classes may be offered at different levels by a college or a society, nearby or through correspondence. Be sure that your objectives for taking the program match the course outline. A class is an excellent way to build a knowledge base, and if it is held locally, you will meet like-minded people and learn about local resources. The local society's library collection is likely to be built around the most pressing needs of the membership, and the society probably receives many journals on an exchange basis.

The staff of libraries and archives, at home or away, can provide some assistance. More and more institutions, however, are charging for these services. In any case, staff time is limited so be sure that your question clearly states the information you seek. When writing or e-mailing, enquire about genealogical guides or finding aids for sale. You can phrase future enquiries or directions to a professional researcher more precisely when the information outlining the records is at hand.

Scottish family history societies are an excellent source of assistance. New members contribute the names they are researching to the list of members' interests. Additions are checked against those already submitted and printed in the journal. Consider contributing an article to the journal, another effective way to tell others about your research. Support can also be found through an e-mail discussion group; check with the society or a site such as RootsWeb. For publications, societies offer bookstalls and online shops and some accept credit cards. A society may issue its own publications in print, on fiche or CD-ROM, generally associated with the locality.

Professional assistance will be necessary from time to time, either for some specialized skill, such as reading Latin, because you cannot travel to view a record yourself, or because you require assistance in planning the approach to a difficult problem. Find an affordable researcher in terms of rates, amount of advance payment required, and maximum expenditure permitted before reporting. Membership in a Scottish society is one way to identify researchers; another is to contact the Association of Scottish Genealogists and Record Agents or the Association of Professional Genealogists. Members must meet a standard of service and observe a code of practice.

Help from others comes on a more casual basis. Family historians are always eager to share stories and research tips. Attending a conference, talking after club meetings, chatting via the computer—these are ways to exchange information. Whatever you do, and fun though it may be, remember that all this talk can take time away from actual research.

Build Knowledge and Experience
Libraries and Archives

How well do you know your local public library? Even if it is small, do you know whether it has interlibrary loan service, a microfiche reader, or a microfilm reader? These three items mean that materials can be brought in from any institution that is part of the interlibrary loan system. You can obtain some records on microfilm, and many societies now publish finding aids or sources such as directories on fiche. How close is the nearest library of a substantial size? Can you visit it from time to time? Is it worth your while to pay the yearly fee for nonresidents to obtain borrowing privileges? If you practice the library skills outlined in the previous section you may be pleasantly surprised at what is waiting to be discovered among books, periodicals, and the unclassified materials in vertical files. Is there a university or college library nearby? Is history, in particular Scottish history, represented in its collections? Museums usually have reference collections associated with their respective themes. If places in your vicinity have Scottish connections, find out about the library holdings of historical museums.

How far is it to the nearest LDS Family History Center? Centers vary in size, but all of them have a copy of the Family History Library Catalog (FHLC), Scottish Church Records©, and the International Genealogical Index™ (IGI; see appendix A). Items available in the Family History Centers on an indefinite loan basis are those most heavily used by local patrons. You may be able to contribute to building this stock by borrowing certain types of records for an extended period.

Family history centers often convert long-term loans of popular items to permanent stock. Take time to discover all the patron services, such as copying, publications for sale, introductory videos or classes, and computer tutorials.

The public and university libraries of major cities are likely to be the best hunting grounds for the drop-in traveler. Vancouver and Seattle are two excellent examples of cities with large public libraries. Seattle's has an extensive genealogical collection. Vancouver's downtown library, which opened in May 1995, is a stunning piece of architecture, and a very patron-friendly facility. Some smaller centers may provide surprises because of special collections. In Canada, there is a very fine collection of Scottish material at the McLaughlin Library at the University of Guelph, Ontario. If you are planning a trip, find out in advance about the libraries near your destination. Your local library is a good place to begin enquiries about repositories at a distance. Also, more and more libraries and archives can be accessed via the Internet, and if you do not have this capability at home, your community library may have public terminals. If you happen to arrive at an unfamiliar library unprepared, it is not a serious problem; catalog knowledge and a floor plan (usually free at the information desk) will get results.

Broadening your knowledge of the collections at libraries and archives located at a distance from home serves several purposes. You will increase your awareness of available records. You will usually discover any records that have been published, indexed, or otherwise made more readily accessible. You may resolve a thorny research problem because information about the holdings of a library or archives reveals the existence of a record not otherwise known. A great deal of information is available about libraries and archives in Scotland and their collections. This can be found in print and using the Internet. Four helpful resources are listed here (see also the bibliography and the list of websites).

- *Tracing Your Scottish Ancestors* (Sinclair, 1997). Remains an invaluable resource for the National Archives (formerly the Scottish Record Office).

- *Exploring Scottish History* (Cox, 1999). For those who like their library outlines in print, this is excellent.

- Scottish Archives Network. This is the Internet portal for Scottish archives working to improve records access, and provide helpful resources to historians, genealogists, etc.

- National Archives of Scotland. This site includes sixteen fact sheets in PDF format, ready to be printed or downloaded.

Has it been done before or is someone else working on the same line of research now? There are ways to find out, beginning with online databases and search tools. Major commercial sites such as Ancestry.com offer free searches to databases built up from user contributions. They may contain only a small portion of Scottish names, and origins of the material must be carefully checked, but the chance of finding a useful lead makes the search worthwhile. Origin Search™ offers a one-stop way to check free sites for names. FamilySearch™, the genealogy website of the LDS Church, includes Ancestral File, vital information on millions of individuals world wide organized into family groups and pedigrees. In addition, at this same site you can search the FHLC by surname or purchase sets of CDs in the Pedigree Resource File, a collection of pedigrees submitted to the Family History Department of the Church (over forty-five CDs and a million names on each one).

The Internet provides a platform for society members, or any group, to exchange research information; Genuki and RootsWeb offer access to message boards and e-mail lists.

Another form of surname index is the *Genealogical Research Directory* (GRD) (Johnson & Sainty, 2002). Contributors submit entries, usually surnames but sometimes topics, along with geographic area and approximate date. You do not have to submit in order to consult; however, the fee for submission includes the price of a copy of the GRD. Runs of five years of the GRD are sold as a consolidated database on CD-ROM. The index is in alphabetical order by name being researched and refers you to the name and address of the individual who made the submission. Some submit topics of study, not names.

You may be aware of a connection to a prominent Scot, in which case look up the name in the *Dictionary of National Biography*, and in the series of volumes *The Scottish Nation; the surnames, families literature, honours and biographical history of the people of Scotland* (Anderson, 1863). This series is widely available in larger general-reference libraries and at the FHL. If the family had some social standing, you might check for the name in either work. It only takes a moment and may produce a reference. However, this advice comes with a warning. Do not jump to hasty conclusions without proof of a connection; it may send you on a wasted search. File anything of interest in case it subsequently proves to be useful. To find out whether printed works on the family exist (again you must be sure it is your family), consult *Scottish Family Histories Held in Scottish Libraries* (Ferguson, 1986) and *Scottish Family History: A Guide to Works of Reference on the History and Genealogy of Scottish Families* (Stuart, rep. 1994). These volumes are available in many libraries. About fifty works on Scottish names are listed in *Scottish Personal Names and Place Names* (Torrance, 1992).

If you have the time and the opportunity to browse through less common sources, look for volumes of *Scottish Notes and Queries*. The questions and answers in each issue frequently contain genealogical information; indexes have also been produced periodically. *Scottish Texts and Calendars: An Analytical Guide to Serial Publications* (D. & W.B. Stevenson, 1987) contains informative notations on the contents of the publications of private historical societies. Over the years, these societies have printed volumes of primary and secondary sources. It is worth thumbing through back issues of the *Scottish Historical Review* and the *Scottish Genealogist*. These publications can be found at the Society of Genealogists in London. If you are there and unable to make the journey north, visit the Society's library. It has all the periodicals previously mentioned, and it has its own unique document collection housed in row upon row of sturdy file boxes containing the miscellaneous contributions of members and nonmembers over the years. It is arranged alphabetically. Finding something is purely good luck, but the collection does include the McLeod papers—the very extensive files of a genealogist working primarily in Scottish families.

The Records

This is one situation where familiarity does not breed contempt. Better knowledge of the records will contribute to better results and suggest alternative sources when an ancestor continues to elude detection. Never pass up a chance to scan a different bibliography or a guide to the contents of a record office (many are noted in the bibliography). Venture beyond the most common sources; if a book or record type catches your attention, investigate.

There is nothing to lose except a little time. The experience will be useful, and there is always the possibility of finding new information. No one will ever produce a complete list of sources for Scottish genealogy; materials remain uncataloged, and unique searches require source material no one has yet thought to consider. So, you can never stop learning about records.

For researchers outside Scotland, it is really important to know and distinguish between what exists, what is in the FHL, what is in print or other formats (film, fiche, CD-ROM, the Web), what is in Scottish repositories, and what has been indexed or calendared (a calendar is a descriptive list, essentially a précis of the documents in a class of records). The FHLC Locality Search describes the records collected for a particular place, be it parish, burgh, or county, according to a list of record categories. Helpful as this is, there is a drawback; reading through the listed items you cannot tell whether these FHL holdings are all or part of what exists, and if none is listed, you cannot tell whether any survive at all. To make a meaningful comparison you need to study the FHLC, some of the better source guides such as *Tracing Your Scottish Ancestors* (Sinclair, 1997) or *Exploring Scottish History* (Cox, 1999), and specific record office guides. The FHLC can be consulted in Family History Centers, found online at FamilySearch, or purchased on CD-ROM. Information about record office holdings is best sought online using the SCAN catalogs section, the SRA Summaries of Archival Holdings and the websites of individual archives or libraries.

Additional dividends may be derived from an awareness of how the custodian of the original records describes them. Each classification or record group in the National Archives of Scotland (NAS) has its own descriptive listing of the contents in summary form. The types of headings and descriptions to expect are shown in chapter 5, figure 5-5. You will hear of or see a classification guide variously described as a repertory, an inventory, or a calendar. Even if you never visit the NAS, the guides can help because you learn about the material and better understand the extent of the holdings of the FHL. Some repertories and inventories are referred to in this book, including whether they are available through an LDS Family History Center. If you want to look for the listing in the FHLC, use the Locality Search heading "Scotland – Record type." For further information, take a look at the NAS website, which is regularly improved, and currently offers a series of information sheets on several sources.

Guides to the contents of regional or local record offices and libraries serve a similar purpose and make it possible to compare what is accessible with what exists in total. Making yourself aware of this comparison should deter you from abandoning a search too soon. Content guides and finding aids will also assist in the planning of a research trip to Scotland. Some archives, notably the NAS, are moving increasing amounts of material to other sites with a resultant wait of at least twenty-four hours for production of some material. The NAS recently underwent renovations and no doubt other archives and libraries will make changes. Construction can disrupt access, move records to temporary storage, or cause a temporary closure. If you are coming from a distance, call ahead to check on access in general and for record classes of particular interest. Planning ahead means knowing about the facility as well as its contents.

Historical Context

Genealogy and family history in the truest senses of the words are not synonymous. Family history implies an interest in what was influencing the lives of long-dead ancestors, even if they had no way of knowing it themselves. It also implies building a picture of daily lives and immediate surroundings.

For Scotland, reference to dictionaries of dates and annuals of significant events will be disappointing. Scotland gets lumped in with Britain, which tends to mean that not much is reported. *Harrap's Book of British Dates* (Castleden, 1991) mentions major political events such as the Union of 1707, and the dates of publication of the novels of Sir Walter Scott, but not much else. Nevertheless, this and similar volumes will at least provide perspective on what was going on in the rest of the world at any particular time.

Figure 2-2 is a retrograph. The life spans of several individuals (they could all be members of one family, or each from a different family) are drawn against a list of national/international events and a list of regional/local events. The only requirement is that at least a decade of someone's life falls within the selected 100 years. Choose the events for the twenty boxes on the basis of your knowledge of the chosen individuals. Of course, the regional/local events should be for the area where the listed individuals lived. This diagrammatic summary can become a talking point with relatives or other researchers, or it can be a window on history that leads you to investigate something more thoroughly.

Figure 2-2. 100-Year Family History Retrograph for the Russells and Rennies of Denny.

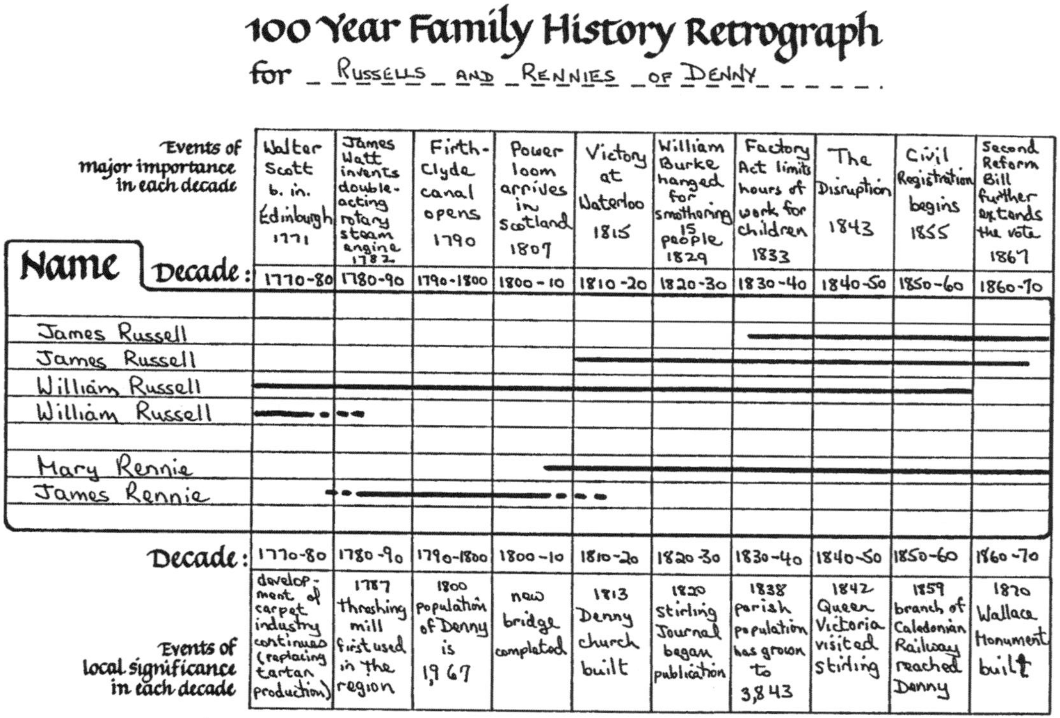

Note: Dotted-line extensions to life-span lines indicate that exact years of birth and death are not known.

The first step then is to read some Scottish history. Start at your public library to ascertain what is available. Poke about in used bookshops where you may find older histories or school and college texts. If you want to expand your knowledge of some aspect of Scottish history, the bibliographies found within general histories will suggest further reading. For books on a local region, once again, used bookstores are worth scouting. Out-of-date travel guides come cheaply and can be informative. You can obtain suggestions for current titles from the regional family history society and by writing to the local libraries, which may sell something themselves.

A picture of an ancestor's surroundings can be created partly through the research you perform. Census returns are very helpful provided you read beyond the listings for the immediate family and look at the neighbors and the neighborhood. Additional information can be found in the preliminary descriptions in directories, in gazetteers, and in the first two *Statistical Accounts of Scotland* (1799 and 1845)—the third one, too, if a mid-twentieth century view is desired. The first *Account* was under the direction of Sir John Sinclair. Each minister in each parish was asked to provide a verbal illustration, discussing such topics as numbers of births, marriages and deaths, emigration, agriculture and industry, and characteristics of the local population. Some reports were brief, but many included the personal opinions of the author on matters as diverse as drunkenness, irregular marriages, the ague, and the prejudices of the lower orders regarding inoculation against smallpox. Sinclair's own analysis of the reports that came back makes fascinating reading and could be useful. It might be important for your research, for example, to know that the inclement summer of 1782 was followed by severe and calamitous cold at harvest time. In Cabrach in Aberdeenshire, heavy snow flattened the crops on September 14th, and this was not an isolated report.[1] References to the *Statistical Accounts*, accessible in print and online, appear throughout this book.

For information on the dress, food, clothing, and housing of your ancestors, look for a social history or for books of people in particular locations or occupations. Good ideas can be found in the extensive bibliographies in *Scottish Local History* (Moody, 1994) and *Scottish Family History* (Moody, 2000). Shire Publications has several titles of interest in these areas including *Discovering Scottish Architecture* (West, 1985) and *Scottish Agricultural Implements* (Powell, 1988).

Books on description and travel occupy a grey area that straddles history and geography. They have a very strong appeal and, if written before 1939, for all but the large urban centers, they are describing scenes not much changed from a century before. Your prospecting may unearth such unusual treasures as the privately printed *Around the Ancient City* (Ryan, 1933), which extols the beauty and history of the area around Brechin. The books nearly always include a map and photographs or drawings.

Geographical Context

Maps are one of the delights of family history research. There have been some fine mapmakers, and their story is told in a fascinating book issued by the Scottish Library Association, *The Scot and His Maps* (Wilkes, 1991). Spatial perspective, topographic detail, man-made features of the landscape, boundaries, and names—maps depict and explain all these things. It is very important information.

Maps can also be created around an economic, social, or political theme. They can be found in atlases, books on historical geography, and histories. You might decide to make your own. You can use a map to plot the distribution of a surname or color code shifts in population, or mark points of departure for ships taking emigrants overseas. Whatever interests you or whatever will graphically represent a vague idea and perhaps turn it into a valid hypothesis is worth depicting. Some examples of sources for data to create your own maps are the *Statistical Accounts of Scotland*, the population summaries of the census returns, or any of the church record indexes described in chapter 5.

Pay attention to boundaries. Always identify the correct parish and county. In some counties it is useful to know that they were also divided into districts. If you are looking for a probate prior to 1823, then a special jurisdiction, the commissariot, should be identified. The Aberdeen and North East Scotland Family History Society produces an inexpensive series of county plans with parish boundaries and the date of earliest entry in the parish register. The revised edition of the *Phillimore Atlas and Index of Parish Registers* (Humphery-Smith, 1995) includes maps showing parish and commissariot divisions.

Several counties have undergone name changes. The most usual form is that used between 1890 and the reorganization of local government in 1974, when the old counties disappeared and were replaced by regions. Archives have been established on the basis of these regions. In 1996 Scotland has again undergone local government reorganization, and some pre-1974 names are back. There should not be any immediate, serious impact on archival collections, although the names of some archives may change and some decentralization of records may occur (i.e., some materials may be moved to smaller local repositories). As for county names, six counties had a name change at some point in time:

- West Lothian was Linlithgowshire
- Mid-Lothian was Edinburghshire
- East Lothian was Haddingtonshire
- Angus was Forfarshire
- Elgin was Morayshire
- Shetland was Zetland

Figure 2-3 shows the boundaries of the counties prior to 1974; the numbers on the map correspond to the counties listed below.

1. Shetland Isles (SHI)
2. Orkney Isles (OKI)
3. Caithness-shire (CAI)
4. Sutherland (SUT)
5. Ross & Cromary (ROC)
6. Inverness-shire (INV)
7. Nairnshire (NAI)
8. Morayshire (MOR)
9. Banffshire (BAN)
10. Aberdeenshire (ABD)
11. Kincardineshire (KCD)
12. Argyllshire (ARL)
13. Perthshire (PER)
14. Angus (ANS)
15. Dunbartonshire (DNB)
16. Stirlingshire (STI)
17. Clackmannanshire (CLK)
18. Kinross-shire (KRS)
19. Fifeshire (FIF)
20. Renfrewshire (RFW)
21. Lanarkshire (LKS)
22. West Lothian (WLN)
23. Midlothian (MLN)
24. East Lothian (ELN)
25. Buteshire (BUT)
26. Ayrshire (AYR)
27. Peebleshire (PEE)
28. Berwickshire (BEW)
29. Wigtownshire (WIG)
30. Kirkcudbrightshire (KKD)
31. Dumfriesshire (DFS)
32. Selkirkshire (SEL)
33. Roxburghshire (ROX)

Figure 2-3. Counties of Scotland, 1890–1974.

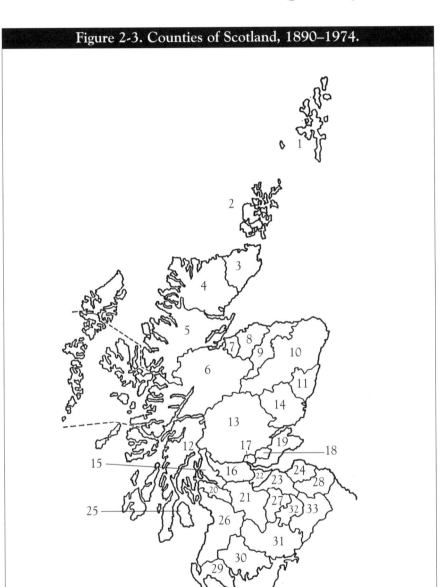

Figure 2-4 indicates the location of the Highland Line. The distinction between the Highlands and the Lowlands involves significant cultural and linguistic differences, but there is also an identifiable geological demarcation between the two. The Highland Line in the illustration runs east across Angus and then north. Geologists call it the "Highland Boundary Fault," marking the visible difference between older, harder Highland rock and the younger, softer, sedimentary deposits of the Lowlands. Whether discussing geological or cultural differences (which do not divide so sharply), the important point to remember is that the division is not a straight east-to-west one, and that the entire east coast is in the Lowlands.

Make it a matter of habit to locate a new place of interest on maps of different types and scales. On a map of the country, where is it? On a map of a county, which parish is it in? On a detailed regional map, what is the lie of the land and what nearby features can be noted? The best maps of Scotland have been issued by the Ordnance Survey. Reprints of the 1890 series can be purchased (1 inch = 1 mile), and modern Ordnance Survey maps have three commonly used scales, all with topographic features. The larger the scale, the smaller the geographic area on the page and the more detail (i.e., 1:2500 is very detailed for a small area, and 1:200,000 is much less detailed for a large area).

Even when you practice good habits, locating some places can be a challenge for reasons other than those discussed in chapter 1. The place may simply be too small to be shown on most maps, or it may have completely disappeared. Whenever this problem arises, work your way through the following suggestions before admitting defeat:

1. Check an atlas with a gazetteer and a scale of one inch = four miles (1:200,000).
2. Look up the name in the *Ordnance Gazetteer of Scotland* (Groome, 1883-85; also on fiche in some Family History Centers and on CD-ROM).
3. Check an area map with a scale of 1.25 inch = one mile (1:50,000), or better (maps at 1:25,000, 2.5 inch = one mile are available).

Figure 2-4. The Highland Line.

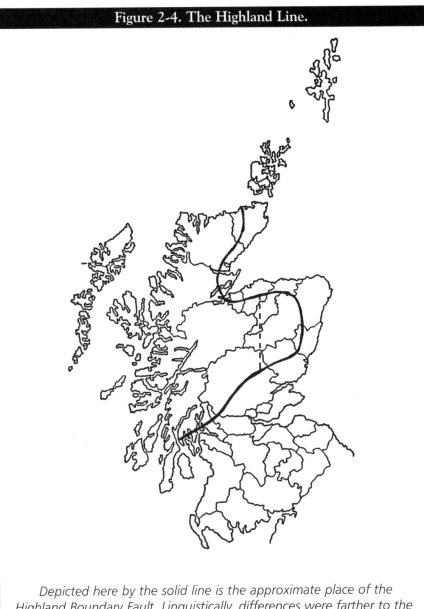

Depicted here by the solid line is the approximate place of the Highland Boundary Fault. Linguistically, differences were farther to the west about 200 years ago—in the vicinity of the dashed line.

4. Check a map contemporary to the time of the ancestor.

5. In urban areas check a street plan, both present day and historical, contemporary to the time of the ancestor.

6. Try the online gazetteer at Scots Origins, which is a database of all the Scottish place, estate, farm and street names in the 1881 census.

7. Look up the place in the *Directory to Gentlemen's Seats, Villages, etc. in Scotland* (Findlay, 1843) and/or in *A Directory of Land Ownership in Scotland circa 1770* (Timperley, 1976), and/or in the place-name index volumes of the Sasine Abridgements, which begin with 1780 and are available through LDS Family History Centers. All these sources contain small place names or estate names that may not appear anywhere else. Remember that your ancestor did not have to own an estate to call it his or her home.

Help might also be found in one of the hundreds of books on Scottish place names identified in *Scottish Personal and Place Names—A Bibliography* (Torrance, 1992). However, the availability of any listed titles is unknown; an online catalog search or interlibrary loan request would have to be tried.

Building a Reference Library

For most of us, book-buying is dictated in part by budget constraints. If cost is a concern, buy books that will serve a useful purpose and be referenced often enough to make ownership more sensible than occasional consultation at a library. If you are working in only one county, it does not make sense to buy a guide to sources in every county of Scotland. Select something regional or county specific. If your ancestors left Scotland prior to 1840, do not buy a book that focuses mainly on civil registration and census returns. The entries in the bibliography include comments, with these points in mind, on content or usefulness.

A good, basic reference collection should include the following:

• An outline history of Scotland.

• A pre-1974 atlas of Britain, scale four miles to the inch.

• At least one how-to book that matches your search needs.

- A book or pamphlet that outlines the contents of archives and libraries in the area(s) of interest.
- A map of the region at a more detailed scale of 1:50,000.
- A map of the parish boundaries in the area of interest.
- A regional or local history.
- The key finding aids and bibliographies that you will refer to again and again; some will be in print, others on CD-ROM, and others may be bookmarked sites in your Web browser.
- Your own bibliography of books, finding aids, and articles that you have found useful, including those you own and those you don't; this bibliography can be on index cards sorted into regional sections, and then by author or subject, or it can be in a computer database (keyword access would be a bonus).

Note

1. Sinclair, *Analysis*, 1826, p. 41.

Summary—Research Essentials

1. Visit local libraries to become familiar with the cataloging systems, layout, and services such as interlibrary loan and periodical indexes (many libraries offer patrons access to online resources).

2. Establish a filing system (paper or electronic) that incorporates ready reference, correct bibliographic details, and a standardized format.

3. Take time to formulate research objectives, and review them as you progress.

4. Join at least one family history society, preferably two—one close to home and the most appropriate one in Scotland.

5. Check—has the work been done before?

6. Do not neglect a background study of the records or the historical and geographical contexts of your research.

3 • Civil Registration

onsider yourself fortunate if you have ancestors or close collateral relations recorded in the Scottish civil registers of birth, marriage, and death. Scottish civil registration is much more informative than its counterpart to the south. Record keeping may have started nearly twenty years later than in England and Wales, but the information about parents on each and every type of certificate more that makes up for the tardy start.

If a search for a record of birth, marriage, or death is the start of your research, consult several maps before you begin. You will need some familiarity with the applicable part of Scotland, in particular the county name, the names of neighboring towns, or the neighborhoods of a major city. Map work is even more important if you must choose between several civil registration entries for the same name clustered close together in time and in place.

From your pedigree chart or your family tree, determine the events for which you need to acquire civil records. Keep in mind that registration began 1 January 1855. Are you fortunate enough to have specific details? Will it be necessary to search over a period of several years? Can the search be limited geographically? In other words, do you need only to watch for entries that fall within a particular county or district? Lack of information may dictate that you collect all of the entries for one particular name (and obvious variations of the name) over a number of years and a fairly wide geographic area. Such considerations will influence the search method you select.

Details

The information on the paper forms for birth, marriage, and death extracts was changed three times. The details are spelled out in Tables 3-1, 3-2, and 3.3. These differences should be clearly understood because you will want to take advantage of the more comprehensive forms whenever possible.

Not so essential, but still useful, is to be aware of changes n the indexes to vital records. Those who continue to use the microfilm version of the indexes in the FHL and Family History Centers should review the details and everyone can benefit from thinking about what facts to gather before a search.

For the first ten years the indexes were handwritten and after that they were printed, until the introduction of computer indexes. Arrangement was

Table 3-1 Details of Statutory Records—1855

Birth	Marriage	Death
• name	• names	• name
• date and time	• date	• date and time
• place	• place	• place
• sex	• form (i.e., rites)	• sex
• father's name, age, occupation and birthplace	• ages and birthplaces	• age
	• occupations	• occupation
• mother's name, maiden name, age, and birthplace	• present residence	• where born
	• usual residence	• name of spouse plus occupation for husband
• date and place of parents' marriage	• condition	• any other marriages
	• signature or mark	• name and ages of issue in order of birth
• no. and sex of other issue, living and dead	• relationship if related	
	• any former marriage if applicable	• father's name and occupation
• was informant present?	• no. of other issue, living or dead	• name and maiden name of mother
• was place lodgings?	• names of parents	
• name of informant	• occupation of father	• cause of death and name of medical attendant
• residence of same if not place of birth	• maiden name of mother	• place of burial
	• witnesses	• signature of informant, relationship, and address if different

by year, then alphabetically according to surname, given name, and finally in date order where names were the same. Male and female listings were always separate, sometimes within the same volume and sometimes in different ones. Events were indexed according to when registered—check the following year for events that occurred in November or December.

A page of a birth index will show the name, the parish or district of birth, and the entry number of each event. From 1929 on, the maiden surname of the mother appears in the index.

Table 3-2. Details of Statutory Records—1856-60.

Birth
- name
- date and time
- place
- sex
- name of father
- occupation of father
- name of mother and maiden name
- signature and quality of informant and residence if different

Marriage
- names
- date
- place
- form (i.e., rites)
- ages
- addresses
- conditions
- occupations
- name and occupation of fathers
- name and maiden name of mothers
- witnesses

Death
- name
- date and time
- place (and home address if different)
- age and sex of deceased
- occupation
- condition
- name and occupation of father
- name and maiden name of mother
- cause of death and name of medical attendant
- burial place
- signature of informant, relationship and address if different

Table 3-3. Details of Statutory Records—1861 and After.

Birth
- name
- date and time
- place
- sex
- name of father
- occupation of father
- name of mother and maiden name
- date and place of parents' marriage
- signature and quality of informant and residence if different

Marriage
- names
- date
- place
- form (i.e., rites)
- ages
- addresses
- conditions
- occupations
- names and occupations of fathers
- names and maiden names of mothers
- witnesses

Death
- name
- date and time
- place and home address if different
- age and sex of deceased
- occupation
- name of spouse (plus occupation of husband)
- parents' names and occupations
- cause of death and name of medical attendant
- signature of informant, relationship, and address if different

Marriage indexes similarly indicate the name, the parish or district of the marriage, and the entry number of each event. Names of brides and grooms are in the indexes but some of the details change. For nine years, from 1855 to 1863, a woman's married surname appeared in brackets. If a woman was married more than once and if the registrar was informed (which was usually the case), all her surnames were indexed with her other names in brackets. This fact can be a real bonus when there has been no evidence that a woman was married more than once or when you are trying to distinguish your ancestor of a common name from many others. In 1864, the other names in brackets no longer appear, but for 1864 and 1865, the indexes show a maiden surname for a woman married previously, and she is indexed under both names. No further changes occur until 1929, when the surname of the spouse is shown.

In the death indexes the basic name, place, and entry number information is supplemented from 1866 with the addition of the person's age at death. Before long, all General Register Office (GROS) computer indexes, 1855 to 1865, will have this detail added. For women, also from 1866, entries are indexed by maiden name and by married name or names, if the woman married more than once. A widow might be indexed only under her maiden name, if she reverted to that name after the death of her husband.

All GROS computer indexes include the registration district number; microfilm copies of the original index volumes do not. One other small point, which you will probably notice for yourself, is always to watch for names beginning Mc or Mac in both forms; the original index volumes list these forms separately.

Twenty years of Scottish civil registration indexes have been incorporated into the International Genealogical Index (IGI). The IGI contains both marriages and births from 1855 to 1874 inclusive (no deaths), coinciding with the consecutive run of years of register copies in the Family History Library (FHL). The information in the IGI is more helpful than what you see on a microfilm copy of the index volumes or in GROS computer indexes because it includes the names of the father and mother.

As you may conclude by now, there are three or four ways in which to consult the civil indexes to vital events. It is time to consider these in more detail, both how they function as well as their strengths and weaknesses.

Searching in Edinburgh

At New Register House, the location of the GROS, there is a daily access fee. At present this is £17, a bit of a shock when other such research facilities (e.g., the Family Records Centre in London) have no admission charge to view the index volumes. On the other hand, the computer equipment, instant results, low cost of digital images, and the amount of work that can be accomplished in one day transform this charge into a reasonable figure. New Register House is a very busy place and visitors are advised to reserve a seat in advance or to arrive early for the few unreserved seats that are kept free each day. You can choose to research for a half-day instead and some advance bookings in the winter cost less; details are at the GROS website.

Every work station has all the equipment you will need, including a computer terminal and a flat-screen monitor. Presently, users have access to the index that has been in place for several years and the partially completed DIGROS system, which stands for the Digital Imaging of the Genealogical Records of Scotland's People. At present, it is necessary to do a computer index search and then examine microfiche copies of vital records. After the transition a reduced number of microfiche sets will be retained for back up.

This conversion should be complete by late 2003 and thereafter the DIGROS system will be used to access the indexes and the digitized images of births, marriages, and deaths. The cost per image on site is very reasonable, fifty pence or about seventy-five cents; or, you can transcribe the entry into your notes or onto forms (see figures 3-1, 3-2 and 3-3).

Some twentieth century records are subject to statutory limitations for reasons of privacy. All records prior to 1901, the year of the most recent census, will be available using DIGROS; however, one hundred, seventy-five, and fifty year rules apply respectively to birth, marriage, and death records. This means that now, in 2003, open access is for births before 1903, marriages before 1928 and deaths before 1953; as each year goes by, another will become available. Official extracts of more recent births, marriages, and deaths can be ordered in person at New Register House, from the local registrar where the event occurred, and by telephone or fax. GROS staff will search among the historic records only for straightforward searches where most facts are known. Further details about official extracts and staff searches are at the GROS website.

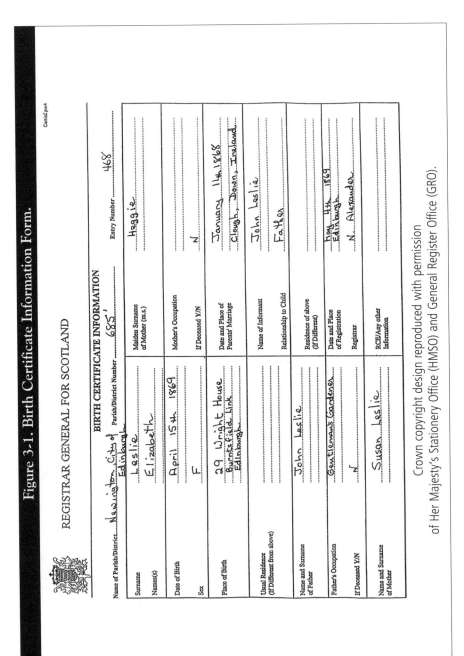

Figure 3-1. Birth Certificate Information Form.

Crown copyright design reproduced with permission
of Her Majesty's Stationery Office (HMSO) and General Register Office (GRO).

Figure 3-2. Extract from Register of Deaths.

006012

1861 – 1965

Extract of an entry in a REGISTER of DEATHS

Registration of Births, Deaths and Marriages (Scotland) Act 1965

No.	1 Name and surname, rank or profession and whether single, married or widowed	2 When and where died	3 Sex	4 Age	5 Name, surname, and rank or profession of father, Name and maiden surname of mother	6 Cause of death, duration of disease, and medical attendant by whom certified	7 Signature and qualification of informant, and residence, if out of the house in which the death occurred	8 When and where registered and signature of registrar
129	Jean DUNSMUIR	1865 November Ninth 11h 0m p.m. Shettleston Lanark	F	63 Years	James Gray Coal Miner Deceased	Hypertrophy Six Months As certified by Wm Young L.F.P.S.G.	*Signed* James Dunsmuir Son Residing in Shettleston	1865 November 11th At Shettleston
	Grocer				Jane Gray m.s. Allan Deceased			
	Widow of William Dunsmuir Colliery Manager						Present	*Signed* Andrew Garrand
								Registrar

The above particulars are extracted from a Register of Deaths for the .... District .... of .... Shettleston

County .... of .... Lanark

in the ....

Given under the Seal of the General Register Office, New Register House, Edinburgh, on 14th January 1988

Crown copyright design reproduced with permission of HMSO and GRO.

Figure 3-3. Marriage Certificate Information Form.

Cert inf.pm4

GRO RECORDS ENTERPRISE

MARRIAGE CERTIFICATE INFORMATION

Name of Parish/District.....................   Parish/District Number ....   Entry Number ....

Date of Marriage	Age	Occupation ....
Place of Marriage	Marital Status	
According to the Forms and Rites of	Father's Name & Surname	Occupation ....
	If Deceased Y/N	
Name and Surname of Groom	Mother's Name & Surname/ Maiden Name	
Usual Residence	If Deceased Y/N	
Age .... Occupation	Witnesses	
Marital Status	Addresses	
Father's Name & Surname	Date and Place of Registration/ Registrar	
Occupation		
If Deceased Y/N		
Mother's Name & Surname/ Maiden Name	Any Other Information	
If Deceased Y/N		
Name and Surname of Bride	R.C.E.	
Usual Residence		

Crown copyright design reproduced with permission of HMSO and GRO.

Searching at Home with ScotlandsPeople

The Internet and personal computers bring Scottish vital records into your home in the form of the ScotlandsPeople website (complete) and the International Genealogical Index (partial) at the FamilySearch site. ScotlandsPeople is the official pay-per-view website for all records in the care of the GROS. In this chapter only the vital records part of the site is discussed—the indexes and the digitized images of birth, marriage, and death records that start in 1855.

Before making any payment, it is possible to get a feel for your chances of success using the free surname (Soundex option 'on') and date-range search. If you are curious about the number of hits for a surname only within statutory registers, then you must set a date range that begins with 1855 or later. There is a table of results indicating the number of records found in the three categories of vital record indexes.

1. Old Parochial Registers Index and Statutory Registers Index—combined total for christenings and births if the date range entered crosses 1855, and in one or the other if the date range does not;

2. Old Parochial Registers Index and Statutory Registers Index—combined total for marriages if the date range entered crosses 1855, and in one or the other if the date range does not;

3. Statutory Registers Index—lists deaths in the statutory registers only but eventually OPR deaths will be included.

To avoid confusion when searching in the middle 1800s, you may want to do two free searches, one range set at no later than 1854 and the other beginning with 1855. The free search is of little or no use with common names unless the range of years can be set to a narrow limit. No other information can be supplied or retrieved from the search.

Once you have registered at the website and paid for access, you will be able to select a search in the vital records of births, marriages, or deaths. The £6 charge gives you thirty page-credits and a forty-eight-hour time limit; no credits are deducted without your confirmation. A results page can show anywhere from one to twenty-five index entries; in other words, the thirty pages of credit can produce from thirty up to 750 items. Viewing the image associated with an index entry consumes five "page credits." Indexes available online match the open records at New Register House: births 1855 to 1902, marriages 1855 to 1927, and deaths 1855 to 1952.

For births and marriages, select the source: statutory records. At present this is the only option for deaths. Before beginning your search, select Help and read the advice provided to find out about required information and the steps involved. Flexibility is built into the search, the broadest being a search of all three statutory record indexes for all of Scotland, and the narrowest, one event for one individual in a specific district. The input page includes lines for surname, forename (two names for marriages), sex, year range, place (all of Scotland if no place entered), and for deaths only, age range. The surname is required and must include at least two characters, but the given name may be omitted or may be as brief as one letter, in which case all names beginning with that letter are found. The search tool accepts two wild card symbols: '?' for a single letter and '*' for one or more, and can be told to use Soundex logic. If you do not select these options, the system defaults to exact spelling. Computers can check things for you and do calculations; a marriage search is simpler because is not necessary to recall the changing details of indexes over the years, and a death search can sort out unwanted listings, e.g., deaths of children when searching for an adult.

Not yet available but coming shortly to ScotlandsPeople is an additional geographic search option, a county search. It will be possible to search a specific county or several in turn. You may have difficulty recognizing the district names as you fill in the search fields and as you examine the tables of results. Keep a map handy and know the reference number for the parishes in the area; generally registration district and parish numbers are the same (they start at the north and get larger towards the English border). Refer to the list online at the GROS website, which includes the start and end dates for each district name. Alternatively, there are lists in print: *The Parishes, Registers and Registrars of Scotland* (Spiers, 1993) or The *Key to the Parochial Registers of Scotland* (Bloxham and Metcalfe, 1979). Another place to find parish numbers is within the parish entry in the Family History Library Catalog (FHLC).

If you are satisfied that the number of hits indicated is what you want to view, the next screen will show a table of results summarizing several details in each record. Buttons at the right of the screen let you select to see the image (with zoom features) or to place an order for an official extract. The lists of results viewed during a session, index pages and images, are saved in a password-protected area of the website to which you can return later at no charge, after your time has expired. Results can also be printed and downloaded. At the ScotlandsPeople homepage, check "What's in the Database" for current details of available images (1855 images will be last).

Figure 3-4. ScotlandsPeople: Facts in Index Search Results

Birth Result: surname, forename, year, sex, district, county, GROS reference

Marriage Result: first surname, forename, second surname, forename, year, district, county, GROS reference

Death result: surname, forename, mother's surname (where available), year, sex, age, district, county, GROS reference

---

Figure 3-5. Results of a Search for Thomas Strachan, 1855–1875.

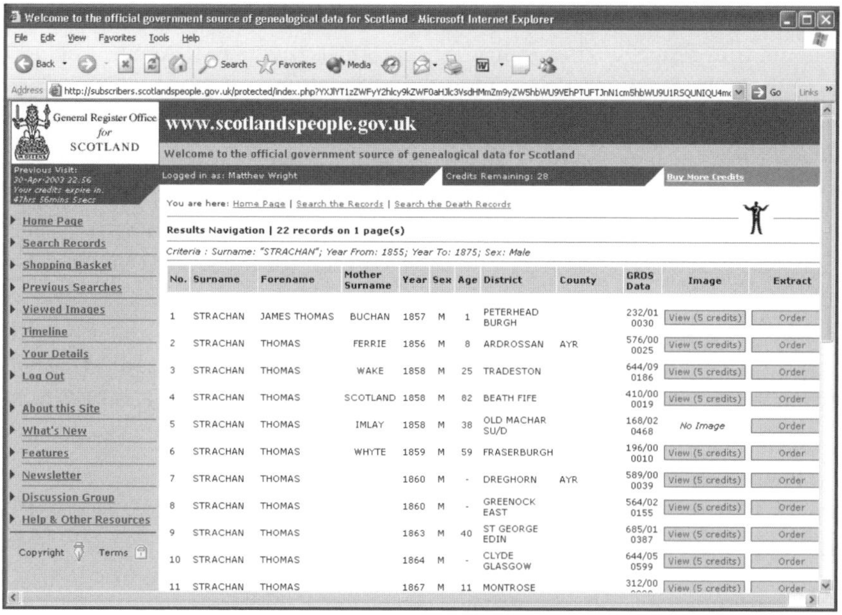

Resources at FamilySearch

Turning now to the FamilySearch website, you find free access within the IGI to the first 20 years of civil registration indexes of birth and marriage. A search result contains considerable information: individual's full name, parent(s) or spouse, gender, event, date, place, and microfilm references. The input screen offers flexibility as to how much precision is wanted in the search; read the instructions because some combinations do not function. Names can be searched on exact spelling or according to the system of standardized spellings within the IGI. By the way, the logic for this is different from the Soundex and wild card options that can be used at ScotlandsPeople, which is perhaps a reason for trying both indexes when an event is proving elusive.

Any of you lucky enough to have an odd first name in the family can search on first name only. It is possible to get a result with the following fields filled in: given name, event, date range, region, and county. If you take out the given name, insert the surname and leave all other fields the same, this search will not work; you get notice in red telling you why.

Slightly different approaches to the online IGI search can be found at Hugh Wallis' website for IGI Batch Numbers and at Scots Origins; the significant difference is the ability to search at the parish level. The LDS Genealogy Department filmed the registers in batches or sections, and these alternate sites use this information to make parish level searches possible. The Scots Origins site has a simpler interface (see the descriptions in appendix A) but both of them present search combinations not possible through the FamilySearch site itself. Scanning the numbers for the county of Angus, you will see there is usually one batch for the twenty years of civil registration marriage entries and two for births.

If a result is found in the online IGI, then you can choose to view the microfilm copy of the register volume (the index provides the number); the FHL holds copies for 1855 to 1874, 1881, and 1891. Alternatively, you can opt to use ScotlandsPeople to access the digital image, place an order with the GROS, contact the specific registrar or engage an agent in Salt Lake City or Edinburgh. Online orders can also be placed at Scots Origins, who originally held the contract with the GROS to put their records online (websites and addresses are in appendix D).

Manual Searches

Fully manual searches of indexes remain possible. The rapid expansion of online access is a boon to most of you, but others may not have made the technological transition. Microfilm copies are not going to disappear overnight. All the indexes (this includes deaths) up to the middle of the twentieth century are on microfilm in the FHL; some Family History Centers have extensive microform index collections. Libraries in the UK, Canada, Australia, and elsewhere may have collections of indexes as well. Family history societies are good sources of information about local resources.

It is always wise to think about pitfalls, and the fastest route to a result, particularly when working your way through rolls of microfilm. Look for the sibling with the unusual given name or for the bride if her name is less common than the groom's. Bear in mind that in the death indexes, a woman may appear under her maiden name *and* married name; it is also possible she may have reverted to her birth name if left a widow. Geography remains a hazard; consult maps and lists of parishes to become familiar with the region, place names, and parish numbers (see page 44).

Selecting a Search Method

The computer literate among you will use the IGI, or its alternate batch-number access points, and ScotlandsPeople, according to inclination or necessity. There are no death indexes at the FamilySearch website, the indexed births and marriages are for a limited period, and although the index entries have plenty of detail, there is no immediate access to digital images. For those with access to New Register House, three days of online access is just about equal to one day on location. If few names are involved, one day via the Internet is probably more economical.

Some people are comfortable with familiar methods, and those who are close to a Family History Center will find that the routine and reasonable cost continues to be attractive. In many cases it will come down to what is at the Family History Center, what facts you have to work with, and your comfort level with a Web-based search. Should you decide to use a professional genealogist, there is some competition among service providers, both individual research agents and small companies. Contact details for a considerable number of these can be found online at Cyndi's List in the Scotland section under the category labeled *Professional Researchers, Volunteers and*

Other Research Services, in the list of agents at ScotlandsPeople, and from the professional associations listed in appendix D.

Thinking It Through

Remind yourself of the date 1 January 1855 whenever you consider the tactics to be utilized in a search. Make a note of those persons who were born, married, or died since that date. All register entries, where the facts were known, include the names of the mother and father. Do not think only in terms of the direct line, for the record of a brother, sister, aunt, or uncle could be equally illuminating. The death entry of an elderly maiden aunt in the late 1850s could provide key details to launch a search in parish registers for your direct line. You might extract similarly useful data from the marriage records of siblings of an emigrant.

The best feature of Scottish vital records is the inclusion of parents' marriage details (i.e., date and place) in a birth record. It is quite possible that a birth recorded in the first fifteen years or so of civil registration includes marriage information that predates the introduction of statutory records and perhaps even the first nominal census of 1841. This leap across time is extremely valuable, more so if the surname is common or if the marriage occurred in a secessionist church (see chapter 6). There is a hitch. For the five years from 1856 to 1860, this marriage information was omitted. If your ancestor was born within that period, you must seek a sibling's birth record for the marriage details. If you are among the unlucky few who do not find any births outside those years, you must rely on a search in the marriage indexes.

Set your search parameters with some flexibility, and maintain a certain level of skepticism. The name spelling is not fixed. The dates are always open to question, and places named have been known to differ among records. Sometimes you will see "deceased" after a parent's name on a marriage record, but its absence does not guarantee that the person was alive at the time of the event. Think hard about what could be done to a name by the registrar or the person involved. Pronunciation may be the cause of a radically different appearance in the register. Poor handwriting created problems, and names are often misindexed because of reversals, transpositions, and omission of one name. With a surname-style middle name, an entry could conceivably find its way into three places. Where information is scarce, begin by assuming that people could marry at a very young age, or become parents at an unusually advanced age, or live to be ninety plus. As for places, keep the map handy, and be prepared to find the name of a town you know from family notes to be several miles from the obscure village that was the true birthplace.

When you obtain the register details, pay attention to all of them. What do they tell you? Do they match information in other records such as census returns? If this is the first record obtained, where else should you look for corroboration? Who was the informant for a death? Errors are actually more common on death certificates, either because the informant was not a close relative or because the details became vague over time. Do the names of witnesses to a marriage mean anything? Even if they don't, jot them down for future reference. Finally, assess the facts found in the new information to see how they will advance your research.

Watch closely for the possibility of finding a family member, any family member, within the very informative entries for 1855. The birth record adds the ages and birthplaces of the parents and other issue, either living or dead. The marriage record includes present and usual addresses, any previous marriages, and any issue. The death record adds where the deceased was born, details of all marriages, and the names and ages of issue, in order. These additional facts can bridge years, help in the identification of a family, and facilitate the transition to parish registers.

The date an event was registered, and the type (i.e., birth, marriage, or death) will tell you if you can continue the search in the records of civil registration. Always note how closely an event falls to a census year. Moving back and forth from vital records to censuses is good strategy as the details complement one another and confirm family structures. This process may prove difficult if a family moved frequently and had a common name, in which case you must consider what other finding aids or records might assist you.

Whenever a record of birth, marriage, or death fails to turn up, consider in turn the standard cautions. Are the basic facts accurate? Have you checked both Mc and Mac? How might the name have been altered? (It is unlikely that an illiterate informant would have taken any interest in what the registrar wrote). Did the event take place in Scotland? Might the family have moved between birth and registration? When ages are found in the death indexes (from 1866 on), have you allowed for the fact that the information may have come from an unreliable source?

Two features of Scots law may be behind missing entries. An illegitimate child was legitimized by the later marriage of the parents, so consider a search under the maiden name of the mother. Also, divorce has always been possible in Scotland, so a missing death record may not be missing at all. You may simply be looking under the wrong married name. Be sure to search under the woman's maiden name.

Repeating the search is an option, with some alterations in the way you watch for possibilities. Alternatively, you may decide to seek additional information from some other record. Census returns have already been mentioned, and it is not long before all of them, 1841 through 1901, will be indexed and their digital images available. The GROS will later add minor civil records (e.g., army, marine, and consular lists) and the details in the Register of Corrected Entries to their database, the latter changes cross-referenced to the original extract. Another useful option is the index to testamentary records at the Scottish Documents website.

Conclusion

Civil registration records are a good place to begin Scottish research. If you can find a connection, even on a collateral line, it could be a wise strategy to examine their entries. The registrars requested parental information for all records, including deaths; in other words, the extract for someone who died in the 1850s can give you facts for people alive in the 1700s. These records are easy to consult and can be worked together with a search in census returns—work in one feeds off the other. The results should build a sound basis of fact for working your way further into the past.

Summary—Civil Registration

1. Select the name, date, and place guidelines for the search. If you are sure of the facts, view the image via the Web, place an order with the GROS, use an agent in Edinburgh, or write the district registrar. For the years 1855 to 1874, 1881, and 1891, microfilm copies of the registers are in the FHL.

2. Find the location on a map and note names of neighboring parishes or districts.

3. Search the indexes for the appropriate years—at ScotlandsPeople, in the IGI for the first 20 years, on microfilm at Family History Centers, or with the help of an agent in Scotland. An event may not have been recorded at all, or recorded with errors or recorded outside the date and place ranges selected for the search. Check all the indexes because they utilize various types of search logic and different people prepared them.

4. Once an entry is found, the extract can be obtained using the same options mentioned in item 1 above.

5. When you have acquired results, note every new fact, compare dates against census years and the start of civil registration, and determine the next step. Also, consider whether locating civil records for other family members would be useful (e.g., a possible 1855 event).

4 • Bridging Decades and Centuries

cottish research is unusual in that there is a very sharp break where civil records end and centrally collected church records begin. Many records straddle the critical year of 1855. Census returns, voters' lists, directories, and newspapers all can enhance the knowledge gained in civil records and provide a link to earlier church records. These sources can also provide useful clues about people who left Scotland before civil registration began, but who had identifiable relatives who did not leave.

Pay attention to dates to assess what resources you can consult. Nominal census returns were taken every ten years and are available from 1841 to 1901. Note that the census returns for 1841 and 1851 predate the start of civil registration in Scotland, which can make them exceedingly important. Electoral rolls begin in 1832, but for many areas the start date is considerably later. The existence of directories and newspapers varies from place to place, but generally they exist from earlier dates in larger towns and cities.

When, What, and Where

The combination of household groupings, relationships, birthplaces and occupations found in all but the earliest nominal census returns means that they are wonderful resources and problem solvers. Seven censuses are available for study, 1841 through 1901. For earlier returns, only statistical reports were to be submitted to the authorities. Some enumerators recorded names, but most of these lists were destroyed or lost. More information on surviving fragments is provided later in this chapter.

Wonderful as they are, census records are not perfect. There are gaps and misleading entries because our ancestors did not always tell the truth, and the enumerators were not infallible. Nevertheless, the census was taken in the same manner everywhere and stored centrally afterward, so it survives as a nearly complete, well-organized and accessible record of the nineteenth century. Census records less than one hundred years old are accessible only to lawyers dealing with inheritance problems.

The method of enumeration was built around enumeration districts and sub-districts. Enumerators wrote a short account of district boundaries and these appear at the beginning of every section of the census; the descriptions contain interesting physical detail, and occasionally, genealogical clues. Generally districts correspond to parishes, but not always. Furthermore, districts were not identical through every census and if a district straddled a county line the returns were put with one county only. Geographic knowledge is therefore important for everyone except perhaps those seeking people with rare names; computer indexes find them anywhere and you can check the map afterwards.

Districts are smaller in populated areas; and where they are small and close together selecting the right ancestor is more difficult. Until all censuses are indexed, you may have to search several districts. If you have an exact address for a family in a community of 40,000 or more, perhaps from a birth records, you can consult a street index.

The content of the 1841 census is sufficiently different from the others to warrant a separate description. The columns show the location (i.e., village name, street name), the names of everyone in the household, their occupations, approximate ages, and whether or not they were born in the county. The ages recorded were supposed to be the actual ages of anyone fifteen years old and under; for everyone else, the actual age was rounded down to the nearest five years. There was lots of room for error within these instructions. Some enumerators rounded up. Anyone who fibbed a little (e.g., was actually fifty-two but said he or she was forty-nine) ended up way off the mark. The rather vague birthplace question resulted in cryptic responses noted as Y (yes, born in the county), N (no, born in another county), E (born in England/Wales), I (born in Ireland), or F (born in foreign parts). Think about these possibilities as you check the place location against the location of the county boundary or the border with England. An answer could mean a few miles away, at the other end of Scotland, or at the other end of the kingdom. Another serious drawback of this census is that it does not reveal relationships. This means, for example, that a man, woman, and child living together could be a family or a brother and sister caring for a young relative. Similarly, a houseful of people with several surnames could be landlord and lodgers or members of one family. There is some compensation in the fact that where more than one household resided in one dwelling, the enumerator distinguished between them by using a double slash (//) between dwellings and a single slash (/) between family units.

The value of the 1841 enumeration lies in two factors. This is the first census for which nominal lists were retained for the entire country, and it predates civil registration by fourteen years. Relationships and birthplaces may be obscure, but the household groups still can assist with family reconstruction.

To a greater extent similar benefits can be found in the 1851 census, also nominal and also predating civil registration, but with the addition of relationships and accurate ages and birthplaces (figure 4-1). It, and succeeding returns, are therefore considerably more useful. The enumerator requested the actual present age of each individual and did not round off the response. Neither was the birthplace reduced to a minimally useful single letter, although the answer recorded may be less precise the further away it was from the place of enumeration. For those born locally, the parish and county should be indicated; otherwise, only the county name or the other part of Britain, such as Ireland, might appear. An important addition is the relationship of each person to the head of the household, so you can now distinguish between the family members and the lodgers and servants (some terms, e.g., in-law, were not always used in the clearly defined sense that is understood today). Marital status is also given, and in those instances where gender is not obvious from a name, the ages are noted in separate columns for males and females. As with the 1841 census you will

Figure 4-1. Census Information Form.

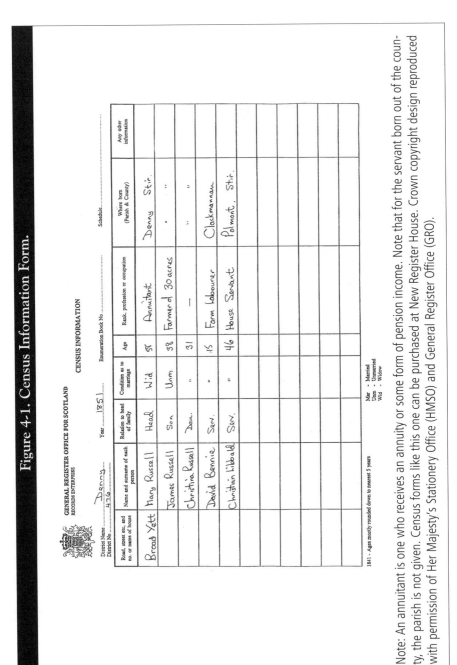

Note: An annuitant is one who receives an annuity or some form of pension income. Note that for the servant born out of the county, the parish is not given. Census forms like this one can be purchased at New Register House. Crown copyright design reproduced with permission of Her Majesty's Stationery Office (HMSO) and General Register Office (GRO).

find the address, sometimes with the street number, and the occupations of those in the household. Some additional pieces of information change in the various censuses. These supplementary bits and pieces, together with dates of enumeration, are summarized in table 4-1.

Table 4-1 Census Dates, Additions, and Deletions	
Date of Enumeration	**Changes**
7 June 1841	
31 March 1851	Accurate ages given Marital status added Details of birthplace included Relationship to head of household added Whether blind, deaf, or dumb added
8 April 1861	Whether blind, deaf, or dumb removed No. of children 5-15 attending school added No. of rooms with 1 or more windows added More detail in the parish description added
3 April 1871	Whether blind, deaf, or dumb restored Whether imbecile or idiot or lunatic added Whether unemployed added Age range of children in school (or educated at home) altered to 6-18
4 April 1881	Scholar now recorded in the occupation column Even more parish details added
5 April 1891	Notes Gaelic and English speakers Employment status is shown (employer, employee, self-employed)
31 March 1901	No change in major details

As you consider the research that you will undertake in census records, remember to investigate the possibility that fragments of pre-1841 returns survive for your places of interest. In some instances, the local enumerator (usually the schoolmaster) went beyond his instructions and zealously recorded all names, places of residence and occupations. To check whether any of these fragments survive for a selected area, consult one or more of three finding aids: *Local Census Listings 1522-1930* (Gibson and Medlycott, 1997), the first two appendices to *Pre-1841 Censuses and Population Listing in the British Isles* (Chapman, 1992), and "Pre-1855 Communion Rolls and Other Listings in Kirk Sessions Records" (Bigwood, 1988). Approximately fifty communities from eighteen counties have some surviving parts of the 1801-1831 returns.

Table 4-2 lists counties with no surviving fragments. Compare any entry of interest to the appropriate heading in the Locality section of the Family History Library Catalog (FHLC) under "Scotland – County – Place – Census. "To discover what exists in local custody, write or e-mail the nearest library or archives to inquire about any pre-1841 returns.

Table 4-2. Counties for Which No Pre-1841 Official Census Fragments Survive

Argyll*	West Lothian (Linlithgow)*
Bute*	Nairn
Caithness	Peebles
Clackmannan	Ross*
Cromarty	Selkirk*
Dumbarton*	Shetland*
Kinross	Stirling*
East Lothian (Haddington)	Wigtown*

*Indicates that other local returns (e.g., Communicant Rolls) survive.

This summary is based on listings in Gibson/Medlycott (1994), Chapman (1992), and Bigwood (1988).

The abstracts—or summaries—of the part of the statistics gathered from parish registers in the initial 1801 census can be viewed on microfilm.

The abstracts make for interesting reading because they give an indication of the growth or decline of an area. Each parish was to report the numbers of burials, baptisms, and marriages in various formats since 1700. Sadly, the odds of examining this for your parish are one in ten. The officials reported that no more that 99 parishes out of the 890 parishes in Scotland which made returns actually had regular registers. For more on the value of statistical evidence, see *Census Records for Scottish Families at Home and Abroad.*[1]

Some sailors and fishermen of coastal communities may appear to be out of place. If on a vessel that is in its home port, they will be found in the shipping lists recorded at the end of the district and not at home. If at sea they will be recorded with the shipping lists of the next port of call, and if already in another port, they will be in the lists for that location. You may experience difficulties using census returns that are not yet indexed; indexing will mitigate or remove the problem entirely if you have enough facts to identify the ancestor. Sailors of the Royal Navy or merchant navy on board ships in foreign waters on census night were enumerated from 1861. The FHL created an alphabetical index to all people on British ships in 1861, about 120,000 names, with an accompanying list of ship names. In the 1881 census index these returns were treated as a distinct section. An interesting bonus for ships on the high seas is their exact position, i.e., longitude and latitude, at midnight on census day.

The census returns for Scotland are found in the Family History Library (FHL) of The Church of Jesus Christ of Latter-day Saints (LDS) in Salt Lake City and can be ordered on microfilm to be sent to any Family History Center. Census returns are also in the General Register Office (GROS), New Register House, Edinburgh. In addition, regional archives and many libraries in Scotland, particularly the main library in a town or district, have the films for the local area. The holdings of any archives or library can be ascertained by consulting *Census Records for Scottish Families at Home and Abroad* (Johnson, 1997), *Census Returns 1841-1891 in Microform* (Gibson and Hampson, 2001) and *Exploring Scottish History* (Cox, 1999). Guides issued by regional family history societies are another source of information on local holdings.

Using the GROS Census Records

In Edinburgh all census returns are in the GROS, New Register House, not the National Archives next door. Charges are the same, £17 per day, as was outlined in chapter 3. Three censuses, 1881, 1891 and 1901 are indexed and digital images are available for 1891 and 1901, transcripts for 1881 (images to follow soon). Over the course of 2003–2004 as part of the DIGROS project, digitized images of all earlier nominal censuses, 1841 through 1871 inclusive, will become available. Patrons will be able to browse the images in advance of the indexes being ready; to help with searching DIGROS will have computer versions of the existing street indexes available. While the imaging and indexing of the 1841 – 1871 censuses is in progress, researchers should refer to printed and microfiche finding aids. Volunteer members of societies within the Scottish Federation of Family History Societies (SAFHS) have completed a great deal of indexing, particularly for 1841 and 1851. These indexes can usually be purchased directly from the societies. The GROS is working with the SAFHS to incorporate them into the computer indexes for 1841 through 1871.

The computerization of the census records and completion of the DIGROS project does not mean the eventual elimination of census returns on microfilm. Copies will be available at New Register House, although there will be fewer readers. Browsing through the enumerations of a whole neighborhood or parish continues to be a useful genealogical exercise, even if all family members can be found through indexes and images.

ScotlandsPeople, the Web source of GROS records, is making indexes and images available at about the same pace; check under the heading "What's in the Database?" ScotlandsPeople presently provides access, for a fee, to indexes of three enumerations, 1881, 1891, and 1901, transcripts for 1881 and images for the other two. The 1881 transcript of an individual entry within its complete household can be viewed for a single page credit; for images of census books the charge is five credits. If this is to be your first source for census material, check the site regularly for changes and additions or sign up to receive e-mail notification.

Those of you who have already looked for civil records, will find the search routine familiar. You must register and pay the £6 access fee, good for thirty page credits or forty-eight hours. At present it is necessary to search the 1881 census separately. In the search box, the field for the surname is marked as required and must have at least two characters. The forename can be omitted; if only one letter is used, all forenames with that first letter are included. The search engine looks for exact spelling of surnames unless options are selected; i.e., Soundex engaged or wild card symbols inserted ('*' and '?').

The fields for a census search vary slightly depending on the census: surname, forename, sex, and age range are common to all. The 1881 search box has fields for an address, the census place and the birthplace. For 1891 and 1901, you can search one or both together and add the county and district where enumerated but not a birthplace. You are asked to confirm that you want to expend one credit for each page of up to twenty-five index results.

For 1891 and 1901, the table of results that match your search criteria contains the following genealogical facts: census year, surname, forename, sex, age, district, and county. Where available, you may also select buttons for viewing images (5 additional page credits each) and ordering copies. The 1881 transcript includes the same facts as well as dwelling name or address, relationship to the head of the household and birthplace.

ScotlandsPeople includes some information at the site to help you use the indexes and understand the images. There is a glossary of occupations found in the census and another for unusual terms in general. You can also access a page that explains the steps in a search and another describing how to view and print images.

Using Other Census Records

The census returns for Scotland, 1841 – 1891 on microfilm, are found in the Family History Library (FHL) of The Church of Jesus Christ of Latter-day Saints (LDS) in Salt Lake City and can be ordered through any Family History Center. In addition, many archives and libraries in Scotland and elsewhere have partial or complete microfilm collections. Anyone can purchase microfilm rolls at a cost of £35 per film; details are at the GROS website. To find out the holdings of an archives or library check the website or send an enquiry. A listing, up to the 1891 census, is in *Census Records for Scottish Families at Home and Abroad* (Johnson, 1997). Alternatively, the appropriate family history society should have the information.

There are at least two reasons for selecting a microfilm version of the census. One is convenience, because a large collection is close by, and the other is economy because in-depth studies are best done on microfilm, except for 1881 where the CD set is the cheapest method. Microfilm is an option for any search if you are not using the Internet and if you do not mind waiting for the film to reach a Family History Center. It is worth remembering that indexes are not required when the parish or vicinity is known and population density is low, because you can read a film in a couple of hours or less.

If you decide to use FHL resources, the starting point is a place name search in the Family History Library Catalog (FHLC). Census records are listed for every parish with film numbers for each enumeration. In the FHL you serve yourself and in a Family History Center staff will help you place the order. Census returns from 1841 through 1891 can be consulted this way; quite likely many genealogists will continue to do so because they are accustomed to it. All GROS street indexes for large towns and cities are available. Addresses are helpful in urban areas when there isn't an index; they can be found in other records such as directories, birth, marriage and death extracts. As of late 2002 there is no word about being able to access the 1901 census through the FHL.

The many nominal indexes published by family history societies can be used in combination with a microfilm search. If you want to know what is currently for sale watch the society website (see appendix D), join the society or take part in an online discussion group for the county.

The 1881 Census

The 1881 census has so many formats for access it deserves special attention. The index and transcripts are accessible at New Register House and online at ScotlandsPeople. A few years ago the *1881 Census and National Index* for all of England, Scotland and Wales, so detailed to be almost a transcript, was made available for purchase on CD-ROM by The Family and Church History Department of the Church of Jesus Christ of Latter-day Saints. In addition, the 1881 census index can be found on computer at the FHL and in Family History Centers. Look a little harder in centers and libraries and probably you will find the first version of the 1881 census index, on microfiche in four different arrangements. Last of all, there are microfilm reels in the Family History Library and other repositories.

The two formats that can be used at home deserve a closer look to compare features and search techniques. The ScotlandsPeople 1881 search form requires that you enter a surname (of at least two letters) or an exact address (street name or house name). You may also specify census place, birth place, age range, and gender.

The CD set has a national index on eight discs and sixteen regional disks; there are two of the latter for Scotland, Highlands and Lowlands. The information that can be provided for the search, and that you see in the results of national and regional sections, are not the same. Use the National Index if you cannot find the family in Scotland and want to check whether they went to England or any other part of mainland Britain, the Isle of Man or the Channel Islands. Looking at a CD-ROM regional index, the most unusual aspect is that the search works whether or not a name is entered; e.g., you can call up a list of everyone aged 30 born in Banff and living in Banff. Also, it is possible to search for a given name only; not possible at ScotlandsPeople. Unless the "exact spelling" box is selected, the CD search tool ignores middle names. It is not apparent in the search window, but one wild card symbol, the asterisk, can be used. The age range option does not go beyond five years, i.e. a maximum search of a stated year plus or minus five. It is possible to be specific about birthplace and/or census place. This requires cautious use because the enumerator did not always record the parish of birth, especially if across the border in England. It is worth saying again that all of Britain— England, Scotland, Wales, the Isle of Man and the Channel Isles—are in the CD set. This makes it easy to go looking for migrant ancestors.

Figures 4-2 and 4-3 show the results that appear in response to your search input; in this case a search for John Duncan, aged 75 to 80. At ScotlandsPeople you see a list of possible results. The next step is to choose the most likely entry and use one credit to view the image. With the *1881 British Census and National Index*, click on the name of interest and a summary of household information appears in the bottom half of the window; select the 'details' option from the tool bar and further information appears. the gender option at ScotlandsPeople is useful, but it was possible for the sex to be recorded inaccurately. With both versions, you have the option of restricting the search according to the birthplace of the individual.

Those of you with Scotland—Canada or Scotland—USA connections have a bonus for this time frame at the Family Search website. You can check for families that moved to North America. The 1881 census index for England, Wales, the Channel Islands, and Isle of Man is part of a much larg-

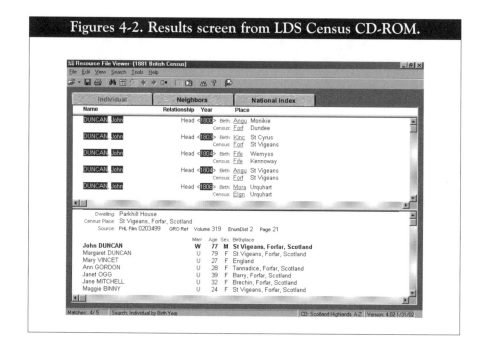

Figures 4-2. Results screen from LDS Census CD-ROM.

Figures 4-3. Results screen from ScotlandsPeople.

er index that includes the 1881 census of Canada and the 1880 census of the USA. The British data matches what is on the CD-ROM; however, Scotland is not online at Family Search because of the ScotlandsPeople online system.

Strategy, Tips, and Pitfalls

Embark on a census search with an objective. Understand whether it is a fishing expedition to catch all entries of one surname, a broad-based search for a specific person, or a specific check defined by name, date, and location. Answering several questions can help you to sort this out:

- What name or names are to be noted, and what are the possible spellings?
- Is a name common in the search area?
- On what basis was the census year selected? Is it the best choice?
- On what basis was the location selected and with what degree of certainty?
- Is the place or area selected made up of one or more parishes? Which ones?
- How much is known about the individual or the family in this census year?

If the search is based somewhat on conjecture, you may have to repeat it using different parameters. Where information is lacking, you must establish limits for the search—the year or years, the geographic area, the names to be listed, and whether other limiting factors must be created to make the search manageable, such as only certain ages or occupations for anyone of a particular name.

The selection of a location to search may generate some thought and planning. Those who find their ancestors residing in the same parish in Scotland through three or more census returns are fortunate. Scottish ancestors moved about, often to search for work in a neighboring parish. In large cities, they moved from one lodging to another. They went to Ireland or England and returned, or they emigrated overseas and didn't bother to tell anyone from whence they sprang.

Begin with what is known and attempt to build upon it. If starting from an overseas location, be sure to exhaust all possible sources that might reveal the place of origin. Censuses are particularly valuable as Canadian entry in figure 4-4 indicates. If no place can be discovered that way, consider what you know about the family that emigrated. How many family members might appear in church registers or civil registration records in Scotland before departure? If the surname is common, can the combination of several Christian names coupled with that surname in a family unit be used to improve the chances of recognition? Remember that civil registration indexes begin in 1855, and that the Scottish Church Records index, the Old Parochial Register Index©, and the International Genealogical Index (IGI; see chapter 5 and appendix A) are all excellent national finding aids. Are any identified family members known to have remained in Scotland around whom you could form a research plan?

Figure 4-4. 1861 Census Return, Brockville, Ontario.

CENSUS RECORD SHEET

date of census _1861_   Ref.No. _C1044_

Province: _Ontario_   County: _Leeds_

Town or Village _Brockville_   Road/Street/etc. _East Ward_

Date of Search _23 Oct '95_ Scope _East Ward only_ Condition of Record _good_

Name and Surname of Each Person	Rela-tionship	Status	Age of M	Age of F	Occupation	Birthplace	Religion
WARDROP John	head	m	43		Contractor	Scotland	Free Church
Catherine	wife	m		38		Scotland	"
Euphemia	dau.	s		18		Scotland	"
Robert	son	s	16			Ireland	"
Janett	dau.			14		Ireland	"
Alexander	son		12			Scotland	"
Catherine	dau.			8		Scotland	"
Margaret	dau.			6		Scotland	"
Ellen	dau.			4		Canada	"
John	son		1			Canada	"

Common names and vague geographic clues combined with having to work in a census that is not yet indexed make the search more difficult. Before embarking on a lengthy and possibly futile search through many census returns, examine the usefulness of other records. Once again, the most obvious ones are the indexes to civil registration and the parish register indexes. Directories, valuation rolls, and tax records may also help. Some cities or towns have unique records which could be of use. The Glasgow poor records are an excellent example (see chapter 10). In other words, pause long enough to do your homework, and be sure it includes consulting maps. Obtain a map of the parish boundaries and one for the abutting counties. Be alert to the fact that some parishes straddle county boundaries, but the enumeration for the entire parish will be within the county which included the larger part. In circumstances where you need to build a list of possible names, select a focal point and work methodically outward from there.

Always try to follow a family through more than one census over two, three, or four decades to compare their answers each time. Watch for inconsistencies in ages, children born in different locations, or the presence of a elderly relative, whose birthplace may be a bonus clue. The accuracy of any record is only as good as the information supplied by the informant. If the head of the household gave the answers for other members in one census and got it wrong, you could be working from incorrect data, which may have been given accurately to the enumerator of a subsequent census.

There are several possible explanations as to why an expected record fails to turn up. The individual could have been away census night. The authorities did not ask about absentees as these people would be enumerated at the temporary lodging. For a few locations, a return may simply not exist or the ink may have faded to the extent that the return is not readable. You may have missed the entry because you did not recognize it. Reconsider the possible spelling variations and name alterations. Include in this consideration that a single mother and her child will appear under different names in two returns if she married in the intervening period. Are you looking in the right place? Be prepared to go forward or back one census, to alter the scope of the search, or to check other sources.

If your own direct ancestors are proving elusive, it may be possible to work through the family of a sibling or other close relative. It may be easier, also, if a relatively common surname is offset by an unusual Christian name.

It is difficult to recommend one way to proceed; consider all the facts that have been discussed here as well as your computer equipment and skills and search options nearby. It will not be long before every census is accessible, index and images, for a reasonable charge from home or in some sort of research center. Some searches will cost little or nothing because the location is certain and the film can be viewed directly. A combined search, online and using microfilm, may sometimes be the best choice. Whatever you do, remember that you are the one person with the knowledge and instincts to recognize what fits, so do as much as you can yourself.

Directories and Electoral Rolls

Directories first appear in the major centers of Glasgow, Edinburgh Aberdeen and Perth. By the 1830s there are general trade publications for all of Scotland as well as a variety of regional, county and town directories. Directories published before the mid-1800s name prosperous farmers, merchants and manufacturers, civil and military professional people, landowners, and the nobility. These people either paid to be included or subscribed to purchase the publication. One useful example, referred to earlier, is the *Directory to Gentlemen's Seats, Villages, etc., in Scotland* (Findlay, 1843), which offers two different arrangements of people and places (see Figure 4-5). It is not until the 1870s that there is a really significant rate of inclusion of residents in what came to be known as post office directories.

The most obvious fact found in a directory is the address. Other information includes occupations, home and business locations and descriptions of each community. The details and styles of their arrangement vary. Some directories provide, for each town, a list of people by trade or occupation and an alphabetical list; others offer maps or guides to streets. You usually find information about churches, schools, burial grounds, markets or fairs, and transportation—times and routes of coaches, trains and coastal vessels.

By the time of the first census returns there are enough people entered into directories that they should be considered a likely source for checking family locations between census returns. Directories also can be used for the comparison of address information found on certificates of birth, marriage and death. With the help of a map, you can pinpoint a location, identify

Figure 4-5. Directory to Gentlemen's Seats, Villages, etc. in Scotland (by James Findlay, Edinburgh, 1843).

By Place

Villages, Seats, &c.	Post-Town.	County.	Occupants, &c.
Delnies	Nairn	Nairn	Mrs C. Simpson
Delvine House	Dunkeld	Perth	Sir J. M. M'Kenzie, Bt.
Demain	Inverness	Inverness	William Baillie
Denbie House	Ecclefechan	Dumfries	Richard Hetherington
Denbrae House	St Andrews	Fife	Mrs Wemyss
Denboig House	Newburgh	Fife	Mrs Stewart
Denhead	St Andrews	Fife	Village
Denhead	Coupar-Angus	Perth	David Duncan
Denmore	Aberdeen	Aberdeen	George C. Moir
Dennylolin	Killironie	Ayr	William Knox
Denny	Denny	Stirling	Village
Denock	St Andrews	Fife	T. E. MacRitchie
Derndleugh	Aberdeen	Aberdeen	William Simpson
Denny Mains	Denny	Stirling	Rev. John Dempster
Desorin	Denny	Stirling	James G. Adam
Dens	Peterhead	Aberdeen	William Arbuthnot
Dereulich	Dunkeld	Perth	Alexander Stewart
Derwig	Ballochroy	Argyle	Village
Desery Cottage	Mozart	Aberdeen	Sir F. Stovin, Bart.
Desery Shiel	Tarfund	Aberdeen	Sir F. Stovin, Bart.
Deskford	Cullen	Banff	Rev. George Innes
Deskin	Ballinalloch	Banff	James Stewart
Deuchar	Forfar	Forfar	James Marnie
Dewaha	Aberdeen	Aberdeen	John Blackie
Devon	Alloa	Clackmannan	Village
Devonshaw House	Dollar	Clackmannan	William Patton
Devnaside	Tillicoultry	Clackmannan	Village
Dewartown	Ford	Mid-Lothian	Village
Dhuurnig	Strazhaven	Lanark	Rev. Walter M'Leay
Dichmont	Uphall	Linlithgow	Walter Paris
Dillar Burn	Lesmahago	Lanark	Village
Dingleton	Melrose	Roxburgh	Village
Dinvin	Portpatrick	Wigtown	John Murdoch
Dinwiddie Lodge	Lockerbie	Dumfries	A. Maxwell
Dirleton Manse	Haddington	Haddington	Rev. John Ainslie
Dirnanean	Kirkmichael	Perth	Patrick Small
Disblair	Summerhill	Aberdeen	Rev. Dr Geo. Morrison
Disblair	Summerhill	Aberdeen	William Stephen
Dochfour	Inverness	Inverness	Evan Baillie
Dochgarroch	Inverness	Inverness	David Fraser
Doda	Leader	Berwick	Alexander Nisbet
Dollar Manse	Dollar	Clackmannan	Rev. Dr Andrew Mylne
Dollarfield	Dollar	Clackmannan	Robert Haig
Dollerie	Crieff	Perth	Anthony Murray
Dolls (Distillery)	Messtry	Lanark	M'Nab, Brothers, & Co.
Dolphinton Manse	Noblehouse	Lanark	Rev. Dr Afton
Dolphinton House	Dolphington	Lanark	Richard M'Kenzie
Dolphinston	Tranent	Haddington	Village
Don Cottage	Old Aberdeen	Aberdeen	Patrick Pirie
Donibristle (Colliery)	Crossgates *	Fife	Village
Donibristle	Aberdour	Fife	Grieve & Nasmyth
Donibristle Park	Aberdour	Fife	Earl Morny
Doonholm	Ayr	Ayr	Peter Murdoch
Doonpark	Castle Douglas	Kirkcudbright	John F. Ireland
Doonside	Ayr	Ayr	David Crawford
Dores	Inverness	Inverness	Rev. D. Fraser
Dorin	Strontian	Inverness	Rev. Ranald Rankin

By Occupant

Occupants, &c.	Villages, Seats, &c.	Post-Town.	County.
Russell, James	Newtown of Lathirsk	Freuchie	Fife
Russell, James	Aden House	Mintlaw	Aberdeen
Russell, James	Kinraid	Linmig	Inverness
Russell, Rev. Robert	Yarrow Manse	Selkirk	Selkirk
Russell, Rev. Robert	Hayston	Cupar	Fife
Russell, Robert	Seggie	Milnathort	Kinross
Russell, Walter	Kincraig House	Elie	Fife
Russell, William	Glenduckie	Newburgh	Fife
Russell, Miss Isabella	Kincraig	Elie	Fife
Rust, Rev. James	Kootyholm	Canonbie	Dumfries
Rutherford, Rev. G. B.	Manse of Slains	Ellon	Aberdeen
Rutherford, George	Howran Manse	Kelso	Roxburgh
Rutherford, Rev. James	Sunnyside	Melrose	Roxburgh
Rutherford, James	Violet Bank	Lauder	Berwick
Rutherford, Miss J.	Channelkirk	Annan	Dumfries
Rutherford, A.w. M.P.	Ashintilly Castle	Kirkmichael	Perth
Rutherford, Wm. Oliver	Craigiehall	Cramond	Linlithgow
Ruthven, Lord	Edgerton	Jedburgh	Roxburgh
	Freeland	Bridge of Earn	Perth
Sadler, Thomas	Norton Mains	Ratho	Mid-Lothian
Sage, Rev. Donald	Resolis Manse	Cromarty	Cromarty
Saltoun, Lady	Philorth	Fraserburgh	Aberdeen
Saltoun, Lady	Ness Castle	Inverness	Inverness
Samuel, James	Broom House	Winchburgh	Linlithgow
Samwell, Thomas F.	Broomhill House	Lasswade	Mid-Lothian
Sanderson, David	Kirkwood House	Ecclefechan	Dumfries
Sanderson, Mrs	Augusfield	Aberdeen	Aberdeen
Sandford, E. D.	Balmuto	Kirkcaldy	Fife
Sandlands, Capt. W.	Barneyhill	Dunbar	Haddington
Sandlands, Wm. N.	Couston	Bathgate	Linlithgow
Sandison, William	Auchenelech	Skene	Aberdeen
Sanda, Thomas	Swanbister	Kirkwall	Orkney
Saugster, Rev. John	Gervald	Haddington	Haddington
Sawers, Peter	Nether Kirkfield	Haddington	Haddington
Scarlett, Hon. R. C.	Inverlochy	Fort-William	Inverness
Scarth, Robert	Papdale House	Kirkwall	Orkney
Schoular, Arthur	Over Inins	Kilfhuan	Argyle
Scobie, Mrs Mackay	Toynhead	Durness	Sutherland
Scobie, Miss H. C.	Keoldale	Loanhead	Mid-Lothian
Scoon, William	Andver	Durness	Sutherland
Scotland, John	Greenwells	August	Roxburgh
Scott, Adam	Glendouglas	Melrose	Roxburgh
Scott, Alexander	Tulloch	Jedburgh	Roxburgh
Scott, Rev. Andrew	Glasshillie	Fort-Augustus	Inverness
Scott, Andrew	Craiglockhart	Lockearron	Ross
Scott, Carteret George	Bonkle Manse	Slateford	Mid-Lothian
Scott, Charles C.	Etrick Bank	Walston	Lanark
Scott, David	Makey	Selkirk	Roxburgh
Scott, David	Hawkhill	Balerno	Mid-Lothian
Scott, David	East Dalry	Edinburgh	Mid-Lothian
Scott, Donald	Newton	Largs	Ayr
Scott, Fitzmaurice	Inverquarry	Chance Inn	Mid-Lothian
	Seggieden	Inergory	Forfar
		Perth	Inverness
			Perth

cross streets and pick out features of a neighborhood. They are, in other words, helpful either as back up or as pointers to other records.

Directories are worthy of consideration because, although not numerous for Scotland, they are quite accessible. They are found in local collections in archives and libraries in Scotland. They are also found in significant numbers in the FHL on microfilm and microfiche (do a place search and then find the "Directories" topic); and many are online. The databases at Ancestry.com include a set of material titled *UK and US Directories 1680 to 1830* and it includes directories published in Scotland up to 1830. Places listed in the description of the Scottish contents are: Aberdeen, Angus, Ayr, Dundee, Edinburgh, Glasgow, Greenock, Paisley and Renfrewshire. Some of these place names are towns and cities and others are counties. There are usually more places included in the individual titles, such as Leith within Edinburgh volumes.

When consulting directories be sure to ready the full description of the contents in the front, examine the layout, and remember that there was a time lag between when the information was collected and when it appeared in print. In addition, keep in mind that not every household or building is listed—you should rely on the census or the post-1855 valuation rolls for more complete listings.

Another possible method of checking the presence of an ancestor in a particular community is to consult the voters' lists. The first parliamentary reform bill was passed in 1832. This was a very tentative step toward universal adult suffrage. It took two more such bills in 1868 and 1884 and the Householders of Scotland Act of 1881 to significantly extend the list of male voters and to put women on any lists at all at the local and county council level. Universal suffrage did not occur until 1930. Before 1832, those who were entitled to vote in parliamentary elections were required to meet a property value qualification, which excluded most of the population. The first change in 1832 set the property limit at £10.

Despite the limitations in their scope, voting lists can be useful. First, they were made up on an annual basis; thus, they provide a means of checking how long someone remained in one place. Before 1918 the register explains the qualification to vote. You will find the occupations of those named, whether they are owners or tenants, and property descriptions.

Women, able to vote in local elections from 1882, were listed separately. They had to meet the property qualifications and be either unmarried or not living with their husbands.[2] If you are interested in more detail on the reform bills and changing qualifications, read the introduction to *Electoral Registers Since 1832* (Gibson and Rogers, 1989).

From the Union in 1707 until the first Reform Bill in 1832, the vote in the countryside (as opposed to the burghs) was much more restricted in Scotland than in England and Wales. There were fewer than 3,000 voters in 1788 and every one of them, along with the way each voted, was listed in *A View of the Political State of Scotland in the Last Century* (Adam, 1887), which can be found in the LDS collection on microfilm. Similar volumes described the results in 1790, 1811, and 1820. Who voted and how they cast their ballots could be recorded because the vote was public. The secret ballot was not introduced until 1872.

The names of electors may appear in lists of freeholders, in lists of voters, or in poll results. Some are regarded as national resources and others as local, so the FHLC Locality entry may appear under either the county or the burgh name, with the topic heading of Voters' Registers. To assess the survival and availability of these records in Scotland, use the resource guides found in the bibliography.

For the purposes of some searches, the need to consult these sources may appear to be minimal; the dates don't fit or your ancestors were unlikely to have been tradesmen or merchants, voted or owned property. Do not dismiss them too readily because you do not know everything about your ancestor and his ups and downs, or collateral members of his family. There are other lists of inhabitants or heads of households that better fall under the heading of taxes; they are discussed in chapter 9.

Newspapers

Newspapers have long been used for their fund of factual information. Dipping into old newspapers is akin to lifting the lid of an ancient trunk in the attic. There is a fascinating mix of fact, opinion, and odd detail which throws considerable light on the lives and viewpoints of our ancestors and their communities. Content and opinion, dictated as they were by a desire to sell newspapers, can become an object of study in themselves.

The first national papers of significance were the *Edinburgh Evening Courant*, 1718, and the *Caledonian Mercury*, 1720; the first regional paper was the *Glasgow Journal* 1741. Substantial news reporting was slow to develop until spurred on by the French Revolution and issues like electoral reform. By 1800 Edinburgh had seven newspapers. Scottish publications are described in detail in *The Waterloo Directory of Scottish Newspapers and Periodicals 1800-1900* (North, 1989). This is available in the FHL, or check for it at major university libraries. Comments on the content and point of view of a newspaper may run to several hundred words, and publication dates, present locations, and publishers and editors names are all given.

The *Directory of Scottish Newspapers* (Ferguson, 1984) indicates the location of surviving newspaper files, and The National Library of Scotland maintains a list of the periodicals which it holds. Any one of these sources will guide your search for relevant publications, and an inquiry to the local library in Scotland will produce information on local holdings. Some journals and papers have been indexed. Two examples are: the FHL holds a copy of the index to *The Stirling Journal and Advertiser,* and *Family History Sources in Kirkcaldy Central Library* (Campbell, 1994) mentions a microfiche index to names from the *Fifeshire Advertiser* 1845-1865. Many libraries maintain indexes or clipping files for the local newspaper. A singular incident, or the name of a prominent person, or the construction of a significant building, these are the sorts of things that would have been classified and clipped for deposit in a file. The other source in the United Kingdom for Scottish newspapers is the British Library newspaper collection at Colindale in the north of London. This is a heavily used facility and you should opt for doing newspaper searches in local libraries when that is possible.

Scottish newspapers on microfilm can be found in reference libraries around Scotland and the UK as a whole and in countries where there were many Scottish immigrants. Check online library catalogs for holdings. The Internet Library of Early Journals includes at least twenty years of the Edinburgh publication, *Blackwood's Magazine*.

Many of you may be familiar with the *Scots Magazine*; its modern format dates from 1929 and copies sometimes turn up in used bookstores. Early issues are harder to find. In the first place, publication was not continuous and there was a break of 50 years in the 1800s. It began publication in 1739, and for a long time included a section of birth, marriage and death announcements. Copies are in major libraries; Colindale in London and the FHL (1739–1817 on microfilm) being two locations outside Scotland.

Another possible source of information can be found within the pages of genealogical journals. On the simplest level, you could consult the journals collected by the library of the genealogical society where you live. You may have subscribed for some time to the journal of a family history society in Scotland. Have you recently checked your back issues or the index? Most journals issue one every two or three years. Finally, there is the PERiodical Source Index (PERSI), published by the Allen County (Indiana) Public Library Foundation in cooperation with the Genealogical Department of the Allen County Public Library. This index is in two parts, 1847-1985 and 1986 onward. It is based on subject and uses three basic categories, locality, research methodology, and families. It could save time and effort, either through a direct reference to your family or through a how-to article which addresses an important issue. PERSI is available on microfiche at most Family History Centers (a research outline is available).

Finally, current newspapers can be of assistance. Editors usually publish letters from overseas requesting a reply from descendants of a local person. Addresses are obtained by reference to *Willings Press Guide*, widely available in reference libraries.

Conclusion

Any one of these resources has the potential to create crucial links with other records and to provide basic genealogical facts. The inhabitants lists may be used to focus on place and time, to check how long someone remained at a location, or to confirm whether or not you are tracking the right person. The records together, and some of them alone, span a considerable period of time, and also provide insights into social history. This in itself is reason enough to incorporate them into your research whenever possible. By the time you have read the *Statistical Accounts*, a book on the history of the town or county, consulted maps and gazetteers, and gleaned what you can from these records, you will have the evidence to recreate a meaningful impression of the lives and times of your nineteenth-century Scottish ancestors.

Notes
1. Johnson, 1997, 1-2.
2. Sinclair, 1997, 127.

Summary—Census Returns

1. Select the name(s), place, and census year to be searched.

2. Does the search require the use of an index? If so, for which year or years? Is the index at ScotlandsPeople, on CD, or available in some other form, e.g., on microfiche from a society? Check the society web page and/or the appropriate page at Genuki.

3. Decide whether to view census records at New Register House, as online images or transcripts or on microfilm.

4. IF not using the GROS resources, check what is available through a local Family History Center and/or libraries and archives.

5. If using FHL microfilms, 1841 to 1891, begin with the FHLC, using the place search to find the entry for the parish/district and select the "Census records" topic and then the appropriate year. The 1881 index provides the film reference.

6. For densely populated areas, 1841 to 1871, watch the GROS website for information about more indexes becoming available.

7. When the subject fails to appear in the expected location verify that all finding aids have been examined, all search options used (e.g., wild card symbols) and then reassess your facts. A survey search of all people with the same surname may be an option.

8. Other useful tactics include searching for a collateral relation who had an unusual forename, reading the returns immediately before and after for the same place and browsing through the rest of the district.

Summary—Directories, Voters' Lists, and Newspapers

1. Jot down the specific reasons for seeking these records and add whether electoral rolls, directories, or newspapers may supply the desired information. Pay attention to starting dates.

2. Investigate what has survived and what is readily accessible; the options include the holdings in the FHL, items in online databases (some may involve access charges), items sold by family history societies or genealogy publishers.

3. Consult other source lists such as the relevant Gibson guide (see bibliography), newspaper lists, and websites of libraries and archives. For newspapers include the online catalog at the British Library Newspaper Library, Colindale, and for other sources check the Scottish Archives Network.

5 • Records of the Church of Scotland

f your ancestors emigrated prior to 1855, the Church of Scotland registers and their finding aids are the first resource to consult. The records of baptism, marriage, and burial of the Church of Scotland—the Presbyterian Church—are referred to as the Old Parochial Registers or the Old Parish Registers (OPRs). You may have heard that access is a simple matter, particularly for births and marriages. This is so because the central collection is located in New Register House, and its computer search routine is user-friendly. The index, and the digital images to which it will soon be fully linked, is available online for a fee. OPRs are also a part of The International Genealogical Index (IGI), available free on the Web, in the Family History Library (FHL) and Family History Centers. Yet another version, Scottish Church Records, is on computer in the FHL and Family History Centers. Several microfiche indexes exist and can be found in many record offices and libraries. Access is not an issue, nevertheless, problems are not entirely eliminated: some records were lost, others have gaps, some entries are very brief, secession church records are not included, and human error remains a factor. This chapter will help you deal with the difficulties.

Historical Background

Until the middle of the sixteenth century, Scotland was a Roman Catholic country. Bishops, abbots, monasteries (some of you may have seen the magnificent ruins at Jedburgh and Melrose), dioceses, and church courts were the order of the day; however, the church was corrupt and unpopular. The catalyst for change was the return of John Knox from Geneva in 1559. Many years of turmoil followed during the reign of Mary, Queen of Scots. When she went into captivity in England in 1568, the new Protestant religion was firmly established. The Roman Catholic Church had been abolished in 1560. As had been the case in England and Wales a generation earlier, the dissolution of the old system meant massive destruction, including the loss of nearly all the records, paintings, and illuminated manuscripts.

James VI acceded to the Scottish throne in 1567 and that of England, as James I, in 1603. His reign was relatively peaceful, although not free of dispute. King James was a confirmed Protestant who nonetheless believed that the church should be governed by bishops. Astute politically, he accepted for a time in Scotland a system of synods and general assemblies. Once he became king of England as well, James sought to reduce the authority of these organizations and to increase the number of bishops. He died in the midst of this struggle over church governance.

Turmoil returned with the accession of Charles I in 1625. A devout Anglican, hence a supporter of bishoprics and patronage, Charles wanted to bring the Scottish church in line with the Church of England; however, he lacked understanding of the mood of the country, and he was politically inept. His complete insensitivity to the situation was revealed when he finally visited Scotland in 1633. Charles had himself crowned King of Scotland in St. Giles Cathedral according to Anglican rites and went on to appoint a new Bishop of Edinburgh. A prayer book was commissioned to be written for Scotland, and the presbyteries were abolished. In 1637 in Edinburgh, a riot occurred when the new liturgy was used at St. Giles. Soldiers had to be sent north in an attempt to enforce compliance. The Scots responded with the National Covenant, a document that spelled out the Acts of Parliament, which had created, what was to them, the true religion. The National Covenant initiated a tremendous common cause amongst the Scottish people at home and abroad. Supporters came to be called Covenanters. Insensitive to the consequences of his actions, Charles persisted in the use of force in what came to be known as the Bishops' Wars, which went on long enough to overlap the opening battles of the English Civil War in 1642.

The role of Scotland in the English Civil War was complex and is outside the scope of this discussion. Suffice to say it was the Scots who turned Charles I over to Oliver Cromwell. Charles was executed in 1649, and by 1652 Cromwell was in control of Scotland. His intention was to allow freedom of worship to all except Anglicans (known in Scotland as Episcopalians—"episcopal" means "by bishops") and Roman Catholics, a position that angered the General Assembly of the Presbyterian Church. For the people of Scotland, the discontent was directed at the military administration of the country, and when that ended with the restoration of Charles II in 1660, the response was enthusiastic. This good will was short lived. All Scottish legislation back to 1633 was abolished, and rule by bishops returned. Three hundred ministers refused to recognize this action and abandoned their churches. Illegal services, or Conventicles, were held anywhere people could meet. Resistance grew, and positions hardened. The insurrection of the Covenanters was countered severely by the authorities. The 1680s came to be known as "The Killing Time."

Political expediency produced a solution. William and Mary came to the British throne in 1689 at the invitation of Parliament after James II had fled into exile. (James had succeeded his brother in 1685 and was openly a Roman Catholic.) Under William, the Presbyterian system was restored and the established Church of Scotland assumed control of church lands. Episcopalian incumbent ministers were permitted to remain in place if they took the new oath of allegiance. None of the bishops did. In the west of Scotland, two hundred ministers were turned out of their churches with no means of support. In other areas, where Presbyterian sentiment was less strong, transition to new ministers took much longer. The Episcopalian Church of Scotland is considered to date from 1690.

It is interesting to note that the Established Churches of Scotland and England were different, and both repressed the other faith on either side of the border while at the same time being governed by one monarch and one administration in London. This situation was not altered by the Act of Union in 1707, which guaranteed that Presbyterianism was the established Church of Scotland.

In the wake of the two Jacobite rebellions of the eighteenth century, persecution of Episcopalians, who were regarded as supporters of James III (the Old Pretender) and Bonnie Prince Charlie, grew. It was not until one hundred years after it began, and six years after the death of Bonnie Prince Charlie, that the repression finally came to an end in 1792.

The Presbyterian Church experienced internal difficulties in the eighteenth and nineteenth centuries. In a nutshell, the dispute centered around the issue of patronage and whether or not the local church could select its own minister. A number of churches seceded in 1733, and in 1843, a large number of congregations broke away to form the Free Church of Scotland. So significant was this breach that it became known as the Disruption. These splits had a considerable impact on the comprehensiveness of the records of the Presbyterian Church of Scotland. For the twelve years prior to the introduction of civil registration, the OPRs are unreliable because a large percentage of the population belonged to a secessionist or nonconformist church and did not record their baptisms, marriages, or burials in the OPRs. Not until 1929, did these groups reunite, when the British Parliament at Westminster gave up any authority over the Church of Scotland. A flow chart of church formations, mergers, advances, and declines first appeared in *A Church History of Scotland* (Burleigh, 1960) and has since been reproduced in several other volumes including *Tracing Scottish Ancestors* (Bigwood, 1999) and *Collins Encyclopaedia of Scotland* (J. & J. Keay, 1994).

Major Indexes—On Computer

Now, in early 2003, there are more ways than ever to explore the data in Scottish Old Parochial Registers. Looking only at the biggest indexes, your options on computer are the indexes at New Register House, their online counterpart at ScotlandsPeople, the IGI online at FamilySearch, and the IGI and Scottish Church Records on computer at LDS facilities. You therefore have plenty of opportunity—at home, in a record repository, or anywhere there is a computer—to use several comprehensive index resources. It is not accurate to describe them as clear-cut choices because there are slight differences and you may have to refer to more than one.

No matter how hard you have tried to discover a place, or even a county of origin, you may be starting your search with only a name and an approximate date, one that is much earlier than 1855, the start of civil registration. In this situation, computerized indexes to the OPRs offer a chance of success. All of Scotland can be searched at once for an individual or simply the surname; there is no need to guess the county or parish, or to plod through all counties one at a time. At ScotlandsPeople by the end of 2003 you will be able to search an OPR burials database as well.

The IGI and Scottish Church Records make use of their own system of similar names. When you are using the IGI online at FamilySearch, there are many rules associated with combinations of search criteria. You are advised to read the "Tips on How to Search the International Genealogical Index," a link that can be found on the search page. The use of exact spellings provides a good example; if selected, middle names are taken into account but you are not permitted to add the person's parents or spouse, the year or the event. In spite of the many forbidden combinations, the IGI at FamilySearch permits a search for a given name alone; test this out with any unusual one such as Balthazar or Valentine; you can also limit dates and specify a county.

The ScotlandsPeople system is less complex. The search engine assumes that exact spelling is to be used unless the Soundex option is selected or wild card symbols are incorporated into the name. Soundex, by the way, is the option to choose when a Mc or Mac name is involved but it is not available at New Register House. No matter which computer system you are using, read about surnames in advance (see chapter 1) and check available help sections. What this all means is that name searches and the logic behind them vary. This can trip you up but it also can work to your advantage. Be prepared to try different indexes and try the different name options that each version offers.

At ScotlandsPeople you must always keep the page credit system in mind. Fortunately, the number of hits is indicated first and you are asked to confirm the expenditure of credits. Up to twenty-five listings appear on a single page and a page consumes one credit regardless of whether it has one name or more on it; credits are purchased thirty at a time. At FamilySearch, where the IGI online is found, 200 entries appear at a time; if there are more, then "next" can be selected to view additional listings, also up to 200 at a time. Before beginning your search, verify that your search is specific to the IGI and not across all resources together.

Searches can be made with more focused parameters. A first name can be added, the parish can be specified and dates narrowed. The ScotlandsPeople search system permits a search of the whole country or a specific parish; soon the "county" option should be added. Also in the planning is a vicinity search. This will focus on the named parish and others adjacent to it—useful because it covers an area regardless of county lines. At FamilySearch you can specify a search of one county but not of one parish unless you find the batch number first. Scots Origins and Hugh Wallis' site make this easy; see appendix A. Using the DOS-based IGI or Scottish Church Records indexes in a Family History Center, you can perform a search across one or several counties.

All computer databases have some mechanism for linking the principal name to that of another individual. ScotlandsPeople has a field for a second surname, labeled a "parent name" (i.e., the mother's maiden name). The IGI and Scottish Church Records indexes make the link to the given name or full name of the spouse or parents, and call the feature a "parent search." When a marriage or a baptism has been selected, it is possible to ask for all children of parents with the same names. This phraseology is deliberate since it is possible that two or more sets of parents had the same names, in which case you must sort out the families. Bear in mind that a child may be missed if either parent is listed differently in one entry; it is best to begin with the full name of the father and the first name only of the mother. You can create a variation of this type of search at ScotlandsPeople, but it is less precise because you cannot give the full name of the father and the second name is the surname only. Results in all cases include the full names of both parents, provided this information appears in the register entry.

Collecting entries for baptisms and marriages, and utilizing the parent search feature, you can construct a possible line of descent, putting some stress on the word *possible*. None of these indexes links events[1]. You will see no indication that the individual baptized, say in 1751, is the same one with the same name who married in the same parish twenty-five years later. Neither do these indexes point out that a child died before reaching adulthood. All a search accomplishes is a match of data to search criteria. The index search is a preliminary step. To be sure of your conclusions and to be sure that you have all the information contained in the parish register, you must look at a copy of the entry. You should go beyond that and, particularly where there are several possibilities, bring them all forward in time to find the fit. The eventual appearance of a burial index at ScotlandsPeople will help but looking at copies of the register remains the best way to solve a puzzle and get the full picture.

Major Indexes—Other Formats

The discussion to this point has focused on computer databases of one kind or another. You need to be aware of the non-electronic formats as well, the IGI and the Old Parochial Registers Index on microfiche in Family History Centers, the FHL and in many society and public libraries. Microfiche sets will be kept at New Register House as well. If entries cannot be found with a computer, something may turn up on fiche. Content is not appreciably different; the benefits come more from the alternative views and the different arrangements they provide. Their main characteristics are described here; for more details see appendix A.

Until a few years ago everyone used the IGI on microfiche. The edition in Family History Centers is dated 1992, but age is not an issue because newer editions contain more submissions from individuals and not from official extraction work. Scanning fiche, arranged by county, can in some circumstances be quicker than a computer search. This format shows baptisms and marriages together, making it possible to view all entries for one surname in one county. The frames or pages on the fiche can be copied and later highlighted, and you can then plot name frequency or distribution.

The OPR Index is another interesting option. The layout of information on each fiche is similar to that of the IGI. There are, however, four sets of fiche for every county: surname index to christenings, given-name index to christenings, surname index to marriages, and given-name index to marriages. Content is focused on the OPRs with no entries submitted by individuals, and the data was taken from a better and more recent filming. This fiche format given-name arrangement is easy to work with, an alternative to the online search in the IGI.

Other Finding Aids

Indexes and/or transcriptions to limited selections of OPRs can be found in the *British Vital Records Index* (2nd ed., 2002), in society publications, for sale on CD-ROM, at a few geographically specific websites, among the collection of parish register copies at the Society of Genealogists in London, and through some pay services such as Ancestry.com.

The *British Vital Records Index* is a collection of miscellaneous records, mainly baptisms and marriages, from England, Scotland, Ireland, and Wales. The Scottish portion consists of nearly 2.5 million events, only 41,080 of which are marriages. Some counties have lots of data, notably Midlothian (over half a million), Lanark and Ayrshire, while others have just a handful, four from Nairn, twelve from Kinross, and twenty from Sutherland. It is possible that some of the entries are also in the IGI. Despite these detractions, the size of the database, the flexibility of the search tool and the inexpensive price make it an attractive resource for most people researching in Scotland. It contains a mix of entries from the Church of Scotland, secession and other congregations.

People have been transcribing parish registers for a long time. The Society of Genealogists has a huge collection and Scotland is quite well represented. At their website you can check the dates for christenings, marriages and burials for each parish in a series of online lists, arranged according to county. The volumes of transcripts, some indexed and some chronological, can be consulted in their library in London. Published records turn up in many other libraries too, in fact, almost anywhere. Look at catalogs for reference libraries near you. A check of the FHLC will show you that some are in the FHL.

On the Internet, use the county pages at the Genuki website and the Scotland vital records section of Cyndi's List to look for church register transcripts and finding aids. Ancestry has some parish register transcripts within their online database subscription service; these can also be purchased on CD-ROM (*Scottish Church Records*, 4 vols., 2001). At the website a free search, particularly using the advanced option, gives you some idea of the number of hits for a particular name.

A Scottish National Burial Index is in progress. The intention is to incorporate all pre-1855 deaths and burials from the OPRs as well as mortcloth (see definitions on page 87) entries within OPRs (perhaps a few from kirk sessions as well); about 65 percent of Scottish parishes have some surviving records. Member societies of the Scottish Association of Family

History Societies are doing the work according to their own priorities. Some county lists have appeared and are for sale by the society involved. Other societies are hard at work and a few have not yet started. The Federation of Family History Societies sells the first edition of a similar project for England on CD-ROM; as many Scots moved south, this may be worth consulting.

Thinking about Indexes

No matter which index you start with or which one becomes your favorite, every successful search depends on several factors. To readily identify the most likely entries, you need an unusual name or some identifying details—a middle name, the mother's maiden name, a narrow date range, and the names of siblings, place of residence, or occupation. It is important that you keep track of the parameters used in each computer or microfiche search and of all the facts associated with each noted event. It may also be necessary to use other records to find the vital details or to solve some relationship problems.

Computers appear to remove boundaries because you can search across the entire country; nevertheless, the need to be familiar with boundaries never goes away. When a record isn't there or when there are two almost identical entries located a few miles apart, it is essential to have a spatial awareness of the problem. For every search you should look up the names of adjacent parishes and counties. With a targeted area, you can do this in advance but with a general search you consult the maps after finding likely entries. If you are searching methodically across a growing area the structure of parish and county lines can be used to define the stages of the search; along the way, remember to note dates of surviving registers. These details are in the Family History Library Catalog (FHLC) entry, at the GROS website, and in the *Key to the Parochial Registers of Scotland* (Bloxham and Metcalfe, 1979).

There will be times when thoroughness does not produce a result. It may be lack of records, selecting search parameters that don't quite fit or human error in the indexing. It is also possible that the event happened but was never recorded in the registers of the Church of Scotland. Turbulent times in the 1600s and 1700s may have interrupted record keeping; and, although the Church of Scotland minister was supposed to record events in the lives of local families who worshipped elsewhere, this did not always happen. In addition, in large urban areas in the 1800s, many people never went to church. In some instances the event happened but was recorded much later. This delayed recording happened mainly though not exclusively, with births, which were subsequently registered in retrospect after the beginning of civil registration. They can be found in the Register of Neglected Entries, in the computer index at New Register House, and online at ScotlandsPeople. A copy of the register is in the FHL; many neglected entries are within the *British Vital Records Index*.

With extensive searches you should review the contents of all the indexes and the advantages each has to offer. Some things can be done with one and not with another, and it is wise to consult more than one index or more than one format. This discussion began with the largest computer databases available because, for most people, a search starts on the Internet at home or in a Family History Center; however, bear in mind that occasionally the perspective gained from a fiche search can help. More discussion on these indexes can be found in appendix A.

The Registers

The earliest Scottish parish registers date from the sixteenth century, but only a very small number have survived from that era. Twenty-one parish registers contain entries before 1600; 100 years later, the number of extant registers increased to more than a third of the more than 900 parishes in the country. The starting dates are earlier and the survival rate is greater for Lowland parishes.

Entries in the registers vary from the virtually useless to the extremely valuable, incorporating details of occupation, address, and relationships. Ministers were never given any directives regarding what was to be noted in the registers. This omission left procedures open to interpretation and personality. A selection of entries illustrating this variety appears in figure 5-1.

Generally, you will find that a baptismal or birth entry (remember to note which it is) provides the date of the entry, date of birth or baptism (sometimes both), the name of the child, and the names of the parents. Occasionally occupation is provided; in the registers of the parish of Dun, among the nine entries for the children of William Ford, only once was his occupation mentioned. Sometimes relatives are named (for example, the

---

Figure 5-1. Sample OPR Entries.

Burial, in the parish of Montrose:
With the year noted at the top (1825), three columns gave date, name, and age, but for children only the date and name were given:

April 29	James Ford	61

Marriage, in the parish of Montrose:
With the year noted at the top (1759), two columns gave date and parties:

July 29 And^r Ford, Mariner and Katharine Ritchie both of this Parish were contracted

Baptism, in the parish of Dun:
With the name in the margin, entries were extensive:

James Ford of Finhaven had a daughter born of his wife Catharine Aitkin from the Island of St. Croix at Broomley Parish of Dun on the 5th February and baptised there on the 28th of said month by the Rev. John Aitkin Mrs. Ford's uncle of North Tarry, Minister of St. Vigeans named Margaret Cornelia Ford

These three transcripts are good examples, showing as they do very little detail in the burial, a fairly typical marriage entry, and the bonus detail that sometimes appears.

---

sponsors), and the relationship is shown. In nearly all marriage entries, the parishes of the bride and groom are included, along with their names, the date of proclamation, and/or the date of the marriage. Occasionally you will find the occupation of the groom, the name of the bride's father, and (rarely) the name of the groom's father. The unlucky researcher will find merely the name of the groom and the fee paid. In those parishes that recorded them, and many did not, burial entries are pretty much as you see, or you may find reference to the fee paid for the mortcloth (a pall used during burial service, although not for small children, often donated by a prosperous parishioner). The kirk session collected a payment for the use of the mortcloth as a means of raising money for the poor.[2] There is better hope of finding useful information in a monumental inscription.

Missing records, gaps caused by more than the slow start, are also a problem. Fire, vermin, and damp took their toll, but there were other reasons for a lack of record entries. First, there were the dissenting and breakaway congregations that did not record events in the mainstream registers. After 1843, there were more of these than not. Second, there was the eleven-year period when the Stamp Act was in force over the whole of Great Britain (1783-1794). The fee was set at three pence (3d) per entry, and ministers who failed to collect it were liable to be fined. There was a loophole, however. If the minister simply stopped recording in his register, he could not be fined for failure to collect. This was precisely what some ministers did. Third, there was the period from 1633 to 1689, from the first attempt by Charles I to impose the Episcopalian church structure and form of worship to the accession of William and Mary. The uncertainties of war, uprisings, and changing doctrine interfered with the regular keeping of registers.

Viewing microfilms of OPRs is a good idea though the numbers of researchers doing this is going to decline with the arrival of online index entries linked to register images. Those with a Family History Center nearby can order films on loan and scroll through the register page by page. As you become accustomed to the handwriting you will be able to pick out entries that might have been indexed incorrectly. Whatever method you choose to find register entries, be certain the search within a parish is thorough and for all members of a family. It may even be necessary to work out the structure of more than one family of the same surname to identify the correct line. Watch for and note any occupations, locations, or addresses.

Sometimes after collecting entries from one or more registers, there is no lack of information, but rather too much, and imprecise information at that. Again, considering the family of Fords in Forfar, the problem is apparent. Figure 5-2 shows a summarized list of entries found in three different registers.

Resist the temptation to draw conclusions not founded on fact. In this list, it would be tempting to conclude that Andrew is the son of William Foord and Elizabeth Manne, and likewise, that James, son of Andrew and Katherine, born 1765, is the same person as the father of all those children baptized at Dun. These facts may be used as the basis for further search, but more work must be done to prove such points conclusively.

Many of the registers reveal additional information, such as the lengthy baptism entry shown in figure 5-1. The register volume may also

Figure 5-2. Ford/Foord Entries from Three Parishes.

1728, June 6	William Foord and Elizabeth Manne (St. Vigeans)
1729, 28 Sep.	David, son of William Foord & Elizabeth Manne, St. Vigeans
1738, Oct. 29	Mary, dau. of William Foord & Elizabeth Manne, St. Vigeans
1759, July 29	And^r. Ford, Mariner, and Katherine Ritchie both of this parish (Montrose)
1760, Aug. 2	David, son of Andrew Ford & Katharine Ritchie, Montrose
1765, May 14	James, son of Andrew Ford & Katharine Ritchie, Montrose
1766, Feb. 14	Jean, dau. of Andrew Ford & Katharine Ritchie, Montrose
1768, Dec. 21	George son of Andrew Ford & Katharine Ritchie, Montrose
1804, 26 Feb.	James Ford & Catharine Aitkin, Montrose*
1804, 28 Feb.	James Ford & Catharine Aitkin, St. Vigeans*
1805, 30 Jan.	Charles, son of James Ford & Catherine Aitkin, Dun
1806, 28 Feb.	Margaret Cornelia, dau, of James Ford and Catharine Aitkin, Dun
1807, 18 Aug.	William, son of James Ford & Catherine Aitkin, Dun
1808, 26 Dec. Dun	Cornelia Beckman, dau. of James Ford & Catharine Aitkin,
1810, 13 June	Georgina, dau. of James Ford & Catharine Aitkin, Dun
1813, 5 Feb.	Catharine, dau. of James Ford & Catharine Aitkin, Dun
1814, 27 April	Elizabeth Duncan, dau. of James Ford & Catharine Aitkin, Dun
1816, 10 Jan.	James, son of James Ford & Catharine Aitkin, Dun
1816, 27 Feb.	Maria Hartley, dau. of James Ford & Catharine Aitkin, Dun

*Proclamations of marriage were commonly read in the parish of the bride and the groom.

Note: These are point-form summaries of the register entries. Among sources to consult next to help sort out these families are kirk sessions for the parishes of Dun, Montrose, and St. Vigeans; testaments; services of heirs; and burgh records for Montrose.

incorporate burials, another possible source of help in family reconstruction. When you have finished, but before you decide that you have extracted every possible baptism, marriage, or burial entry, return to the indexes. Enter the names of couples in a parent search and check your list-ings against what appears on the monitor. You may have missed an entry or a child may have been born in another parish or county. You never know when a sibling may prove to be the important link to an earlier generation.

Monumental Inscriptions

Visiting graveyards is a common pastime among family historians, and when a visit is impossible, a search for the list of monumental inscrip-tions becomes the substitute. All graveyards have not been transcribed; many stones have been removed, broken, and worn smooth before their messages could be noted. However, much has been done and is being done to record the cemeteries of Scotland. To learn more about Scottish grave-yards, their history, and the types of monuments, look for a copy of *Understanding Scottish Graveyards* (Willsher, 1995).

Churchyards have stories to tell other than those of the deceased. The churchyard area was put to good use, perhaps as grounds for a trade fair or to graze the minister's cow, and many churchyards witnessed the actions of the body snatchers—those who stole the bodies of the recently deceased to sell for anatomical and medical examination. Body-snatching became such a problem that many parishes took steps to foil the criminals. They built high walls or morthouses (where the body could be locked away before the service), installed watchtowers, or used mortsafes (a locked cof-fin case buried with the coffin and removed much later once decomposi-tion was well under way).

The most informative gravestone inscriptions are found in the Lowland parishes. The majority of Highland stones were carved only with initials and dates. Burial within the church itself came to an end with the Reformation. Nevertheless, the titled and the wealthy still found ways to create their special monuments, perhaps by adding an aisle or building a vault against the church. The poor of the parish, the "stranger poor" (e.g., an unknown vagrant), and the unbaptized were usually buried on the north side of the churchyard.

Monumental inscriptions (MIs) are not hard to find. The Scottish Genealogy Society publishes a series of volumes for gravestone inscriptions that predate 1855, and they have a list of those volumes that can be pur-chased. Sample text is shown in figure 5-3. They will also check for an indi-

---

Figure 5-3. Text of a Monumental Inscription.

upon a flag s. side of the church. Wm. Ford esq. 3.8.1728 19.6.1816 New Style (see Jervise ms 530 SAS Lib. p. 905): Fords were at one time extensive linen manufacturers here, one of them, possibly a son of the above, bought estate of Finhaven disposed of by his trustees in 1817—his sister married first Mr. Renny Strachan of Seton, next Mr. Duncan of Parkhill

Extracted from *Pre-1855 Gravestone Inscriptions in Angus, Vol. 2, The Environs of Arbroath and Montrose*. Alison Mitchell. Edinburgh: Scottish Genealogical Society, 1979-84.

---

vidual entry for a fee. This series is in the FHL. The same society issues a leaflet, *A List of Published and Unpublished Monumental Inscriptions Held by the Scottish Genealogy Society* (S. Fleming, 2002), as a guide to the contents of its own extensive collection. For other published inscriptions, consult the family history society in the area (the Aberdeen and North East Scotland Family History Society publishes more than sixty volumes for the northeast). The family history society and the library may also be able to advise you on the existence of unpublished recordings of MIs. The Mitchell Library in Glasgow maintains a typescript index to the MIs in its possession.

Not exactly MIs, the death notices in the *Scots Magazine*, 1739-1833, may be similarly useful, although the people listed are mainly from the professional and landed classes (see chapter 4 for more information about this magazine). The magazine is of course available in Scottish libraries, in some collections in other countries; it has also been filmed by the LDS Family and Church History Department.

You may find that some communities (Glasgow is an example) have what are called "bills of mortality." These are statistical statements regarding deaths in a community. They are interesting and sometimes important if they provide clues about epidemics, crop failure, etc., and thereby suggest reasons for some sudden change in the pattern of an ancestor's life. If your investigation of local sources shows that such reports exist, you should note it for possible reference. Sir John Sinclair, in his *Analysis of the Statistical Account of Scotland* (1826)[3] some years after that survey was taken, was very much in favor of the registration of burials and the maintenance of bills of mortality. A few of his reasons are given here, as they give some emphasis to the shortcomings of burial registers.

- All who die are not put upon the register, but only those for whom the pall or mortcloth is required. This happens only when the funeral takes place in the parish burying ground.

- It has been the custom to use the mortcloth solely for persons above ten years of age.

- As soon as it was known, that the act imposing a tax on registers, did not oblige any person to record the death, and that the only penalty for neglect was the nonentry of the name, the register of deaths, in many parishes, was totally given up.

- In a medical view, such inquiries (i.e., bills of mortality) would suggest the cause of many diseases.

- With a view to morality, the information furnished by bills of mortality would point out the effects of moral and licentious habits, the situations in which they are most frequent, the circumstances that occasion suicides, and perhaps the means of rendering such disgraceful events more rare.

Kirk Sessions

The kirk session was the lowest administrative level of the Church of Scotland. In descending order, the others were the General Assembly, the Synod, and the Presbytery. They all acted as both courts and administrative bodies. Just as in other parts of the United Kingdom, the parish was the logical unit for local administration, so the kirk session took on many civil responsibilities, in particular, care of the poor. Many duties were shared with the heritors, local landowners who because of their greater wealth provided the financial support for community welfare. The session also cooperated with the commissioners of supply in rural areas and with councils in the burghs (see chapter 9).

The records of the kirk session may provide considerable information on your family and on the social history of the parish. The session was the overseer of the morality and discipline of the parish; it repaired the church fabric, kept lists of communicants, distributed relief, and maintained a careful account of fees and fines collected or disbursements paid. Some are available through the FHL collections, although these tend to be the session records that contain baptism and marriage details. Use a locality search in the FHLC under "Scotland – County – Parish – Church records."

In Scotland, surviving records are available at regional archives or at the National Archives of Scotland (NAS). The NAS is turning many of these records over to local authorities, and for many it has retained microfilm copies.

Because of the potential interest and value of session records, every effort should be made to determine what survives for any given parish. If possible begin with the CH2 repertory at the NAS (an older edition is on microfilm in the FHL cataloged under "Scotland – Church records – Inventories – Registers – Catalogs"). Here the NAS holdings of kirk sessions are spelled out (figure 5-4). If you are researching from some distance and an entry has been found in the FHLC, it is still necessary to determine what is in Scotland; more may exist than has been collected on film. Another guide to check is *Kirk Sessions and Other Material Found in the OPRs*. It is online at the GROS website within the Family History section and contains a summary of information apart from baptisms, marriages and deaths, that appears in records at New Register House. You may also come across *Records of the Church of Scotland and Other Presbyterian Churches* (see figure 5-5), a set of microfiche produced by the NAS that lists kirk session material in the NAS. Facts about survival and location of records are important when planning your research, whether they are used to guide an agent or as timesaving preliminary steps prior to a trip of your own.

There is another partial listing of kirk sessions in the *Scottish Genealogist*. Rosemary Bigwood compiled "Pre-1855 Communion Rolls and Other Listings in Kirk Sessions Records" (June, 1988). Her prefatory remarks tell you that some communion rolls may list only heads of families; others give occupation, residence, or even reason for leaving the parish.

Perusal of the accounts or minutes of the local sessions soon makes it apparent that parish administrators were chiefly occupied with morality and revenue and expenditure. Often the two were related. A particular interest in the behavior of parishioners frequently led to the identity of an illegitimate child's father—who could then be pressed to pay for support. Fines imposed for "antenuptial fornication" were a regular and reliable source of parish income until the early 1840s.[4] Where a parish register is missing or particularly brief and uninformative, check the records of the kirk session for such things as the payment of the fee for the proclamation of banns or the rental of the mortcloth, which indirectly gives at least the date of the event you are seeking. In some parishes, for some years, a separate record of

Figure 5-4. CH2 Repertory—The Entry for Elgin.

```
Reference
CH2       145. ELGIN Kirk Session


1.   Minutes    1584-1598
2.              1598-1605
3.              1613-1622
4.              1622-1629
5.              1629-1640
6.              1640-1648
7.              1648-1675
8.              1682-1712
9.              1712-1733
10.             1733-1770
11.             1767-1779
12.             1780-1783
13. Collections 1697-1711
     Minutes    1717-1724
14. Accounts    1780-1825
15.             1827-1843
16. Poor Distribution 1842-1849
17. Young Men's Guild minutes 1892-1901
18. Sabbath School Library Register
19. Ladies' Association for female missionaries
          in N. India 1844-1857
```

Note: This example includes a very long run of Minutes and, for some years, separate listings of Collections, Accounts, and Poor Distribution; there is enough information to help you decide whether to make the extra effort to access it. National Archives of Scotland. Repertory of Church of Scotland Records, 1976.

Figure 5-5. Sample Format of Entries in Records of the Church of Scotland and Other Presbyterian Churches.

* Edinkillie, CH2/432 [Moray]
Ednam, CH2/841
Edrom, CH2/1133
Edzell North, CH2/627[1]; OPR 285
    South, CH3/543
Eigg and Canna, CH2/780

Anything with a CH2 reference has kirk session records; those for Edinkillie have been transferred to the regional archives; there is a footnote for Edzell North with further detail; the CH3 reference is for records of a secessionist congregation. From Records of the Church of Scotland and Other Presbyterian Churches. Scottish Record Office: Edinburgh, 1994.

distributions to the poor was maintained. Penance of a couple who had gone through an irregular form of marriage was also recorded here.

Irregular Marriages

In Scotland, it was possible to marry without the proclamation of banns or the blessing of the minister. The Church of Scotland denounced these irregular or clandestine marriages and further showed its disapproval by barring the couple from Church privileges. Suitable repentance, such as sitting in church on the "repentance stool" in front of the entire congregation listening to a stern admonition from the pulpit, and the payment of a fine, usually restored the couple to full acceptance. For some, the toleration of irregular marriages was inexcusable (see figure 5-6).

In parts of Scotland the notion of a trial marriage for a year was accepted as normal. Such arrangements were usually made on one of the Term Days—2 February (Candlemas Day), 15 May (Whitsunday), 1 August (Lammas Day), and 11 November (Martinmas Day). Sometimes this was called hand-fasting. If a fine was paid at the time the marriage was regularized, often when the first child was born, it would show in session records. By Scots law, provided the parents were free to marry at the time of birth of an illegitimate child, the child was legitimized by the subsequent marriage of the parents. An individual might have gone by the mother's surname at birth and later in life by the father's.

> ### Figure 5-6. A Commentary on Irregular Marriages.
>
> In former times, too great facilities were given to irregular marriages by the magistrates of Rutherglen, who frequently received a fee for their trouble, and even at this day a Rutherglen marriage is too easily obtained. The form is simple. The couple go before a magistrate, and acknowledge that they have been married without the proclamation of banns by a person unauthorized by the church whose name they do not recollect, and in consequence of this irregularity, they acknowledge a fault, and subject themselves to fine and imprisonment; on which the magistrate fines the parties, remits the imprisonment, and gives an extract of their acknowledged marriage, which is binding in law.
>
> Extracted from "Report for Rutherglen in Lanarkshire," *New Statistical Account of Scotland*, Vol. VI, Lanark. Edinburgh: W. Blackwood, 1845.

When Lord Hardwicke's Act was passed by Parliament at Westminster, it applied to all parts of Great Britain and Ireland except for Scotland and the Channel Islands. Marriage could not occur without the reading of banns or obtaining a license, and only Church of England, Jewish or Quaker forms of marriage were legal. Some Presbyterians in England came north for the marriage rites of their faith. Others eloped to Scotland, since that clandestine marriages were no longer legal or binding south of the border. The most famous destination was Gretna, but hasty marriages also occurred at several other places. This phenomenon ended in 1856, and it may have been a concern for the impact of the railway that led the authorities to eliminate this quick marriage option for English runaways. From that date on, it became necessary for one of the parties to the marriage to have been resident in Scotland for at least twenty-one days. This was by no means the end of the appeal of Gretna, which was revived as a marriage mart in the twentieth century. If you are interested in the places and dates for surviving records, the GROS website is able to help once again. Within the Family History section can be found *Irregular Border and Scottish Runaway Marriages* (Robert Nicholson, 5th ed., 2000).

Conclusion

The records of the Church of Scotland are the single most important resource for pre-1855 research, and genealogists are fortunate that there are so many options for access. These records are indexed several ways and in several formats, digital imaging is nearly complete, and microfilm copies are reasonably accessible. All of this is available at very little cost.

Two things are essential for researchers to keep in mind. Become familiar and at ease with the computer and microfiche formats of the indexes. Then, be certain to identify and know the location of all surviving records of the parishes in your research, whether these records are in the FHL or in Scotland. You can then plan an effective and thorough strategy. When you require the assistance of an agent, this information will mean that you can give specific directions and better assess results.

Be careful about drawing conclusions, or considering the research complete because several generations can be readily followed in the indexes. The indexes are subject to error and you may have identified the wrong person. Always go to the registers and look for corroborative information elsewhere.

Notes

1. At the end of 2002 the IGI online acquired a new linking feature. Some people are connected into families and can be displayed in family group sheets and charts. The IGI, you should recall, is not derived only from indexing films of original records but also from submissions of individuals. This means it is important to regard any added linkages with a healthy skepticism and to verify the information.

2. Lindsay, 1975, 128.

3. Sinclair, 1997, 189, 192.

4. Lindsay, 1975, 123.

Summary—Church of Scotland Records

1. Identify the name or names (and variations), the time period (be flexible), and the place (as accurately as possible). Is the place a parish or within a parish of another name? Does it straddle a county boundary? What are the neighboring parishes?

2. Decide which index to consult first and review its search fields, minimum requirements, etc. If the search is limited to one parish or a group of parishes, check for the dates of surviving registers using the GROS website or the FHLC. If confined to a county, scan a list of OPRs for the county to get some sense of major gaps and weaknesses.

3. If this search fails to produce one or more possible results, consider selecting another index, one with a different treatment of names, and try again.

4. Look at a copy of the entry, and preferably at the whole register for a number of years on either side of the entry. Look at other events as well. Obtain all possible clues from the register.

5. Go back to the index or indexes to look for collateral relations, try spelling variations, and use any new clues found so far in the search. Be sure you have tried the parent search option of the IGI.

6. If new parishes have been introduced into the search, look up their register details at the GROS site and in the FHLC.

7. Look for other church records of the parish or parishes being searched (e.g., kirk sessions, histories, gravestone inscriptions). You will need to consult the FHLC, the catalog of the local archives and the NAS, and the local family history society.

6 • Records of Secessionists and Other Denominations

he Old Parochial Registers (OPRs) are the records of the Church of Scotland, that is, the established Presbyterian Church. These registers do not include records of other denominations or records of the breakaway Presbyterian congregations.

Through to the end of the eighteenth century, the strength of the Calvinistic faith kept other denominations from gaining much support in Scotland. Other Protestant faiths that came north with the English Armies in the seventeenth century—Independents, Baptists, and Quakers—made little impact at that time. The Episcopalian Church, which was for some years the state-supported established church (see the outline of church history in chapter 5), was left weak and without much following because it was suppressed and persecuted for nearly a century. Roman Catholicism, left powerless at the time of the Reformation, did not return to any prominence until the arrival of so many Irish immigrants in the nineteenth century.

When Episcopalians had the upper hand, there were penal laws directed against Presbyterians and others, designed to keep them from positions of influence and to keep the dissenting churches weak. When the situation was reversed by William III in 1689, these laws were directed against Episcopalians. Outline histories of the dissenting churches and some interesting comments on the situation in Scotland can be found in the *National Index of Parish Registers*, Vol. XII (Steel, 1970). It states:

> As a result of the alternating supremacy of the Presbyterian and Episcopalian elements within the church, with each change the party in power enforced the penal laws against its dispossessed opponents, who had themselves been responsible for the enactment of the statutes under which they were condemned. Whoever was in power made little difference to the Catholics.[1]

Through the eighteenth and nineteenth centuries, the question of patronage versus the will of a congregation to control the appointment of a minister was a serious source of dissention among Presbyterians. Many congregations quietly left the Church of Scotland to find a new meeting house and arrange for the support of the minister of their choice. In 1843, the matter came to a head with a petition to the queen, but there was little change. Four hundred and seventy-four ministers, about one third, broke away, gave up their churches and stipends, and formed the Free Church of Scotland (this event is sometimes referred to as the Disruption). In 1847, a large number of other secessionist congregations grouped together as the United Presbyterians. The religious census of 1851 counted more than 1,300 places of worship among these two groups and more than 2,000 that were not Church of Scotland.[2]

None of this helped record keeping. During the Episcopalian period, 1661-1690, The Covenanters did not want their baptisms and marriages recorded in the registers, and the Seceders felt so strongly against having events written into the register of the Church of Scotland that they sometimes paid the threepenny tax (between 1783 and 1794) but refused to allow the entry to be made. It should come therefore as no surprise that those ancestors who chose to worship in a different manner may prove to be more difficult to find. There is, therefore, a very good chance that a search in nonconformist registers will become necessary.

Finding the Records

When civil registration was introduced in 1855, the records of the Church of Scotland, the established church, were called in. They are now in the possession of the Registrar General. Most of the records of breakaway Presbyterian churches came into the possession of the Church of Scotland at or before the time of the reunion in 1929. Roughly thirty years later, these records were turned over to the National Archives of Scotland (NAS). The NAS has also received many of the surviving records, or microfilm copies, of other denominations. The records of denominations other than the established Church of Scotland can be located in the NAS, in a regional repository, or in the archives of a particular church.

Records of these other denominations are spotty within the collections of the Family History Library (FHL) of The Church of Jesus Christ of Latter-day Saints (LDS). For the majority of parishes, there are only the Old Parochial Registers (OPRs), but frequently some larger places, such as Aberdeen, list several nonconformist registers. Peruse the national, county, and local sections in the Family History Library Catalog (FHLC) using a place name search. At the beginning under "Scotland – Church records" is a reference to Quaker sources.

Roman Catholic records remained in local control but the NAS has a collection of register photocopies, the earliest is dated 1703 (listed in RH21). There are not many Catholic registers from before 1800. A number of Catholic registers are in the FHL. The *British Vital Records Index* includes names from a few (e.g., 600 entries from the cathedral in Edinburgh, 1780 to 1811).

It is quite probable that you will need to search the registers of a breakaway congregation. The NAS has an extensive collection, both originals and copies; some originals have been moved to local archives. There is a series of repertory guides describing the records, CH3 and CH10–16 (see Figure 6–1). The collection in the NAS is incomplete but microfilm copies are added from time to time. A recent guide, *Registers of the Secession Churches in Scotland* (Baptie, 2000) summarizes what records survive, their locations, and references; also, information on items among the records at New Register House can be found at the GROS website. If you regularly use a Family History Center, investigate the holdings of the FHL; also, much of this collection is within the *British Vital Records Index*. A list of contents for a parish or a county can be found using any of the CDs in the set and performing what is referred to as a Collection Search; this feature is accessed via the tool bar.

Figure 6-1. CH3 Repertory—The Entry for Motherwell.

```
Reference
CH3
383. MOTHERWELL First U.P. Church
          (later Brandon Street U.F. Church
          and Brandon Church of Scotland)


1. Session Minutes        1865-1889
2.                        1889-1911
3.                        1911-1928
4.                        1928-1939
5.                        1939-59
6.                        1958-69
7.                        1969-71
8.              (scroll)  1928-1931
9. Congregational and     1865-1896
   Managers' Minutes
10.                       1896-1921
11.                       1921-1947
12. Managers' Minutes     1947-71
13. Baptismal Register    1909-71
14. Proclamations         1962-71
15. Communion Roll        1866-1889
16.                       1939-1946
17. Accounts              1962-70
18. Centenary booklet     (Printed)
```

Note: The records of this United Presbyterian Church include baptismal registers, communion rolls, and session minutes.

Repertory of Other Presbyterian Churches, 1971, The National Archives of Scotland.

The place in which you are interested may not be included in any finding aids. Before deciding that there are no records for nonconformist churches, make sure you know what churches actually existed in the area in your ancestor's day. Again, the *Ordnance Gazetteer of Scotland* (Groome, 1885) and the *Statistical Accounts of Scotland* (1799 and 1845) are excellent sources (see figure 6-2). You can check further for surviving registers by consulting

---

Figure 6-2. Larkhall: A Community with Several Churches of Different Denominations.

Larkhall, a Lanarkshire town and *quoad sacra* parish, chiefly in Dalserf parish, but partly in Hamilton. Standing 320 feet above sea-level, ¼ mile from the right bank of the Avon, 1½ from the left bank of the Clyde, and 3¼ miles SSE of Hamilton, the town has a station on the Lesmahagow branch of the Caledonian railway, 6¼ miles S by E of Holytown. With slight exception it began to be built about 1776, and for 15 or 20 years continued to be only a small village. It then was rapidly extended, chiefly by means of building societies, but is less a town, in the ordinary sense of the word, than an assemblage of villages, hamlets, rows of houses, and isolated dwellings. Its inhabitants are principally miners connected with neighbouring collieries, bleachers, and handloom weavers in the employment of Glasgow manufacturers; and Larkhall has a post office, with money order, savings' bank, and telegraph departments, a branch of the Union Bank, gasworks, a *quoad sacra* parish church (1835; 700 sittings), a Free church, a U.P. church (1836; 700 sittings), an Evangelical Union chapel (1876; 420 sittings), St Mary's Roman Catholic church (1872), a subscription library, a masonic lodge, etc. The *quoad sacra* parish is in the presbytery of Hamilton and synod of Glasgow and Ayr; its minister's stipend is £200. Four public schools—Academy, Duke Street, Glengowan, and Muir Street—and a Roman Catholic school, with respective accommodation for 272, 81, 350, 350, and 212 children, had (1881) an average attendance of 284, 81, 422, 501, and 179, and grants of £281, 8s., £50, 11s. 6d., £351, 18s. 6d., £456, 13s., and £147, 10s. Pop. of town (1861) 2685, (1871) 4971, (1881) 6503, of whom 96 were in Hamilton; of *q. s.* parish (1871) 5332, (1881) 7063, of whom 360 were in Hamilton.—*Ord. Sur.*, sh. 23, 1865.

Note: A quoad sacra parish is one that is separate for ecclesiastical purposes only.

From the Ordnance Gazetteer of Scotland, by F.H. Groome, vol. 14, 472, Edinburgh, 1883-85.

the catalogs at the Scottish Archives Network website and the Archival Summaries at the Scottish Records Association website, which summarize contents of archives, special collections, and many museums and libraries.

The Records

Information in the registers for the various Protestant denominations is not very different from what is found in those of the Established Church. Burials are less likely to be found. For some congregations, administrative records, similar to kirk session records, are also in existence.

Where there are both Established Church and secessionist congregations in a parish, if an entry fails to show up in the expected source, always check the register of the other. Bear in mind that a secessionist church may have gone through more than one change of faith yet have continued to use the same book as the parish register.

Roman Catholic registers are usually more informative than most. They include records of death that may show name, age, occupation, cause, and marital status. Some marriage registers indicate the home parish of Irish immigrants.[3] Unfortunately, most do not begin until the nineteenth century. Copies of some are available in the NAS which has been copying pre-1855 registers, but many remain in local custody. Boundaries for Catholic dioceses can be found in *Catholic Parishes in England, Wales and Scotland, An Atlas* (Gandy, 1993). These boundaries were not set up until 1878. If you have Roman Catholic ancestors in Glasgow, particularly of Irish origin, you will be interested in the St. Andrew's Database. This has been formed from the marriage registers of St. Andrew's Cathedral, 1808-1839. Note the dates, which are prior to the Irish famine. For this period there was no record of people departing from Irish ports for Scotland, so it is a valuable bonus that these registers indicate the parish of origin in Ireland. For further information, see "St. Andrew's Database" (Bayne, *Newsletter of the Glasgow and West of Scotland Family History Society*, Spring, 1992) or consult the Scottish Catholic Archives.

It is abundantly clear that for the majority of dissenting churches you must seek the information in Scotland. For denominations unrelated in any way to the Presbyterian Church, there could be as many as four places to check—the NAS, the local library or archives, the archives of the church head office, or the local church.

Notes

1. Steel, 1970, 102.
2. Steel, 1970, 188.
3. Sinclair, 1997, 22.

Summary—Other Denominations

1. As usual, first set the parameters of name, date, and place, noting when to be flexible or alert for variations. Study maps and town descriptions for clues about active church congregations.

2. Identify the denomination(s) of interest.

3. Find out what can be checked using the *British Vital Records Index* and what can be accessed through Family History Centers and the FHL. There are secession congregation, Catholic, Methodist, and military chapel records, etc., within this index.

4. Investigate overall availability of other Presbyterian records using *Registers of the Secession Churches in Scotland* (Baptie, 2000) and online catalogs. An alternative is to send enquiries to the NAS and regional archives; their staff may direct you to church archives or a local minister.

5. Submit a question on the subject to the area family history society or to a county mailing list or message board.

7 • Disposition of Goods and Property

he inheritance of moveable goods and the transfer of ownership of land or property in Scotland, whether by inheritance or sale, introduce unfamiliar procedure and terminology to those new to Scottish research. Until recently, searching has been something of a challenge as well. Fortunately this problem is receding as technology improves access. The greatest improvements are for testamentary records, which can now be accessed through an online index and digital image order service. Records of the inheritance of land, services of heirs, have good indexes and now these are available on CD-ROM. Sasines, which document land transfer, continue to present challenges.

The inheritance of moveable goods was handled separately from the inheritance of land, buildings, and mining rights (known as heritable property). When someone died possessed of both moveable and heritable property, two records resulted directly (though not necessarily immediately): the testament for the movables and the service of heir or *retour* for the property. Another was generated indirectly by property transfers, the record of sasine. The record of sasine also was generated when land or property changed hands as a result of a sale or when it was used as security against a loan.

Many more people had personal possessions, such as furniture, cloth-ing, tools, or jewelry, than had heritable property. People in remote parts of Scotland and those with few possessions more often than not passed things on without recourse to the legal procedure. It follows that more prosper-ous people appear in testamentary records and that Lowland entries are more common than Highland.

Testamentary Records

Begin by considering the likelihood of locating a particular ancestor in testamentary records. When was it? Where was it? Was he possessed of sufficient moveable goods to have generated an official record? Some gen-eralizations are possible. The further back in time, the lower the probabil-ity of finding a record. The percentage of the population making wills before 1800 is very small indeed. The eldest son may not appear in the tes-tament because he received the heritable property. As already suggested, in remote parts, if only a few personal possessions were involved, there seemed little point in seeking out a court when things could be arranged without. Nevertheless, when assessing the individual's financial condition, also ask yourself how sure you are of this conclusion. Do not dismiss the search too readily or forget that you can search for a sibling or other rela-tive instead.

There are two types of testamentary records: a testament *testamentar* included a will; a testament *dative* did not. A testament without a will is more usual. Both types of probate records include inventories that list, in varying detail, personal possessions of the deceased and debts owed or due. Where the executor was identified in a will, the court confirmed his appointment. Where there was no will, the executor was appointed and confirmed by the court. The executor was usually a relative, but was some-times a creditor. Because these *confirmations* show the reasons executors were appointed, any involving a relative are useful. The record should include such details as the name of the testator, occupation, residence, and date of death. If there is a will, it indicates the identity of the executor and any personal wishes of the testator, which are often of genealogical value. After 1823 some courts maintained separate registers for wills and inven-tories and before that date some supplementary documents were listed later; hence it is possible to find multiple entries for one person.

The testator did not have much freedom to do as he pleased with his personal property. If a widow *and* children survived him, one third went to the widow, one third to the children, and one third to whomever the deceased wished. If a widow *or* children survived, one half went to the survivors and the other half to beneficiaries chosen by the deceased.

Research procedures for finding these records can be conveniently divided into three sections: since 1876, 1823 to 1876, and before 1823. This does not mean that for every jurisdiction the local officials stuck to these cut-off dates in their record keeping. Some of the early registers continue beyond 1823. Some volumes of confirmations, inventories, and testaments straddle two periods; however, these divisions are not a cause for concern. The online index for all testaments before 1876 is comprehensive and provides the name of the court.

For the most recent period, 1876 and after, there is an annual index, *The Calendar of Confirmations and Inventories*. This is available at the National Archives of Scotland (NAS) up to 1991 in three formats: printed, microfiche cards, and computer (for post-1984 and found in the Legal Search Room). For the period 1876 to 1936 *The Calendar of Confirmations and Inventories* can be found in the Family History Library (FHL) of The Church of Jesus Christ of Latter-day Saints (on the bookshelves and on film). Many libraries around Scotland have copies of all or part of this, and the FHL films can circulate to Family History Centers.

The text of a confirmation after 1876 is full of information. Notice the use of the term, the Commissariot of Ayr; the commissariots were abolished in 1823 but the term continued in use.

20 July.– Confirmation of Elizabeth Brown or Gilchrist, Greenholm, Parish of Gilchrist, who died 9 July 1876, at Kilmarnock, testate, granted at Ayr, to Janet Cameron Gilchrist, her daughter, Executrix nominated in Will or Deed, dated 7 February, 1876, and recorded in Court Books of Commissariot of Ayr, 2 July 1876. (*Calendar of Confirmations and Inventories*, 1877.)

These calendars are fully alphabetical within each year, though there may be some entries in addenda at the end. A woman is listed under her married name. For each individual listed, the other details are value of the estate, occupation (if known), date and place of death and confirmation, whether testate or intestate, and the name of the executor or executrix, often including the relationship to the deceased. With this information, you can apply to the NAS for a copy of the record, including the will if there was one. If the information as to name, date, and place of death is accurate, it is possible to apply directly to the NAS, dispensing with the index search. There is a handling fee to which copy and postage charges are added.

Before 1876, in fact from the earliest surviving record in 1514, all Scottish testaments have been newly indexed in a computer database. There are no more incomplete sections or missed entries because this index is derived from a new and thorough check of all surviving records. The index can be consulted online through the Scottish Documents website, or accessed from the Scottish Archives Network (SCAN) homepage. In addition, digital imaging of all testamentary records is nearing completion. Simple as this may sound, it remains useful to understand the court system and the way the records were originally stored. This knowledge facilitates the selection of probable entries and is quite important if you opt to look for microfilm copies in the FHL collections.

In 1823 legislation made the sheriff courts responsible for testamentary business. Courts and boundaries changed to coincide pretty much with the counties, although Perth and Argyll had two courts each, and in 1832 a second court was added for Angus. The change in system was not sudden; some sheriff courts took until the end of the decade to complete the change (e.g., Aberdeen in 1827 and Edinburgh in 1829). In a few areas both courts operated simultaneously for some time. This period lasted until 1875.

Up until 1823 commissary courts dealt with testaments. There were twenty-two and boundaries were not related to county lines, but derived from the early Catholic dioceses of Scotland. Before the Reformation, probate had been a matter for the courts of the Catholic Church. You should know the name of the commissariot in which your ancestors resided; these four resources supply the information in various formats.

- *The Atlas and Index of Parish Registers* (Humphery-Smith, 1995) contains color maps of the commissariot boundaries.
- *Tracing Scottish Ancestors* (Bigwood, 1999) lists every parish and the commissariot in which it was located.

- *Tracing Your Scottish Ancestors* (Lewis, 1997) has a list of counties and the name or names of the commissariots that had jurisdiction within each.

- *The Scottish Archives Network* also has a county list and adds the start and end dates of surviving records.

When testamentary business was transferred to the sheriff courts, it meant that the commissary courts were abolished. As already pointed out, the term "commissary" did not disappear. Another factor did not change, the superiority of the court in Edinburgh. It could be used for testaments of people from anywhere in Scotland, and it was always the court for the business of anyone who died outside Scotland. From 1858 to 1900 there was a special list of those dying in England or Ireland with moveable property in Scotland; titled *Probates Resealed*, it is in the NAS. The online index includes the testaments of those dying elsewhere.

The Online Index to Testaments

Searching for Scottish testaments up to and including 1875 recently became much simpler with the arrival of the index at the Scottish Documents website. In the standard search it is possible to search for a surname only (even a partial surname), to include a forename and to decide whether or not to specify a search based on exact spelling. There is also an advanced search with additional input boxes for (a) title, occupation, or place, (b) the court or commissariot, (c) a range of years, and (d) a choice of sort options — forename, surname, or year. You are warned to search Mc or Mac names according to both forms. If you search only on a particular court, check the Edinburgh court as well because it could handle probate for anywhere in Scotland. Results are presented in groups of 50 on each page up to a maximum of 500; if more than 500 are found you are asked to refine your search.

For Scottish emigrant or trading families, a useful tip is to perform a search restricted to the Edinburgh commissary court. This was the court for anyone dying overseas. Using the name Aitken, this search turned up a list of fifty, several in England, a few in the West Indies, and a few in America. In most the place details are fairly specific (e.g., London, St. Domingo, and Kentucky).

Figure 7-1 shows a transcript of the entries resulting from a search for William Ford. You can see that details in the index vary. Some show the occupation and the precise address. The date is expressed according to day, month, and year, and is the date of the probate. Only one of these entries specifically mentions wills.

When you perform an online search you will see another column on the right indicating whether you can view the image online. If you choose to do so, the item is added to the virtual shopping cart. The cost is £5 per testament regardless of the length of the document, which may range in size from a single page to twenty and more. Once you've paid, you can download the image or choose to visit it at the website. Any ordered images remain in your own area, accessible by user name and password. Those of you researching at the NAS in Edinburgh will not be ordering photocopies but copies of the computer images. The use of digital imaging

Figure 7-1. Transcript of Index Entries From the Online Index To Scottish Probate Records, 1500 to 1875.

Surname	Forename	Date	Residence	Court
Ford	William	4/2/1742	in Belnacraig	Aberdeen Commissary Court
Ford	William	18/8/1820	Glass Manufacturer in Edinburgh	Edinburgh Commissary Court
Ford	William	11/3/1859	Plumber in North Berwick	Haddington Sheriff Court
Ford	William	2/6/1870	Esquire of Westwood in Forfarshire reisiding at No. 34 Minto Street in Newington near Edinburgh	Edinburgh Sheriff Court Inventories
Ford	William	2/6/1870	of Westwood in County of Forfar	Edinburgh Sheriff Court Wills
Ford	William	24/7/1873	Draper at Brechin	Forfar Sheriff Court

Note the two entries for William Ford of Westwood, one for the inventory and the other for the will.

means the original volumes of testamentary records will not deteriorate further because they no longer need to be handled.

Some probate records of commissary and sheriff courts are on microfilm in the FHL. In other words, a mixed search, using the online index and films of the probate records, is possible. You can check what is available by consulting the FHLC at the county level and looking under the topic "Probate records." This works even if the name of the court is not the name of the county. In the case of the Commissariot of the Isles, which served the counties of Argyll, Bute, Iverness, and Ross and Cromarty, you will find the records listed in the four areas. These cover the years from 1661 to 1823.

Services of Heirs

Before 1868 it was not possible to bequeath land. All land was considered ultimately to be the property of the Crown, so it was necessary for the heir of a deceased landholder to prove that he was indeed entitled to it. Inheritance followed the law of primogeniture, that is, the eldest son inherited or, if there were no sons, the land was divided among daughters (who are sometimes referred to as "heirs portioner"). Do not give up on a search too soon despite the limited number of land owners. Just as there was often a lapse of time between the death of an individual and the creation of the testamentary record, so also many more years might have passed before the heir actually sought to set the record straight.

The investigation of the proof of the right of an individual to assume the ownership of his deceased kinsman's land was held before a jury. The result of this inquest was sent back to Chancery in Edinburgh—hence the other name for these records, *retours*. This procedure was also used to appoint a tutor, essentially a guardian, of a fatherless child. The records were written in Latin until 1847, apart from the years 1652 to 1659. The indexes from the beginning of the eighteenth century are very informative, but given the extent of detail that may be in the actual retour, it is recommended that you obtain a copy and have it translated. If you would like to read a good example, refer to *In Search of Scottish Ancestry* (Hamilton-Edwards, 1983).

The information found in entries of the decennial indexes to records of services of heirs is shown in figure 7-2. These volumes are for the period 1700–1859; thereafter, there are annual indexes. The listings are alphabetical

Figure 7-2. Sample Entries from the Decennial Indexes to Services of Heirs.		
Names of the Persons Served	**Distinguishing Particulars**	**Date of Recording**
Gourlay, Robert	Merchant, St. Andrews, to his Father, Robert Gourlay, Merchant there - Heir General - dated 9th May 1812	1812, June 3
Graham, Ann	at St. Vigeans, to her Uncle William Graham in Newbigging - Heir Portioner General - dated 20th January 1818	1818, Feb. 3

Extracted from the *Decennial Index to the Services of Heirs of Scotland, 1810-1819*, Edinburgh, 1860.

according to the names of the heirs, otherwise referred to as *the person served*. There is at the end of each volume or ten-year section an alphabetical list of names of *persons served to* where that differs from the name of the heir; this is very helpful if an inheritance involved a distant relative. These Indexes to the Services of Heirs in Scotland are available in large volumes or on microfilm and can be purchased on CD-ROM. The records themselves have been filmed (1586–1901), which means that access to indexes and records is possible through the FHL and Family History Centers. These are Chancery records and were generated by the national government, so the FHLC entry is found under "Scotland – Land and property." If you are convinced that there should be a record but cannot find one, refer to *Tracing Your Scottish Ancestors* (Sinclair, 1997), which mentions two sources at the NAS perhaps best described as "strays": List of Unrecorded Retours and Index of Retours of General Service.[1] As these lists have been placed among post-1900 records, access requires assistance in Edinburgh.

For the earlier years, 1530 to 1700, there is a separate index to the records of services of heirs. First published nearly 200 years ago, it has been reissued in many forms, most recently, on CD-ROM (using Adobe *Acrobat Reader*). Properly titled *Inquisitionum ad Capellam Domini Regis Retornatarum Abbreviatio*, it is, as you might expect, entirely in Latin. Fortunately this is not a problem. A typical entry can usually be understood. Records are in the NAS and on film in the FHL.

You may come across the word *taillie* or *tailzie* in these decennial indexes. This is the Scottish form of the word "entail," by which a landowner stipulated who would inherit the land for generations to come. If you have landed ancestry and you find reference to this, only limited checks can be done outside Edinburgh. The FHL holds *An Accurate Alphabetical Index of the Registered Entails in Scotland from the Passing of an Act of Parliament in the Year 1685 to February 4, 1784.*

A number of other unusual words will turn up in these records. The sample entry in figure 7-3 is taken from *Services of Heirs, Roxburghshire, 1636-1847*, which was published by the Scottish Record Society in 1934. The terms are explained beneath.

Should the opportunity arise, take the time to look through the volumes of the *Scottish Historical Review*. They are on microfilm (this type of browsing is best done onsite) at the FHL, or you may discover that a nearby university library holds the series. The benefit of this is that from time to time in the "Communications and Replies" column of this periodical,

---

Figure 7-3. Sample Entry from Service of Heirs, Roxburghshire, 1636-1847.

Service of Elizabeth Marshall, wife of William Johnstone, residing at Bongate near Jedburgh, to her cousin-german John Waugh, feuar in Kelso, in his half tenement of land as particularly bounded and described, lying within the burgh of Kelso, as also another tenement of land, lying at the Chalk cleugh of Kelso, as also particularly bounded and described, lying also within the town of Kelso (in nonentry since the death of her said cousin on the 16th of July 1831).

Expede 30 July 1836 (Six papers.)   R. 12 Aug.
1836

Explanations:
cousin german: a first cousin
feuar: one who holds land in feu (i.e., in perpetual lease)
cleugh: a ravine with steep sides, usually with water (i.e., a gorge)
nonentry: not recorded

Reference was made to several sources to locate these terms. In addition to the *Scottish Genealogist's Glossary* (Burness, 1990), *The Oxford Dictionary on Historical Principles* (Little et al., 1973) is a useful resource.

printed lines of inheritance appear, with frequent reference to the records of services of heirs. An example is shown in figure 7-4.

Register of Sasines

Property transactions were important, so whenever land changed hands, or even if it was used as security, the action was entered in the Register of Sasines. This register has been maintained continuously since 1617. A General Register was set up in Edinburgh and Particular Registers in the localities—in other words, in other areas of the country. Writs could be registered at either. There were separate registers for the royal burghs. In 1868, the Particular Registers were abolished and the General Register was continued with county divisions. The wording of the documents is generally long and repetitive, but often very useful family details are embedded in them.

Searching for a record after 1780 is actually quite easy, aided by the existence of volumes of Abridgements with accompanying indexes to persons and places. All of these volumes are available at the NAS and through the facilities of a Family History Center or at the FHL. The per-

---

Figure 7-4. The Campbells of Strachur, an Excerpt From The Scottish Historical Review.

Colin Campbell of Strachur died in September, 1743 (Services of Heirs), was father of John, who succeeded, and Janet, of whom afterwards.

General John Campbell of Strachur was served heir to his father, July 27, 1744, and January 29, 1800. He died August 28, 1806.

Janet Campbell, afterwards of Strachur, married C. Campbell of Ederline, was served heir to her brother John, March 30, 1807, and died January 8, 1816.

Dugald Campbell of Ederline was served heir to his father, Colin Campbell of Ederline (died June 1780), dated Oct. 16, 1782. He married Mary Campbell, and must have died before 1816. Was probably father of Colin who succeeded to Strachur.

Colin Campbell of Strachur was served heir to his grand uncle, General John Campbell, April 12, 1816, and to his grandmother, Janet Campbell of Strachur, Nov. 21, 1821. He died June 16, 1824.

John Campbell of Strachur was served heir to his father Colin, January 12, 1825. Extracted from *The Scottish Historical Review*, Volume Four, 234, Glasgow, 1907.

Figure 7-5. Sample Entries from The Sasine Abridgements for Aberdeen.

1783.   ABERDEEN.   179—203

(179)   Jul. 14. 1783.
JANET, MARION, HELEN, & ELIZABETH FOR-
BES, daughters of William Forbes, Minister at Monothugh,
as heirs portioners to William Forbes of Belnabodach, their
great-grandfather, *Seised*, May 23. 1783,—in BELNABO-
DACH, par. Invernettie;—on Pr. Cl. Con. by James, Earl of
Fife, Jan. 6. 1783.   P. R. 30. p. 1. 112.

(180)   Jul. 15. 1783.
JOHN DAVIDSON of Tillychetly, *Seised*, Jun. 25. 1783,—
in CORRACHRIE in Cromer, comprehending Mains and
Nether Corrachrie, Hole, Bruchead, Muirhall, Backside, Clury
& Mill of Corrachrie, par. Logie Coldstone; Milltown of Rip-
pachie or Ardgeith; Rippachy, Ardgeith, Clinnettie & pen-
dicles Ronafea, Whitechael, Craigshen, Parkhead, Bogforlen,
Broomhill and Westkmill of Rippachie, par. Migvie; Over
Kilbatho, Bluefield, Bluesmill, and Monavie, &c. par. Kilbatho
or Towie;—in security of £614. 19s. 4½d.;—on Bond by Robert Lumsden of Corrachrie, Jun. 25. 1783.
   P. R. 30. p. 1. 113.

(181)   Jul. 18. 1783.
CHRISTIAN LESLIE, spouse of Alexander Burnett of
Kemnay, *Seised*, Jul. 12. 1783,—in the Barony of KEMNAY,
par. Kemnay;—in security of a liferent annuity of £135;—on
Mar. Con. Nov. 13. 1781.   P. R. 30. p. 1. 114.

(182)   Jul. 18. 1783.
ALEXANDER BURNETT of Kemnay, as heir to George
Burnett of Kemnay, his father, *Seised*, Jul. 12. 1783,—in
CRAIGERNE, Salmon Fishings in Don, par. Cluny & Kem-
nay;—on Pr. Cl. Con. by Alexander, Duke of Gordon, May
21. 1783.   P. R. 30. p. 1. 115.

(183)   Jul. 22. 1783.
ROBERT HORN ELPHINSTON of Horn & Logie, &
Sir Ernest Gordon of Park, *Seised*, Jul. 10. 1783,—in the
Barony of NEWTON or WRANGHAM, par. Culsamond;
Melkonside & Trinds; Superiority of parts of Williamston,
Mill, &c. & Trinds, par. Culsamond;—on Disp. by Capt.
Alexander Davidson of Newton, Dec. 24. 25. 1782.
   P. R. 30. p. 1. 116.

rony of KNOCKLEITH, par. Auchterless;—on Ch. Resig.
by Alexander, Duke of Gordon, May 30. 1780.
   P. R. 30. p. 1. 121.

(191)   Aug. 11. 1783.
JOHN DUFF of Hatton, *Seised*, Jul. 17. 1783,—in WOOD-
TOWN, Old Mill, part of Mill lands of Seggat, par. Turreff;
—on Con. of Excambion between James, Earl of Findlater &
Seafield, and said John Duff, Feb. 21. May 1. 1767.
   P. R. 30. p. 1. 122.

(192)   Aug. 18. 1783.
ALEX. LUMSDEN, son of Alex. Lumsden, Advocate,
Aberdeen, *Seised*, Jul. 31. 1783,—in parts of GILCOM-
STON, par. Old Machar;—on Ch. Resig. by the Master of
Kirk & Bridge Works, Aberdeen, Jul. 30. 1783.
   P. R. 30. p. 1. 123.

(193)   Aug. 18. 1783.
MARJORY LOGIE, daughter of Andrew Logie, Merchant,
Aberdeen, *Seised*, Jul. 31. 1783,—in part of GILCOMSTON,
par. Old Machar;—on Ch. Resig. by the Master of Kirk &
Bridge Works, Aberdeen, Jul. 30. 1783 (under reservation of
the liferent of Marjory Moir, relict of said Andrew Logie).
   P. R. 30. p. 1. 124

(194)   Aug. 18. 1783.
JAMES CLERK, M. D. Dominien, *Seised*, Jul. 31. 1783,—
in part of GILCOMSTON, par. Old Machar;—on Ch. Resig. by the Master of Kirk & Bridge Works, Aberdeen, Jul.
30. 1783.   P. R. 30. p. 1. 125.

(195)   Aug. 18. 1783.
The Boxmaster of the SHOEMAKER TRADE, Aberdeen,
Seised, Jul. 31. 1783,—in part of GILCOMSTON, par. Old
Machar;—on Ch. by the Master of Kirk & Bridge Works,
Aberdeen, Jul. 30. 1783.   P. R. 30. p. 1. 126.

(196)   Aug. 18. 1783.
GEORGE SKENE, M. D. Prof. of Philosophy, Marischal
College, Aberdeen, *Seised*, Jul. 31. 1783,—in parts of Gilcom-
ston, to be called FOUNTAINHALL, par. Old Machar;—on
Ch. Resig. by the Master of Kirk & Bridge Works, Aberdeen,
Jun. 4. 1783.   P. R. 30. p. 1. 127.

(181)   Jul. 18.1783.

CHRISTIAN LESLIE, spouse of Alexander Burnett of Kemnay, *Seised*, Jul. 12. 1783,—in the Barony of KEMNAY, par. Kemnay;—in security of a liferent annuity of £135;—on Mar. Con. Nov. 13. 1781.

(192)   Aug. 18. 1783.

ALEX. LUMSDEN, son of Alex. Lumsden, Advocate, Aberdeen, *Seised*, Jul. 31. 1783,—in parts of GILCOMSTON, par. Old Machar;—on Ch. Resig. by the Master of Kirk & Bridge Works, Aberdeen, Jul. 30. 1783.

The designation P.R. means this is a Particular Register, helpful when interested in locating the full document. From *The Sasine Abridgements for Aberdeen*, volume 1, 1873, ©The National Archives of Scotland.

sons index covers the period from 1781 to 1868 and the places index, 1781 to 1830. The Abridgements on film are for the years 1781-1868.

To search the Abridgements, make the usual selection of a name, time period, and county. Whether you select the persons or the places index will be determined by the objective (e.g., one particular name or all entries in an area for one or more names). There should be no difficulty making a selection from among the listings of volumes of Abridgements as they are arranged in categories by county and date. The entry reveals enough that it may not be necessary to see the entire original wording (figure 7-5). The complete text of a sasine can be obtained from the NAS. It will be long and repetitive and may include Latin words. This is not the end of the Abridgements, which along with indexes, exist for more recent years at the NAS.

Prior to 1780 indexes are not available for all areas of Scotland or all years. Anyone searching in Edinburgh can consult the indexes that do exist; distance searchers can find a list of these in *Tracing Your Scottish Ancestors* (Sinclair, 1997). Where gaps exist in the indexes, the next best

---

Figure 7-6. List of Royal Burghs.

Aberdeen	Dornoch	Irvine	Pittenweem
Annan	Dumbarton	Jedburgh	Renfrew
Anstruther	Dumfries	Kinghorn	Rosemarkie and
Arbroath	Dunbar	Kirkcaldy	Fortrose
Ayr	Dundee	Kirkcudbright	Rothesay
Banff	Dunfermline	Kirkwall	Roxburgh
Berwick	Dysart	Lanark	Rutherglen
Brechin	Edinburgh	Lauder	St. Andrews
Burntisland	ElginFalkland	Linlithgow	Sanquhar
Campbeltown	Forfar	Lochmaben	Stirling
Crail	Forres	Montrose	Stranraer
Cromarty	Glasgow	Nairn	Tain
Culross	Haddington	New Galloway	Whithorn
Cupar	Hamilton	North Berwick	Wick
Selkirk	Inverary	Peebles	Wigtown
Dingwall	Inverness	Perth	

This list is based on information in the *Ordnance Gazetteer of Scotland* (Groome, 1883-85) and in *A Companion to Scottish History from the Reformation to the Present* (Donnachie and Hewitt, 1984).

option is to consult minute books, meaning the chronological summaries, or diaries, of the court. These are at the NAS, and the FHL holds minute books for Particular Registers from 1599 to 1763. Consult them when you know the county and have a fairly accurate date.

If your ancestors live in a royal burgh such as Paisley or Montrose, it will be necessary to look in the sasines for the burgh. Some parts of these are in the FHL on microfilm. The minute books of sasines for Montrose are listed under "Scotland – Angus – Montrose – Land and property"; others are similarly placed. A list of royal burghs is in figure 7-6. Be sure to look at maps contemporary to the period of the search so that you are aware of the area covered by the burgh at that time. What is part of a town now may have been out in the country then; therefore the records will be part of the main body of sasines already described. The NAS has quite an extensive collection of burgh sasines; however, the availability of indexes is limited mainly to the years after 1808. Consider checking with local repositories for holdings. For example, the sasines of the royal burgh of Crail to 1804 are at St. Andrews University Library.

Some of the indexes to persons for the registers of sasines prior to 1780 are sold by the NAS. Nine of these include years after 1700: Index to the General Register of Sasines, 1701 to 1720; Sheriffdom of Banff, 1617-1780; Shire of Berwick and Bailiary of Lauderdate, 1617-1780; Sheriffdom of Caithness, 1646-1780; Sheriffdom of Dumfries and Stewartries of Kirkcudbright and Annandale, 1617-1780; Sheriffdom of Elgin, Forres and Nairn, 1617-1780; Sheriffdoms of Inverness, Ross, Cromarty and Sutherland, 1606-1780; Sheriffdom of Lanark, 1618-1780; and Sheriffdom of Forfar, 1701-1780 (the last one is on fiche).

The sensible approach is to first consider what you need and then how to obtain it. Logic suggests you begin with the appropriate local record, either the particular or burgh registers, and then consult the General Register, because it was open to anyone from anywhere in Scotland. It may, however, be easier to work the other way around, particularly if you are relying on FHL resources. It has on film the index to the General Registers from 1701 to 1720, as well as an index to those from 1617 to 1700.

Conclusion

The disposition of goods and property in Scotland may not have involved very many people, but those leaving legacies and transferring land were from all walks of life. In addition, these records are well indexed; it is very easy to verify whether or not an ancestor is among them. Finally, copies of testaments, services of heirs and sasines are widely available. All have the potential to provide relationship information that can make up for missing parish records or possibly confirm a weak link. For direct ancestors and for collateral relations, these three classes should all be searched.

Notes

1. Sinclair, 1997, 47.

Summary — Testamentary Records

1. Consider the known facts and their accuracy; next set the range of years and geographic area for the search; also know if this is an individual search or a survey of records for one surname.

2. For testamentary records before 1876, consult the indexes at the Scottish Documents website. For the modern period use the NAS indexes.

3. Copies of documents can then be ordered online; or taken from a FHL film.

Summary — Records of Services of Heirs

1. Consider the known facts and their accuracy; next set the range of years and geographic area for the search; also know if this is an individual search or a survey of records for one surname.

2. Collect the relevant information from the Decennial Indexes and/or the Index to Retours using the CD-ROM, books, or microfilm indexes.

3. If seeking the full record, consider whether the assistance of an agent is required (to 1847 the documents are in Latin).

Summary — Sasines

1. Ask yourself a few questions before starting the search. What points to the conclusion that an ancestor was involved in land transactions? Was the property close to home or farther afield? What was the most likely time frame for registration?

2. For anything after 1780 consult the Abridgements first, using the persons or places index as appropriate.

3. For earlier periods consult *Tracing Your Scottish Ancestors* (Sinclair, 1997) in the Scottish Record Office for information on finding aids. Contact local archives and/or the FHLC to find out about availability and access to indexes, minute books, and records.

8 • Trades and Occupations

iscovering more about the occupations and living conditions of your ancestors, no matter how humble, has become much easier over the past twenty-five years. There is a greater interest in the everyday lives of ordinary people, and in industrial history. Museums of rural life with working farms using old techniques are now found in many parts of Britain. It is possible to take a ride on an old steam train, to see an ancient mill or mine in working order, or to visit a tenement in Glasgow just as it was at the turn of the nineteenth century. There is also an ever-expanding body of knowledge. Not only are there more books and articles, but genealogists are turning their attention to creating finding aids or writing how-to books devoted entirely to trades and occupations (see the bibliography).

An examination of the trades and occupations of your ancestors may lead into the study of different aspects of economic and social history. Economics was at the root of many historical events which affected people's lives. For example, the Union of 1707 had its roots in economics (the failure of the Darien scheme in South America), as did Scottish emigration to North America in the eighteenth and nineteenth centuries. Some of you will dip into the subject area only enough to learn what the occupation was; others will be drawn into histories of an entire industry, into company records, into asking questions about tools, clothing, pay, working conditions, or the impact of new machinery.

An important part of family history research is to understand how your ancestors worked and lived. For one thing, it adds a touch of reality, thus reducing the danger of romanticizing their lives. Taking time to discover what someone ate, wore, slept on, and worked at each day brings you closer to viewing them as real people, and, there is a bonus. This type of research usually turns up clues or even hard facts that can further your research.

The occupation of an ancestor, at least in the past 160 years, is not difficult to discover. It appears in census returns, in civil registration records, in testamentary records, in directories, and sometimes in parish registers. This is not an exhaustive list, but it shows that the most commonly used sources for nineteenth century research will probably reveal an occupation. Prior to the first census in 1841, finding an occupation may involve more work. The records that reveal an occupation, such as services of heirs, sasines, and testaments do not encompass a large portion of the population. You may have to address the problem by a roundabout route. What sort of community was it? Did nearly everyone work on the land or in a linen mill or in the fishing fleet? Was there a large house in the vicinity where some individuals may have worked as servants? What sort of record may supply an answer?

The divisions in this chapter are quite arbitrary. The intent is to supply sufficient information about a range of occupations in order to provide guidance for organizing a framework for your research. There are too many different kinds of occupations and businesses to give information for them all. From what is described here and your own research skills you will be able to delve into the employment history of your ancestors.

Government Employees and the Professions
Civilian Government Employees

Senior British government officials for Scotland, particularly in more recent times, are listed in editions of *Whitaker's Almanac*, which has been published annually since 1868. Here you will find Members of Parliament, judges, school principals, senior officials of government departments, senior administrative officers of towns and cities, trade union secretaries, etc. If you have never examined one of these fascinating volumes, take the time to do so. The facts cover all of the United Kingdom and Northern Ireland. Recent editions are available in most large reference libraries, but the number of back issues they hold varies. Some directories, notably court directories, include senior officials. Otherwise the search for a civil servant will begin most likely in Edinburgh. The National Archives of Scotland (NAS) holds various pay, pension, and government lists (specifically the registers of the Great Seal and the Privy Seal). *Tracing Your Scottish Ancestors* (Sinclair, 1997) provides details on accessing these sources.

For employees of particular government departments, most records do not begin until into the twentieth century. However, if your ancestor worked for the Post Office or Customs and Excise, you are more fortunate. For roughly one hundred years, form 1803 to 1911, there is at the NAS a list of postmasters, postmistresses and letter carriers.[2] Since the finding aid is arranged by location of the post offices, it is necessary to know the name of the town. The NAS hold the records of these two departments up to 1830. This includes a resource in the form of a card index, *The List of Members of the Scottish Excise Department 1707 – 1830*; it has been filmed by the Family History Library (FHL). For the years after 1830, Customs and Excise officials are listed in the documents held by the National Archives at Kew, outside London. Pension records are the most useful source. There is an online leaflet to guide you through the records, "Customs, Excise, Tax Collectors and Civil Servants."

Before reading further about national records, many of which are stored at Kew, you should be aware of the changes being launched in April 2003. The Public Record Office (PRO) and the Historical Manuscripts Commission (HMC), presently in central London, are coming together to form a new organization to be called the National Archives. There will be a new joint gateway website, the HMC will move to Kew and the services of these two organizations will be further coordinated. Address and website information in appendix D reflects this change.

Military and Naval Personnel

A disproportionate part of the British Army was made up of soldiers of Scottish origin. All army records from 1707 are at Kew, and several useful parts of this massive collection have been filmed by the Family and Church History Department of The Church of Jesus Christ of Jesus Christ of Latter-day Saints. There have been sufficient developments in accessing military records to make it possible for anyone to do at least some of the work without specialized knowledge. Before beginning any research read the relevant leaflets issued by the National Archives; e.g. British Army: Useful Sources for Tracing Soldiers, British Army: Soldiers' Discharge Papers (1760-1913), British Army: Soldiers' Pensions (1702-1913), and British Army: Muster Rolls and Pay Lists, circa 1730-1898. There are about twenty leaflets in all and they can be downloaded from the website or picked up at Kew. Unless you expect to visit Kew, next review the British military collection in the FHL. Using the locality arrangement of the FHLC, select "Great Britain" as the place and "Military records" as the topic. For additional details, particularly on the less commonly consulted records, consult a guide devoted to army sources, such as *Army Records for Family Historians* (Fowler and Spencer, 1998).

For most army research you must know the soldier's regiment, or make a calculated guess as to which one it was; the latter course of action may lead to making more than one guess and repeating the search. The records of those soldiers discharged to pension, 1760 to 1854, are the exception. The index to War Office (WO) 97, containing discharge documents, has been completed and incorporated into the online catalog of the National Archives, "Procat." In addition, names of soldiers listed in WO 121/1 to 136 which contains certificates of service of Chelsea out-pensions are also in the catalog. Those who were pensioned were actually listed as outpatients of either of the military hospitals at Chelsea (in London) and Kilmainham (near Dublin). Figure 8-1 is a transcript of the results of a search for Alexander Campbell, restricted to WO entries.

The index details may be enough to positively identify the soldier ancestor and the full record can be consulted, as well as additional documents because the regiment is now known. The proper title of WO 97 is Royal Hospital Chelsea Soldiers' Documents and the material includes information on soldiers discharged to pension prior to 1883 and discharged for whatever reason after 1883. For a discharge before 1873 the documents are arranged by regiment, to 1883 in alphabetical order within each section of the service (Cavalry, Artillery, Infantry, Corps), and thereafter in one alphabetical sequence. There remains, therefore, a short period, 1855 to 1872 when it is necessary to know the regiment. The information in the documents includes what is shown in Figure 8-1 as well as age at enlistment, trade, a physical description, and reason for discharge. Records up to 1854 have been filmed and can be found in the FHL.

Not every pensioned soldier's name has been entered into the catalog; not every soldier was discharged to pension; not all former soldiers received a pension; some died in battle or while still in service; some purchased their way out of the army (records of these soldiers do not survive before 1883). A search within the dates 1760 to 1854 should begin by checking for a name using the catalog, but many of you will have to resort to other sources.

For most other army records the regiment is the key. There are several ways to try and discover this detail. Your soldier ancestor may have

Figure 8-1. Results of a Catalog Search for a Soldier Discharged to Pension.

Document Reference	Title/Scope and Content	Covering Dates
WO 97/514/135	ALEXANDER CAMPBELL Born [Not Known] Served in 33rd Foot Regiment Dischaged aged [Not Known] Years of enlistment and discharge are unknown covering dates give a generic date range only	1760-1854
WO 97/1200/112	ALEXANDER CAMPBELL Born [Not Known] Served in 1st Invalid company 39th Regiment Dischaged aged [Not Known] Covering date gives year of discharge	1781
WO 121/1/275	ALEXANDER CAMPBELL Born Craignish Argyllshire Served in 3rd Foot Guards Discharged aged 41 after 15 years 7 months of service	1787
WO 121/9/226	ALEXANDER CAMPBELL Born Calder Nairnshire Served in 3rd Foot Guards Discharged aged 38 after 20 years of service	1790

been caught in a census and the enumerator may have noted his regiment. At the time of his marriage, birth of a child or his death, the registrar may have noted the regiment. If you are lucky an entry will be found in the registers of regimental births (more on these later). Another possibility is to fit the facts with what can be found in books of military history. Do you know where the ancestor served or have some information about a particular campaign or battle in which he took part? Nearly every battle or skirmish of the British Army has been described somewhere, including the names of the units involved. You could also browse through reference books that provide brief histories and battle honors for each regiment. Not so easy to use, but informative on the service of each regiment is *In Search of the Forlorn Hope* (Kitzmiller, 1987).

Many soldiers who had been posted overseas to parts of the British Empire stayed on when their term of service ended. They may have taken a land grant near to the place of discharge. The clue may be lurking in the local history of the place where your ancestor settled, and this occasionally includes reference to the regiment or regiments in the area at the time.

Once the regiment or regiments are known, turn to the records. Soldiers' records, in some cases, begin at the turn of the eighteenth century. You will depend upon records such as pension lists, description books and muster rolls. Description books, as the name suggests, include a description of the soldier, which was useful to the authorities when seeking deserters. Muster rolls are registers of the officers and men of a regiment present at the muster, which was called on a regular basis. The first muster of an individual includes his birthplace and age at enlistment, and sometimes his trade at the time. Each regimental list is by rank and then by order of joining. Muster rolls are available at Kew.

Some of these other records are in the FHL. There are some additional pension records: Royal Hospital Chelsea Regimental Registers 1715-1857 (WO 120) and Registers of Out-Pensioners of the Army and Militia 1759-1863 (WO 118, mainly from Kilmainham). The Chelsea records are, as the title suggests, arranged by the regiment in which the pensioner last served. The Kilmainham record group consists of entry books (some arranged by date pension awarded), an index to some of the years, and a register of the pensioners resident abroad who were transferred to the establishment of the Royal Hospital Chelsea in 1822. Other sources which can help with pensioners resident abroad are WO 22 (Royal Hospital Chelsea Pension Returns 1842-1882; must know district of residence) and *British Army Pensioners Abroad: 1772-1889* (Crowder, 1995).

Depot Description Books 1768-1908 (WO 67) are a good source of information. They give the physical description of each soldier, date and place of birth, trade, promotions, and the reason why the soldier ultimately ceased to be useful to the army. Some soldiers were not included— those who transferred to one regiment from another, and those who enlisted where the regiment was stationed rather than at the depot. Regimental Description Books (in WO 25) are more extensive but do not begin until the nineteenth century. Some of both of these classes are in the FHL.

Officers are somewhat easier to trace. In the first place, the *Army List* includes every officer indicating his regiment, and how long he has been in his current rank. You can read about it in a National Archives/PRO leaflet and it is widely available in the UK and overseas in reference and military libraries, and on microfilm through Family History Centers. Among the documents, Records of Officers Services (WO 76) are useful and have been filmed by the FHL. This series begins quite early and is extensive in the nineteenth century; however, it does not include all regiments. The organization is by regiment, which is not a problem in the case of an officer since you probably located this information already in the *Army List*. As the title implies, WO 76 provides details of service and ranks held and some additional personal information, such as date of marriage and births of children. It is possible to follow an officer's career, including any time spent on half-pay. Officers did not have pensions; they either went on half-pay (i.e., when not actively employed by the army) or sold their commissions.

Also worth considering is WO 42, simply titled *Certificates of Birth, etc.* If an officer died while on full or half-pay, application was sometimes made by the widow for support or on behalf of the children. This series includes certificates of birth/baptism, marriage, and death; probate records; service records; and personal papers during the period from 1755 to 1908. For about one hundred years, from 1776 to 1881, it is arranged alphabetically. The alphabetical part of WO 42 has been filmed and can be obtained through the FHL or Family History Centers.

The Highland regiments, and other Scottish regiments are well represented among the countless books of military history to be found in public and university libraries, museum libraries, the FHL and for sale from specialist bookshops. The Mitchell Library in Glasgow has a large collection and actually produced a bibliography of Scottish military History, *Wha Daur Meddle Wi Me* (1991). Among resources at the FHL can be found musters to a few pre-1707 regiments, the Blotter Register of the Gordon Highlanders 1803-1881 (births and marriages), and Army Muster Rolls copied from the lists at the NAS for the seventeenth and eighteenth centuries. The 1745 Association has published the muster roll of the Stuart army of 1745-46 under the title *No Quarter Given* (Livingstone, Aikman and Hart, 2001). Other military titles are in the bibliography.

The militia is the reserve force of the army. These soldiers mustered and trained occasionally and were liable to be called up in times of national emergency. To be strictly accurate the militia of the British Army dates from 1797. Other units, which date from earlier times, were volunteer and fencible regiments. The former served at home and the latter anywhere in the British Isles. Militia units had no such restrictions. These records usually give name, occupation and dwelling place; occasionally a birthplace is added. Men eligible for service (aged 18 to 45 with some exemptions) were listed and subsequently mustered according to a ballot system. The list is therefore more complete. It was possible to pay someone to be a substitute at a muster. To locate these records consult *Militia Lists and Musters* (Gibson and Medlycott, 2000) and guides to the records of sheriff courts and county councils at the NAS; a check of the FHLC is also a worthwhile.

Within the collections of the General Register Office in London, there is a group of records, separate from the births, marriages, and deaths of England and Wales, which relates to the army. These are registers of army births and marriages from 1761 and of deaths from 1796. The regimental series of births/baptisms and marriages begins in 1761 for home events and in about 1790 for those occurring abroad. The births/baptisms of children born to the wives of soldiers have been indexed, and these indexes include the regiment. The latter fact is important because it may mean that this resource is a tool for finding a soldier's regiment or it may at least narrow the field to a few soldiers with the same name. You must have some idea of when and where children were born. The marriage records are not indexed, so it is necessary to know the regiment and an approximate date. Another set of vital records is called the Chaplain's Returns, 1796-1880. They record births, baptisms, marriages, deaths, and burials, are indexed (regiment not included), and relate to events abroad.

The Scots also went to sea, although not in the same numbers. If they served with the Royal Navy, the records are available through the National Archives at Kew. Of that massive collection, the FHL has filmed the Continuous Service Engagement Books 1853-1896. The years from 1853 to 1872 are classified as Admiralty 139, and 1873-1891 as Admiralty 188. Arrangement is by seamen's numbers, but separate indexes are available. The entries show date and place of birth, physical description at enlistment, and details of service. Before the middle of the nineteenth century the main source of information is the ships' musters. These are at Kew (1667-1878, Admiralty 36-41); the key to searching these records is the name of the seaman's ship. Determining the ship is a challenge, though not an insurmountable problem, particularly with the help of an experienced researcher. Somewhere between 1828 and 1836 musters acquire "alphabets," which are indexes of surnames grouped by first letter only. About fifty years earlier, a few as early as 1765, the navy pay books (1691-1856, ADM 31-35) have alphabets, and give the seaman's ship. Much of the information in the two record groups is similar (pay books may include mention of next of kin), so that one can be used when the other is missing, or perhaps to speed the search in the other. Research can be hindered by the fact that in the 1700s and 1800s a seaman did not always serve his entire career in the navy, but may have been in and out of it and the merchant service. For more information consult a specific guide, *Tracing Your Naval Ancestors* (Pappalardo, 2003).

Once again, officers present fewer difficulties. A *Navy List* (issued quarterly since 1814) provides rank, date promoted, ship, and the station to which the ship was attached. (The lists of ships attached to each station can help narrow the search for a seaman's ship if a place of service is known.) Every officer of the rank of lieutenant or above had to have passed his certificate. In ADM 107 are volumes of certificates, supporting documents, and baptismal records. There are indexes. Additional records at Kew, which you may want to read more about, are Succession Books

(ADM 11 deals with Lieutenants, Commanders and Captains from 1780 to 1847). They are a record of service for commissioned officers arranged by ship. For other ranks there are Certificates of Service, required by a seaman before applying for a medal, a pension, or for entry to the seamen's hospital at Greenwich. First issued in 1790, some references go back forty years earlier (ADM 73). Other records of seamen are discussed under Ships and Railways later in this chapter.

A few of you will discover that the subject of your research was in the Royal Marines (soldiers who served on board ships), or in the Royal Artillery, or in India. If your ancestor was an officer he will show up in the *Navy List* or the *Army List*; Marine officers appear in both. National Archives finding aids indicate the separate classes for marines and artillerymen and a selection of records of these units can be found in the FHLC under "Military records."

If your ancestor was in India, begin by gaining some understanding of the East India Company, the British Army in India, the Indian Army, and the records at the India Office library. *India Office Library and Records: a Brief Guide to Biographical Sources* (Baxter, 1990) is a helpful tally of sources. At the British Library website there is information on carrying out searches in the Oriental and India Office collections. Their catalog can be searched using the Access to Archives website (see page 208). There is a growing collection of records of the East India Company at the FHL.

Military and naval material proliferates on the Internet. For historical background on regiments, essential because of the changes in army structure, start with the site for the Land Forces of Britain, the Empire and Commonwealth. The National Army Museum, Chelsea, includes historical information and has articles on the Civil War and battles in Scotland. There are no official naval records for Scotland. For the Royal Navy, consult the wonderful resources at the National Maritime Museum, Greenwich; both the main site and the *Port* information site. All these URLs can be found in appendix D.

Professions

The professions include doctors, lawyers, accountants, clergymen, professors, teachers, and engineers, to name the most obvious. Certainly, all occupations such as these have professional associations, some of which have existed for a very long time. As a matter of course check the professional lists in the nearest reference library. There are some in the NAS, the National Library of Scotland has many, there is a well-known collection of professional lists at the Society of Genealogists in London, and a selection in the FHL; to name a few locations. Directories, discussed in chapter 4, are a useful source for names and addresses of professionals. *Whitaker's Almanac* is worth consulting for the name and address of an existing professional association which may retain membership information that goes back a long way.

The initial volume of *The Medical Register* appeared in 1858 and it has been published annually since. Some of the doctors included in that first edition received their degrees before 1800. Copies can be found in all large libraries in Scotland and in the Wellcome Library for the History of Medicine in London, a remarkable repository of books, manuscripts, etc., that relate to almost every aspect of the human condition. Another annual listing is *The Medical Directory*, which has been included in the Index to British and Irish Biographies issued by Chadwyck-Healey on microfiche (see appendix B). The 1856 volume is also in the FHL. For a time before the appearance of the *Register*, address an inquiry to one of the following: Royal College of Physicians, Edinburgh; Royal College of Surgeons, Edinburgh; or Royal College of Physicians and Surgeons, Glasgow (see appendix D).

For lawyers, there is a publication known as *The Law List*, issued since 1848, and also available in main libraries in Scotland. There are several alternative sources. At the top of the legal ladder in Scotland were the judges of the Court of Session and all those from earliest records until 1832 are listed in *An Historical Account of the Senators of the College of Justice* (in the FHL, in book form and on film). Lawyers who could plead at the Court of Session were called advocates. The Scottish Record Society issued *The Faculty of Advocates 1532-1943* (1943); since it is one of their publications, it will be readily available in Scotland and fairly accessible elsewhere. Many solicitors are listed in the pages of *A History of the Society of Writers to Her Majesty's Signet* (in the FHL, in book form and on film) which names everyone in the society to 1832. The Signet is one of the Crown seals of Scotland, and writer is another term for solicitor.

Churches have maintained and usually published the names of their ministers for a considerable length of time. *Fasti Ecclesiae Scoticanae* (Scott et al, 1915-61) is a series of volumes which gives biographical details on all the known ministers of the Church of Scotland. The major breakaway churches are covered by four more titles: *Reformed Presbyterian Church in Scotland; its Congregations, Ministers and Students 1743–1876*, *Annals of the Free Church of Scotland 1843-1900*, *Annals and Statistics of the Original Secession Church*, *History of the Congregations of the United Presbyterian Church 1733-1900* and *Fasti of the United Free Church of Scotland*. The NAS holds an index to ministers extracted from the yearbooks of the Episcopal Church of Scotland. For Roman Catholic ministers make enquiries to the Scottish Catholic Archives. The FHL holds all the listed titles for Presbyterian officials as well as a selection of directories and yearbooks and volumes of church history.

Society tends to respect and honor its architects, so most communities have some record of who designed the library, the town hall, and the finest houses. Edinburgh is a wonderful example of a city that is proud of its architecture. The New Town to the north of the Castle and Princes Street was a major rebuilding project of the late eighteenth century. Nearly every building is listed (i.e., cannot be altered without planning permission), and information on James Craig, who created the plan, and other architects subsequently involved, is readily available.

When searching for architects, those who attained prominence are likely to be found in dictionaries of biography; other sources are professional directories and books of local history or architecture. Plans of buildings may be in local archives or libraries in Scotland or among the extensive collection of plans of the NAS in West Register House; this has an index to architects and surveyors associated with it. Another potentially useful resource is the Royal Commission on the Ancient and Historical Monuments of Scotland. It records and interprets historic sites, monuments and buildings and maintains the National Monuments Record of Scotland; more details and a database are online.

There are sources of information regarding teachers and professors, and their students. Volumes of graduates of various schools and colleges have been published (some are listed in the bibliography), or direct an inquiry to the library in the appropriate region. The Society of Genealogists has many school and university lists and has published a guide to its collection (Society of Genealogists, 1988). *The Growth of British Education and its Records* (Chapman, 1992) includes a chapter on Scottish education records.

Before 1872, local schoolmasters were listed in burgh or town council minutes, as this was the authority which hired them. In rural parishes, decisions to hire masters or mistresses were made by the heritors, so a record of this might survive in the Heritors Records at the NAS. Kirk session records may also reveal a schoolmaster's identity, because in some communities he acted as the session clerk. In the more remote parts of Scotland, teaching was often provided through the Scottish Society for the Propagation of Christian Knowledge. This Society provided schools and teachers in the Highlands from early in the eighteenth century. The masters' names show up in various files, such as school registers, salary books, and inspectors' reports. These records are at the NAS.

Merchants and Manufacturers

This category includes people who operated a business on a larger scale, i.e., were importers and exporters, manufacturers, owners of linen mills or mines, operators of breweries, etc. Some businesses operate to this day. Verify a business' existence by checking telephone directories or by asking the Registrar of Companies at Companies House (address in appendix D). Many records of existing and defunct companies have been deposited with libraries and archives, including the NAS, where they are housed in West Register House. There is a card index. To determine the location of other collections check the catalog listings at the websites of the Scottish Archives Network SCAN) and the Scottish Records Association (SRA), or write to the National Register of Archives (Scotland). Records of small companies may be in local libraries. The University of Glasgow has a Business Record Centre, but the staff prefers that you first ask the National Register of Archives (Scotland) about the location of material. Among their holdings are the Clyde Shipyard records. Board minutes are not very helpful, but from employee records you will learn about such things as wage rates, and indirectly, about standards of living.

Some industries and businesses have been the subject of a study by the government or the recipients of assistance. Others have been described in books and articles. The *Statistical Accounts* of the parish usually include an account of trade and local manufacturing. The account may not mention anyone by name, but it could be very helpful to know, for example, that the local cotton manufacturer was shut down for many months in

1790 at Langholm in Dumfries.² If you become particularly interested in the details of one business, build a bibliography on the subject. Searching through library catalogs and bibliographies will show that much has been written on business history. The linen industry is no exception.

The Ford family, which has been mentioned previously, were usually described as merchants of Montrose. Additional details on their businesses emerged from the Scottish Genealogy Society volume of Angus monumental inscriptions which noted that the family was active in shipping and linen manufacture. It soon became apparent that much has been written about the linen industry in Scotland and that the government took a considerable interest in its development. An examination of the few books on the subject at the university library in Victoria, B.C., revealed the fact that the Ford mill was sold on July 11, 1817, and produced an interesting description of what went on inside the mill:

> Each piece [of sail-cloth or sail-duck] is 38 yards long and numbered from 8 to 1. No. 8 weighs 24 lb., and every piece, down to No. 1, gains 3 lb. in the piece. The thread for this cloth is spun here, not by the common wheel, but the hands. Women are employed, who have the Flax placed round their waist, and twist a thread with each hand as they recede from a wheel turned by a boy at the end of a great room.3

You can conclude from all this that surveying local libraries, reviewing bibliographies and catalogs, and building some knowledge of business records is a worthwhile endeavor. Very likely, either relevant facts or evidence of potentially useful sources will emerge.

Craftsmen and Tradesmen

Some of our ancestors who were in business for themselves in the burghs were recorded in surviving burgh records. Anyone who was a member of a guild or needed a license was mentioned. Small shopkeepers, pedlars, hawkers, and clerks were less likely to appear in minutes and ledgers, but they may be found elsewhere if, for example, they sought poor relief or incurred the displeasure of the authorities. Burgh records are spread about so you will need to check with the NAS and with local repositories. Those using FHL resources can search the FHLC under Scotland, the county and the burgh name, selecting the topic "Occupations" in each case. These records may also turn up under "Public

Records" and "History" but a keyword search would get around this. Among the trades and crafts represented are engravers, pewterers, knitters, potters, and clockmakers.

The burgh council, made up of merchants (or burgesses), was responsible for the affairs of the town. Burghs were originally created to foster trade, but their responsibilities expanded. There was maintenance of, for example, the streets, the bridges, the tollbooths, and the schools. There was administration—organizing the fairs, holding burgh courts, collecting fines, stents (property assessment), and fees and rents. Sometimes the burgh councils got into financial difficulty, borrowed money, fell behind, had to raise fees, etc., and generally became unpopular.

The Scottish Record Society published the lists of burgesses for the cities of Edinburgh (Watson, 1930) and Glasgow (Anderson, 1935). The former are in the FHL and both are in any large library in Scotland. A recently published listing of 8500 names comes from Ayrshire, *The Burgesses and Guild Brethren of Ayr 1647 – 1846* (Lindsay and Kennedy, 2003). Sometimes, you can track several generations. If you are researching from a distance and want to pursue this line of research check the SCAN and SRA websites, or check the catalog of specific libraries; and read the leaflets available from the NAS. The collections of the Angus Archives at Montrose include burgh minute books and trade records for such occupations as shoemakers, bakers, hammermen, and weavers in Montrose, and in three or four different communities nearby. Within the time frame being considered you must browse burgh and guild sources, documents such as council minutes, accounts, licensing records, membership lists and charity records.

Apprenticeships, which bound someone to serve a master for a specified period in return for instruction, food, and lodging, were arranged by private agreement. Survival of the contract is uncertain. There are a few published lists of indentures from the guild records of the large cities, or you may find something in burgh records as was alluded to above. There is, however, another possibility. For about one hundred years, the government at Westminster imposed a stamp duty on apprenticeships throughout Britain, and so kept a record of those who paid. Correctly titled the *Apprenticeship Books of Great Britain* and dating from 1710 to 1811, the records are classified under the Board of Inland Revenue. They are divided into town (London) and county registers and the details recorded were name of the apprentice, date of indenture, name and trade of the master, and duty paid. Until 1754, the parents of the apprentice were also included. These records are at the National Archives at Kew, and they have been filmed for the FHL. The Society of Genealogists has indexed them to 1774 (they are also on film) and part of the index to masters can be purchased in microfiche format.

Ships and Railways

For ancestors who went to sea with fishing fleets or the merchant service, records are scattered. The NAS has some records of whalers (1750-1825) and men in the herring fleets (1752-1896). Local libraries in port communities may hold additional material. Once again, the perusal of the SCAN and SRA websites will help you decide about further research. Try out general search engines as well; one very good example of what can be achieved is found at the website for Tayside: A Maritime History.

There are some merchant marine records, and limited indexes, in the FHL; search using "Great Britain – Military records." The collection includes the Registers of Seamen (Board of Trade 112, 113, 116, and 120). The originals of these records are at Kew, but this is not the only repository for merchant shipping records. Begin your search with the National Archives/PRO leaflets; they include topics like service records, crew lists and the Registrar General of Shipping and Seamen.

The largest collection of merchant service records after 1860 is in the Maritime History Archive at Memorial University of Newfoundland. You cannot simply write to request details about a seaman—there are no alphabetical lists of names. You must know the ship and its number and an approximate date. To find the correct ship number, look in a volume of *Lloyd's Register* at a time the ship was in service. These volumes are in the libraries of maritime museums, in some reference collections and on film in the FHL. They list all merchant ships from 1890 and were published annually. Some of the details to be found are captain's name, port of registry, where built, tonnage and shipping line. Where the ship is unknown, by using these volumes it may be possible to limit the search to a manageable number of vessels. Using what facts there are, ask a few questions. What was the shipping line? From what port did the ship sail or on what regular run was it? Reference can then be made to some of the many books which have been written about shipping lines, and then back to the information to be gleaned from a study of *Lloyd's Register.*

There is a possibility that a seafaring ancestor or his dependents applied for charitable assistance. The records are known as Trinity House Petitions; the originals are in the possession of the Society of Genealogists, London, and microfilm copies are available through LDS Family History Centers. Trinity House has actually been several houses over the centuries, and the organization is known officially as the Corporation of Trinity House on Deptford Strand. It began as a fraternity of mariners and pilots and grew to have broad responsibilities which included lighthouses, light-ships, and marker buoys. The surviving petitions, which are arranged alphabetically, begin in the 1780s and continue to 1854 when the Merchant Shipping Act came into force.

Ships' officers after 1845 can be traced through records of certificates of competency, some of which are in the FHL. In addition, there are Lloyd's Captains' Registers, held by the Guildhall Library in London, with microfilm copies in the FHL (they do not circulate to Family History Centers, except for the fiche copy of the volume for 1869) and in the National Archives of Canada in Ottawa. The registers are alphabetical and include date and place of birth and precise details of certification and ships commanded. A very useful book on the subject of merchant seamen's records is *My Ancestor Was a Merchant Seaman* (Watts, 2002). Other guides to archives holdings are listed in the bibliography.

The surviving records of shipbuilding and shipping companies have, in most cases, been deposited at the nearest library or archives. The Glasgow City Archives has records of shipbuilding on the Clyde, including a detailed index containing information on more than 20,000 ships. The Dundee District Archive and Record Centre has material from the Dundee, Perth and London Shipping Company. For further information contact the National Register of Archives (Scotland). Maritime resources can be found in many places. If you live near one of the major repositories for maritime sources (two examples are Liverpool and St. John's Newfoundland), a maritime museum, or in any ocean port you will find collections of books and other resources.

Two books provide lots of information on railway employees. *Railway Records* (Edwards, 2001) describes the resources at Kew, which cover 200 companies from earliest beginnings to 1948. *Was Your Grandfather a Railwayman?* (Richards, 1997) lists records in other locations as well. The NAS collection of railway records is at West Register House. Staff records relate to the employees of the railway company, not to those who built the railway lines. Some companies are better represented than others in the collection. If you do not know which company employed your ancestor, a little detective work should produce the answer, unless many different lines operated in the location. *The Ordnance Gazetteer of Scotland* (Groome, 1883-85) mentions the name of the line serving any town which has a railway station, or you may find the information in a regional directory. Contemporary maps usually identify the company that owned the tracks.

Farmers and Laborers

Farmers and laborers is a catchall category for those farming a smallholding, agricultural laborers, weavers, mill workers, miners, etc. Finding names and personal details may be very difficult, but there is certainly a wealth of information describing pay, tasks, and working and living conditions. This information shows up in books, periodicals, government reports, and diaries.

To gain an impression of the tools, techniques and conditions of farming or industry in your ancestor's district, begin by reading the *First* and *New Statistical Accounts*. Follow up with research in local histories, gazetteers and directories.

The NAS has received material from the National Coal Board, which includes records of companies in the last century. Some of these sources list names of employees, anyone injured, or those who borrowed money from the mining company.[4] The Gifts and Deposits at the NAS include many estate papers. These records contain a variety of information related to estate management and industry such as, employees, tenants, farm names, crop rotation books, and volunteer-force muster lists. An FHL review will show a variety of books on farms and farming, coal mining, hand-loom weavers (their distress was the subject of much study), and milling. If you are interested in reports made to the British government, locate *Scottish Economic History in the 19th Century: an analytical bibliography of material relating to*

Scotland in Parliamentary Papers 1800-1900 (Haythornthwaite, 1993). Further information on Parliamentary Papers is in appendix C.

Conclusion

This topic is different. It lacks precise definition and finite boundaries. When you find a birth record, you have the facts. When you find an occupation, there is so much more to discover. You may be diverted to an entirely new area of research which is as big as you want to make it. The preliminary work which you did in maps and history books will seem more relevant. If you are not yet comfortable with periodical indexes, this might be the time to become so. And if you are happy exploring library listings on the Internet you may turn up book titles, published original records, or student theses which relate to your studies.

In this discussion, reference has been made to museums. Local history museums, maritime museums, preserved railways, working mills, restored cottages and houses are just some of the institutions that interpret the lives of our ancestors for us. Often, these museums also have libraries and photographic collections. If you cannot plan a trip to do those things yourself, a friend, relative, or agent could visit one to enquire, to buy background material, and to take pictures. A few addresses are included in appendix D.

Remember also that investigating someone's occupation may be the only way to gain enough information to identify an ancestor or to discover his or her date of birth.

Notes

1. Sinclair, 1997, 101.
2. Sinclair, Vol. IV, 370.
3. Warden, 1864, 575.
4. Sinclair, 1997, 122.

Summary—Trades and Occupations

1. Establish the parameters of the search. Who is the subject? What was the ancestor's trade or occupation, or did he or she have more than one? When did he or she engage in this type of work?

2. If you know the name of the occupation, be sure to look up at least a brief definition if you are unsure of what the job was.

3. Why is the search being made in occupational records? To learn about working conditions and/or the local scene, or to find essential facts that did not turn up in usual resources?

4. Assess the resources most accessible to you, list them and check this against information on what is available on the occupation. Refer to the books mentioned here as well as guides and leaflets from repositories with major collections. Be sure to investigate resources on the Internet.

5. Prepare a research plan, noting where you need assistance at another location.

6. Broaden you information base by investigating indexes and databases for periodical and historical publications.

9 • Taxes and Contracts

here are times when basic, indexed, and readily accessible resources do not provide the answers. Typical factors are a lack of good base information, a family move, and missing records. When this occurs, consider alternative sources.

Taxation records are sometimes lumped with descriptions of census and census substitutes. Although they can be characterized as a form of enumeration, they are less informative and less inclusive of the local population; however, these shortcomings should not obscure the value of taxation records. They can help you identify ancestors, and the tax information adds another perspective.

The Registry of Deeds is another set of documents to be aware of when you seek supplementary information or when you seem to have reached a dead end. You can consult indexes for most years since 1660, except for a gap in the middle of the eighteenth century. Embarking on a search is something of a fishing expedition, but the catch could be substantial. The deeds relate to marriage contracts, testaments, and an assortment of rather ordinary agreements, incorporating topics such as trade, drainage, and construction. There is obviously potential to find in these documents individuals from all levels of society.

A Word on Local Administration

The first burgh was established in the twelfth century, and by the beginning of the eighteenth century there were nearly 300—seventy-seven royal burghs and about 200 others, the majority known as burghs of barony. The rights and privileges of the burgh (e.g., the tenure of land and the holding of fairs), were spelled out in its charter. The burghs of barony were much smaller, perhaps not even a town as the word is understood today, created with the permission of the Crown by someone who in Scotland would be referred to as a superior or subject superior. Royal burghs were larger, were established by royal charter, held their lands directly from the Crown, and had representation in the pre-1707 Scots parliament. They had exclusive control over foreign trade and elected a council and the magistrates who officiated at the burgh court.[1]

Heritors were local landowners who were taxed or asked to make donations for the maintenance of the church and support of its parish work. Heritors met to resolve issues of parish administration. Some of their minutes and accounts have survived and are located in a separate class in the National Archives of Scotland (NAS). The commissioners of supply, essentially a committee selected from the landowners, determined the amount of cess, or land tax, to be paid by each landowner. They were gentry (i.e., landowners without titles), rather than nobility. Later, the commissioners were given other responsibilities, such as roads and schools. They worked with the kirk session, as the responsibilities were not clearly delineated. In the burghs, the kirk sessions cooperated with the burgh administration over such matters as poor relief.

Tax Records

The government was hungry for money in the later Stuart period after 1660. In the years prior to the union, the Scottish parliament borrowed some tax collection techniques from Westminster in the form of the hearth tax and the poll tax. After the Union, and especially toward the end of the eighteenth century, a number of different taxes were applied to all of Britain. The years of collection for many of these taxes suggest that they were collected to raise funds for the war with France, which went on from 1792 to the defeat of Napoleon at Waterloo in 1815, with only a short-lived period of peace in 1801 and 1802.

In Scotland, the hearth tax was imposed in 1691. The levy was based on the householders at that time, although in some areas it was several years before the collection was completed. This is after the time the tax was collected in England and Wales; William III abolished this tax in 1689 south of the border where it had come to be regarded as oppressive. This opinion arose, not surprisingly, from the fact that the tax was imposed on the occupant of the home rather than the owner. The records are arranged by county, by parish, and by occupant's name (see figure 9-1). The number of hearths gives an impression of the size and value of a house.

Somewhat more informative are the poll tax records, levied first in 1694. This was a head tax, payable by everyone, male and female. Only people on charity, anyone under the age of sixteen years, or members of a household whose total tax due was thirty shillings or less, were excused. There were some additional assessments on tradesmen, servants, and tenants. Rates were set for each of the levels of the nobility, for advocates, army officers, etc. These records may name each person in the house for whom the tax was payable, indicating relationship to the head of the household. The last year for the poll tax was 1699.

A list of poll tax records in the NAS can be found in the *National Index of Parish Registers*, Vol. XII (Steel 1970). The extensive poll tax rolls for Renfrewshire and Aberdeenshire are worth highlighting. The latter are available in a series of booklets from the Aberdeen and NE Scotland Family History Society. *The Hearth Tax, Other Later Stuart Tax lists and the Association Oath Rolls* (Gibson, 1996) includes listings of hearth and poll taxes in Scotland. The hearth and poll taxes are found for some areas in the Family History Library (FHL) of The Church of Jesus Christ of Latter-day Saints (LDS). Begin by examining the Family History Library Catalog (FHLC) using the topic "Taxation" at all three levels—Scotland, county, and parish.

Of the other levies imposed by revenue-hungry and imaginative mandarins of government, the window tax existed the longest, from 1748 to 1798. The information given is the number of houses in the parish, the

Figure 9-1. Hearth Tax for the Parish of Scoonie.

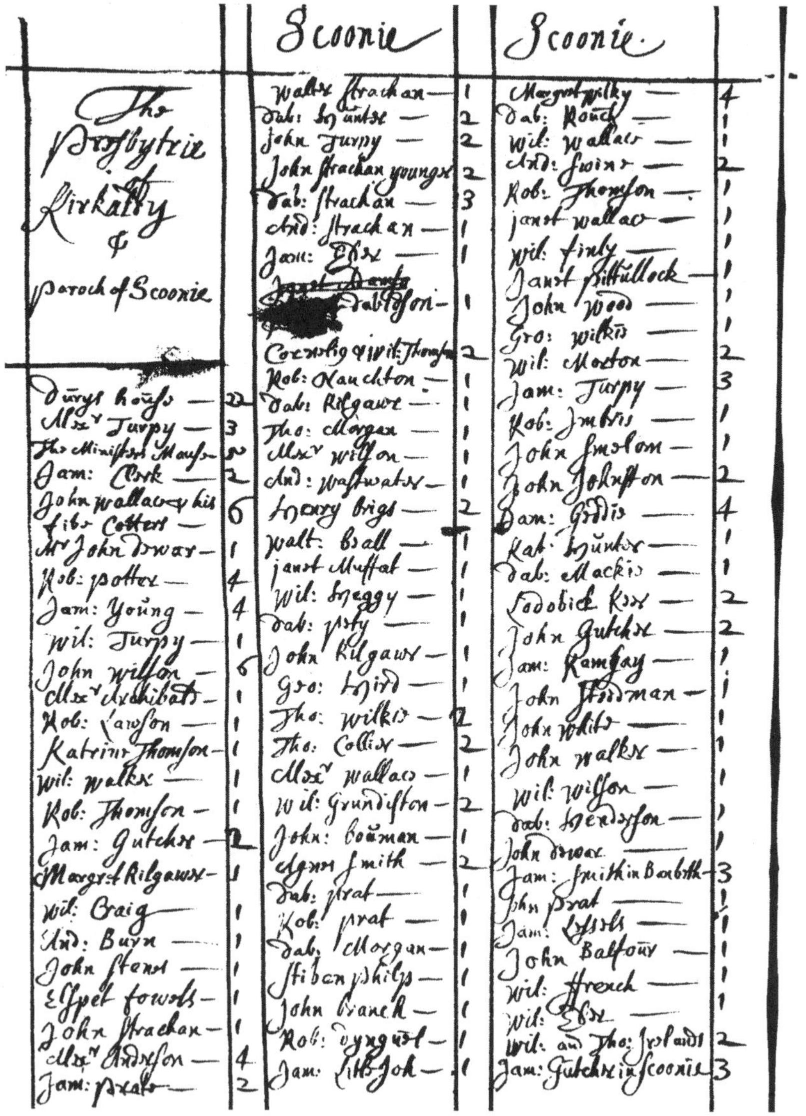

The Presbytrie of Kirkaldy & Paroch of Scoonie		Scoonie		Scoonie	
		Walter Strachan	1	Margret wilky	4
		Dab: Hunter	2	Dab: Rouch	1
		John Turpy	2	Wil: wallace	1
		John Strachan younger	2	And: Swiner	2
		Dab: Strachan	3	Rob: Thomson	1
		And: Strachan	1	Janet wallace	1
		Jam: Elder	1	Wil: finly	1
		~~Janet Dauis~~		Janet Pittullock	1
		[illegible] Dabidson	1	John wood	1
				Gro: wilkie	1
		Coxwlig & wil: Thomson	2	Wil: Morton	2
Durys house	22	Rob: Naughton	1	Jam: Turpy	3
Mr Turpy	3	Dab: Kilgawr	1	Rob: Imbrie	1
The Ministers Manse	5	Tho: Morgan	1	John Smelom	1
Jam: Clerk	2	Mr willson	1	John Johnston	2
John wallace & his fiv Cotters	6	And: Wastwater	1	Jam: Geddie	4
		Henry Brigs	2		
Mr John Dwar	1	Walt: Ball	1	Kat: Hunter	1
Rob: potter	4	Janet Muffat	1	Dab: Mackie	1
Jam: Young	4	Wil: Sneggy	1	Lodobick Kerr	2
Wil: Turpy	1	Dab: Pety	1	John Gutcher	2
John willson	6	John Kilgawr	1	Jam: Ramsay	1
Mr Archibald	1	Gro: Laird	1	John Stedman	1
Rob: Lawson	1	Tho: wilkie	2	John White	1
Katrine Thomson	1	Tho: Collier	2	John walker	1
Wil: walker	1	Mr wallace	1	Wil: willson	1
Rob: Thomson	1	Wil: Grundiston	2	Dab: Henderson	1
Jam: Gutcher	2	John: Bowman	1	John Dwar	1
Margret Kilgawr	1	Agnes Smith	2	Jam: Smith in Balbirnie	3
Wil: Craig	1	Dab: Prat	1	John Prat	1
And: Burn	1	Rob: Prat	1	Jam: Lessels	1
John Stenes	1	Dab: Morgan	1	John Balfour	1
Effpet fowels	1	Stiban philps	1	Wil: French	1
John Strachan	1	John Branch	1	Wil: Elder	1
Mr Anderson	4	Rob: Dyngwel	1	Wil: and Tho: Irelands	2
Jam: prate	2	Jam: Littlejohn	1	Jam: Gutcher in Scoonie	3

National Archives of Scotland, Hearth Tax for the County of Fife, E69/10/2, Presbyteries of Kirkcaldy, Cupar, and St. Andrew's, Parish of Scoonie, 1694. By Permission of the Keeper of the Records of Scotland.

number of windows in any houses with seven or more, and the name of the householder. In some parishes only two or three people are mentioned. To avoid paying this tax, some people boarded up their windows. In burghs it is not usually possible to identify individual houses and their occupants, but in rural parishes this information can often be deduced, particularly for the larger houses. These records are at the NAS.

Tax rolls can be a means of confirming the presence of an individual in a parish. Of the other taxes imposed in the latter part of the eighteenth century, two have a better chance of catching a broader spectrum of the population and, therefore, of being helpful in this regard. The farm horse tax, 1797-98, applied to anyone who used a horse in farming or trade. Carriage and saddle horses were taxed from 1785 to 1798. For a time, the employers of servants were assessed for this perceived luxury. Male servants were taxed from 1777 to 1798. An index of those paying tax on male servants in 1780 is at the Society of Genealogists. Records indicate the name of each servant (sometimes the job as well) and the name of the master or mistress. Female servants were added from 1785 to 1792, with the same information noted.

Other objects targeted by the tax gatherers were carriages, inhabited houses, shops, dogs, clocks, and watches. Sometimes, combined levies were made for two or more taxes. The NAS holds these records, arranged by county, within the collections of the Exchequer.[2]

Land taxes in Scotland have been assessed on a regular basis since the middle of the seventeenth century. Land tax was known as the cess, and after the union, it became an annual tax with valuations of property carried out and recorded under the authority of the commissioners of supply. Whereas the taxes discussed above had a wider application, including occupants as well as owners, the land tax affected only landowners, a much smaller percentage of the population. The existence of valuation rolls before the system was changed by the Valuations of Lands Act in 1855, is very limited and spotty. From 1855, however, the annual valuations are complete and very informative. The property is identified, along with a description of its use, its rateable value, and the names of the proprietor and the occupant, the latter named only if the property was let for more than £4.00 per year (see figure 9-2). These records can be used in conjunction with census returns not only to check back and forth for family locations, but to build up a picture of growth and change in a community.

Figure 9-2. Valuation Roll—Parish of Dun.

375

PARISH OF DUN.

No.	Description and Situation of Subject	Proprietor	Tenant	Occupier	Inhabitant Occupier not rated (48 Vict. cap. 3, secs. 3 & 9)	Ann. Val. of Dwelling-houses of Prem. Inh./Occ. or Proprietary or Ground Ann. of other Subjects £ s. d.	Yearly Rent or Value £ s. d.	Agric. Rating Act, 1896, Pns. of Rent or Value £	No.
	CRAIGO, ESTATE OF	Sir George Macpherson Grant of Ballindalloch, per Claude. Ralston, Factor.							
1	Woods, Glenakenno.			Proprietor			10 0 0		1
2	Shootings, do.	do		do			10 0 0		2
3	Farms and House, Glenakenno.	do	Andrew Spence's Reps.	Tenants			440 0 0	165	3
4	House, Glenakenno.	do			Alex. Martin, Grieve	4 0 0			4
5	do do	do			James Coutts, Ploughman	4 0 0			5
6	do do	do			James Moug, Gardener	4 0 0			6
7	do do	do			Chae. Davie, Ploughman	4 0 0			7
8	do do	do			Wm. Balfour, Cattleman	4 0 0			8
9	do do	do			Mrs. Jane Haddon, Outwkr.				9
10	do do	do			Wm. Webster, Farm Servt.	4 0 0			10
11	House and Croft, Damside of Glenakenno	do	John Clark	Tenant			30 0 0	11	11
12	Farm and Houses, Balvyllo & Balhillo.	do	James Sanson	do	David Rae, Grieve	5 0 0	700 0 0	263	12
13	House	do			Chas. Johnston, Gardener	4 0 0			13
14	do	do			John Beattie, Cattleman	4 0 0			14
15	do	do			Geo. Donaldson, Ploughman	10 0 0			15
16	do	do			Joseph Greig, Farm Servant	4 0 0			16
17	do	do			William Torrie, Ploughman	1 10 0			17
18	do	do			Empty	4 0 0			18
19	do Balhillo.	do			George Walker, Ploughman				19
20	do do	do			George Coull, Cattleman				20
21	do Balhillo.	do							21
22	Shootings, Balvyllo and Balhillo	do	James Sanson, above	Tenant for	Alex. Craig, Porter.		15 0 0		22
23	House and Garden, Bridge of Dun	do	A. J. W. H. Kennedy Erskine of Dun [Dun	Tenant			8 10 0		23
24	Shootings, Disfof Dun, Woodside, Balhillo	do	John Malcolm's Reps.	Tenants			10 0 0		24
25	Farm & Houses, &c., Woodside of Balhillo	do			Peter Leslie, Farm Manager	12 0 0	30 4 0	11	25
26	House do	do			Mrs George Greig.	4 0 0			26
27	do do	do							27
	DUN, ESTATE OF	Augustus John William Henry Kennedy Erskine, per Lindsay, Howe & Co. W.S., 22 Charlotte Square, Edinburgh							
28	Mansion House and Garden, Dun			Proprietor			125 0 0		28
29	Policies do	do		do			25 0 0		29
30	Shootings do	do		do			35 0 0		30
31	House do	do		do	David Wood, Coachman.	4 0 0			31
32	do do	do		do	Andrew Foote, Gamekeeper	4 0 0			32
33	Woods, Dun.	do					11 0 0		33
34	Green Parks, Dun.	do			Andrew Lamb, Overseer.	5 0 0	816 0 0	119	34
35	House do	do			James Gore, Labourer.	4 0 0			35
36	do do	do			John Dundas, Gardener	4 0 0			36
37	do do	do			Alex. Harrison, Labourer.	4 0 0			37
38	West Lodge, Dun.	do			James Crockatt, Labourer.				38
39	Cottage do	do					3 0 0		39
40	Farm and House, Mains of Dun	do	Proprietor for Robert Rodger's Representatives	Tenants	Robert Rodger, Farmer.	25 0 0	750 0 0	282	40
41	Farm House do	do			James Kerr, Ploughman	4 0 0			41
42	House do	do			Empty				42
43	do do	do							43

Extracted from *Valuation Roll of the County of Forfar for the years 1904-1905*. Published by direction of the County Council. Dundee: John Leng and Co. Ltd., 1905.

To use valuation rolls effectively, it is important to refer to maps of the area. This becomes absolutely essential for built-up areas, especially the cities of Edinburgh and Glasgow. If you have access to an index to place names and streets, even if it is for the wrong year for your purpose, it may guide you to the right parish and hence focus your search. For Edinburgh after 1895, it is helpful to know the ward of a particular street; you can find this information in city directories. The difficulty of an urban search is compounded by the fact that the information about a given street may not be located together in an orderly fashion.[3] Even where street name indexes exist, they may not be helpful if they do not explain when name changes occurred. Refer to chapter 1 and the bibliography for a reminder of the maps and other finding aids which may be helpful.

There is a complete set of surviving rolls in the NAS and there are collections in some local repositories in Scotland (e.g., in the Edinburgh City Library). Before visiting a library, check ahead, read the leaflet at the NAS website, and look for information at the Scottish Archives Network (SCAN). Some valuation rolls have been filmed and can be viewed at Family History Centers. Be aware that searches through populated areas in valuation rolls can be tedious, even with maps.

The Registry of Deeds

Any time the parties to an agreement, contract, or transaction chose to ensure the preservation or validity of an undertaking, they sought the backing of a court. The documents or deeds were registered and the volumes of registers of the Court of Session came to be called the Registry of Deeds (the proper term for them was *Books of Council and Session*). There are indexes to the Registry of Deeds, but they are complex. A lack of indexes and few minute books mean that no help can be found in records of other courts where deeds could be registered; this refers to any other court before 1809, the sheriff courts, and the royal burgh courts thereafter.[4]

Would your ancestor have entered into some sort of contract or agreement? That is difficult to predict. He may have repaired the church roof, rebuilt a local bridge after a storm, been party to a marriage contract or been the beneficiary of a testament. It was not necessary to be of high social standing to be a party to a deed. Chances are good enough and results informative enough to justify the search; Gerald Hamilton-Edwards

(*In Search of Scottish Ancestry*, 1983) devotes a chapter to showing how a pedigree can be constructed from details found in deeds. My own research has turned up a marriage contract that revealed the long obscure where-abouts and origins of a female line.

The matter of access and the difficulty of the search will undoubtedly be factors in your decision. If you are working with FHL resources it is quite possible that catalog entries appear confusing—search the topic "Land and property" for Scotland as a whole, select the title "Deeds, minute books and index of deeds and probate writs: 1542-1851" and the details present eight names and various time periods. Scott, Dalrymple, and the rest were at var-ious times clerks of the Court of Session. Only through NAS indexes is it possible to find out which clerk registered the deed that you are interested in; fortunately the indexes are consolidated and include the names of everyone involved in a contract. The indexes for the first thirty-five years, 1661 – 1696, are in the FHL under the same heading and the sub-topic "Indexes" or they can be purchased from the NAS.

From 1696 to 1770, the indexes relate to only a limited number of years: 1696 to 1711, 1750 to 1752, and 1765.[5] These indexes have not been filmed. The records of the unindexed years must be accessed through the minute books (chronological diaries). There are three sets, and you must search all of them. In 1770, a new continuous series of annual index-es begins (in the FHL under the same title "Deeds, minute books and index of deeds and probate writs: 1542-1851"), but this time based solely on the name of the grantor. If it is more likely that your ancestor was on the other side of the table, it presents a problem to the degree that it might deter your search. The odds can be improved by knowing the names of the local landowners because the name of each grantee, though not indexed, is included in each reference. Therefore, by searching for each entry in the local landowner's name, you could check then for the name of the subject of your search. Sources for the identity of landowners include the *Statistical Accounts*, the various published returns of owners of land, directories, gazetteers, valuation rolls, and books on local history.

Conclusion

Taxation lists and details of contracts appear less interesting on the surface, relate to a limited segment of the population and, for the distance researcher, are more difficult to access. Nevertheless, they are worth considering since a number of you will discover an ancestor who qualifies to be found among those named. Compare the years of collection and the details of the various taxes to your own research to determine if any of them might be a source of useful information. Take a little extra time to survey the neighborhood. It may prove useful to try to reconstruct several families within the parish through, for example, the poll tax records, as this may help you sort out the names in the Old Parochial Registers and determine another generation. An interesting account of this technique can be read in the article "William Edward, Identifying an Eighteenth Century Aberdeenshire Miller" (Hinchliff, *Aberdeen & NE Scotland FHS Journal*, Aug. 1994).

Notes

1. Moody, 1994, 54.

2. Sinclair, 1997, 96-97.

3. Sinclair, 1997, 63.

4. Sinclair, 1997, 71.

5. Sinclair, 1997, 69-70.

Summary—Taxes and Deeds

1. Verify the facts associated with the search (name, geo-graphic area, range of years) and from the various tax records and deed indexes, select the relevant records to search.

2. Determine how much of the search you can undertake your-self, based on your location and access to microfilm copies (check the FHLC). If assigning work to someone else, have a good understanding of what is available to the agent and state your purpose clearly. Check the SCAN website to view sample documents (Lanark cess 1724-5 and Kilsyth Heritors' Minutes early 1800s).

3. Take into account the fact that searches over several years in unindexed records can involve quite a bit of time. This is particularly a problem with the records of the Registry of Deeds for much of the 1700s.

10 • Special People

 ome of your ancestors undoubtedly attracted the special attention of the church, the courts, or government of one level or another. They may have needed assistance because they fell on hard times, they may have chosen the wrong side in one of the Jacobite rebellions, they may have appeared in court because they broke the law or because they were of an argumentative disposition, or they may have been the unfortunate victims of violent death. In addition, one or more of your ancestors made the difficult decision, willingly or unwillingly, to leave Scotland and start a new life overseas.

The Poor

Until the middle of the nineteenth century and the adoption of The Poor Law Amendment (Scotland) Act, 1845, two principles guided the system of poor relief. The home parish, or the parish of settlement, of each individual was responsible for that person's assistance, and a distinction was made between able-bodied poor and the destitute. The former required only short-term relief until they could find work; the latter required regular assistance because of infirmity, old age, and the inability of other family members to provide support. Settlement status was acquired by parentage, birth, marriage, or three years residency in the parish. A claimant had to be unable to support him- or herself and be without relatives who could offer relief. The destitute sometimes traveled back to the parish of settlement; records show assistance given to beggars on their way home.[1] On the other hand, the same power of removal that was exercised in England was never exercised in Scotland. Paupers frequently stayed in their parishes of choice, even though their assistance might come from another parish.[2] Assistance was not refused to anyone; however, every parish was conscious of its limited resources and tried to avoid paying support when it was not responsible.

In the countryside, the parish, through the kirk session and the heritors, looked after the local welfare, collecting the funds, managing relief and moving vagrants. Sometimes this involved authorizing those who could go about the parish begging for assistance. Money came from voluntary contributions, fines, fees (e.g., for use of the mortcloth, for marriage, or for renting a pew), bequests, collections at the church door, and from a tax on the landholders. If the funds for poor relief came entirely from voluntary contributions, the heritors rarely interfered, leaving decisions about relief to the discretion of the kirk session.[3] Revenue from fines may have been imposed by the magistrates or the kirk session. In some cases, a condition of being placed on the poor roll was to agree to the consignment of personal effects to the kirk session for sale after the person's death. Kirk session records sometimes carefully note the collections made, as in the following example from Fetlar in Shetland:

1852

December 18   David Petrie at Aithness and Molly Sinclair at Funzie contracted this day and were married on the 23rd December, 1852, by the Rev. David Webster. Pd. 2/- to the poor[4]

In towns and burghs, assistance was a more complicated matter. Sometimes, poor relief was doled out by the burgh, usually through the supervision of the magistrates, sometimes by the local church, sometimes by the guilds or the trade organizations. The town was more likely to have a poorhouse or charity workhouse for the very old, the very young, or the sick. Some people belonged to friendly societies (an association or constituted body for the provision of relief during sickness, old age, or widowhood, usually organized by occupation, e.g., foresters or fishermen). Members made payments when they were working, and received help when they were not, rather like a form of unemployment insurance.

With the passage of the Act of 1845, came the beginning of the shift of responsibility away from such a localized system toward the creation of a state bureaucracy to manage social welfare. It was not an abrupt change. Kirk sessions went on giving out assistance long after, but a new system was developing, built around Parochial Boards. Needless to say, this resulted in a new set of records.

Background knowledge of economic history and local history will help you decide whether or not to consult records of the poor. For example, two factors that affected many people over a wide area of Scotland were the potato failure of 1846 (potato failure was not confined to Ireland) and the decline in the linen trade and hand-loom weaving in the first half of nineteenth century. Hand-loom weaving had brought relative comfort to many and relieved the distress of those affected by the changes in agriculture. This occupation made it possible for the old or the widowed to continue earning some income at home. Some weavers earned as much as £2 in four days.[5] The power loom arrived in 1807, and the subsequent competition from mechanically produced cotton led to the disappearance of spinning by 1840. If your ancestor was a hand-loom weaver after 1820, he or she may have required assistance at some time.

Weather reports are a less obvious example of where to find historical information that might point to a search in poor law records. Newspapers, the writings of diarists, and local history books may draw attention to particularly severe winters or other conditions that led to crop failure, hence to a number of people suddenly requiring relief.

Time spent reading about local and national economic conditions will help you determine whether or not these records might be useful. Dip into volumes of history with the help of their tables of contents and consult the appropriate parish description in the First and New Statistical Accounts.

The Records of the Poor

Until 1845, the kirk session records are the first source to consider. Some sort of poor roll may also be located with the records of the heritors of the parish. If you are fortunate, the lists of payments, whether regular, occasional, or in kind (e.g., clothing) was compiled in a separate list, but it is far more likely that you will have to plod through the accounts. You may have to know your ancestor's parish of settlement (remembering that the parish of latest residence may not be that from which he or she received relief), and to have selected a reasonable number of years for the search. The records of the poor in the burghs vary from place to place depending on how the responsibility was shared.

The National Archives of Scotland (NAS) holds an extensive collection of minutes, accounts and other records for the kirk sessions. In recent years some of these have been returned to the appropriate regional archives; usually the NAS has kept microfilm copies. Those of you researching members of secession congregations and other denominations should also consult the Church of Scotland kirk session records. Prior to the 1845 legislation that reformed the poor relief system, the kirk session was responsible for all citizens regardless of where they went to church. Some independent congregations did have their own form of support so look for that as well. The CH 2 repertory at the NAS lists the collection and it can be found summarized in the microfiche guide, *Records of the Church of Scotland and Other Presbyterian Churches*.

Some kirk session records can be accessed on microfilm through the Family History Library (FHL) and Family History Centers. Kirk session records have been collected by the FHL primarily for the baptism and marriage information they contain, but other documents have also ended up in the collection so it is always worth investigating. The logical starting point is a locality search using the name of the parish and the topics "Church records," "Court records," and "Public records." Also, check the Family History Library Catalog (FHLC) for records of the nearest larger town in case ancestors sought relief there. You will want some idea of the overall extent of the relief records for the time and place of your search. Consult the catalogs and guides available through the Scottish Archives Network (SCAN) and Scottish Records Association (SRA) websites, or write to the county repository.

After 1845, once the change in authority occurred, the location of the records varies. A few are at the NAS, but mainly, they are in record offices, libraries, and perhaps still in municipal halls. You may also find some assistance through the knowledge of members of the area family history society.

Glasgow has a superb resource due to the efforts of the Strathclyde Regional Archives (now the Glasgow City Archives) and many volunteers,

Figure 10-1. Example of Kirk Session Record in the FHLC.

```
            Family History Library Catalog 23 Feb 1996        Page 1
                        **Full Display**

AUTHOR
Church of Scotland.  Parish Church of Carnbee.

TITLE
Old parochial registers, 1646-1855.

PUBLICATION INFORMATION
Salt Lake City : Filmed by the Genealogical Society of Utah, 1979.

FORMAT
on 2 microfilm reels ; 35 mm.

NOTES
Microfilm of original records in the New Register House, Edinburgh.

CONTENTS
Carnbee is parish 413.
                                                      BRITISH
                                                      FILM AREA
Session book (includes Baptisms 1646-1670, ------------------- 1040152
    Marriage proclamations 1646-1699, Mortcloth             item 2-3.
    dues [burial records] 1672-1699); Baptisms
    1662-1674, 1693-1819; Marriages 1726-1752,
    1761-1819; Mortcloth dues 1782-1792; Burials
    1790-1819
Session book (includes Marriage proclamations --------------- 1040153
    1705-1726, Mortcloth dues 1706-1760); Baptisms          item 1-2
    1820-1855; Marriages 1820-1848; Burials 1820-
    1854
    .
    Another microfilm copy.  Salt Lake City :
    Filmed by the Genealogical Society of Utah,
    1951. -- 2 microfilm reels ; 35 mm.
Baptisms (years missing as above) 1662-1855; --------------- 0102171
    Marriages (years missing as above) 1726-1848;
    Mortcloth dues 1782-1792; Burials 1790-1854;
    Session book (includes Marriage proclamations
    and Mortcloth dues as above) 1705-1760
Session book (includes baptisms, marriage procla- ---------- 0103243
    mations and mortcloth dues as above) 1646-1699

THIS RECORD FOUND UNDER
    1. Scotland, Fife, Carnbee - Church records


Family History Library Catalog Copyright © 1987, Aug 1995 by
The Church of Jesus Christ of Latter-day Saints.  All Rights Reserved.
```

largely from the membership of the Glasgow and West of Scotland Family History Society. The applications for poor relief in the parishes of Glasgow (beginning in 1851), Barony (beginning in 1861), Govan (beginning in 1876), and numerous other parishes of the region have all been indexed. This index is accessible on computer in the Archives. Considerable detail about the individual applicants and their circumstances are revealed in the records.

The Parochial Boards established by the Poor Law Amendment (Scotland) Act had the power to tax and the authority to build a poor house. Some rural parishes could not possibly afford to do this and so banded together with neighboring parishes to find the resources. Support for the poor house was based on the number of inmates from each parish, so the records indicate the home parish, as well as the usual name, occupation, and date of admission.

A postscript to this discussion is the topic of health records. I mention these records because voluntary hospitals and boards of health kept track of their patients, who were often people not recorded elsewhere. A voluntary hospital was one supported by donations and bequests. The earliest ones opened in the eighteenth century. They kept records of their patients, their staff (although not usually the female nurses and servants), and their benefactors. Health records are not readily available because they remain in local custody, but this topic is the subject of a booklet available from the Aberdeen and NE Scotland Family History Society, *In Sickness and in Health* (Watson, 1988).

Lawbreakers and Litigants

A few of your ancestors, and many more people in total, may have found themselves in a court of law. They may have committed a petty crime or a capital offense, been negligent, sought legal redress over a contract, or disputed the provisions of a will. For the curious, a day in West Register House or a university law library could prove to be interesting and rewarding.

Various courts dealt with different types of cases. The finding aids are not particularly straightforward, and many records are not indexed; however, if you have good reason to believe your ancestor appeared in court the rewards justify the effort. It is not necessary to become an expert on Scottish legal procedure to enjoy the hunt and to turn up results. This discussion begins with the Jacobite rebels, followed by some ideas for looking for family disputes and criminal proceedings.

The number of people transported after the Jacobite uprisings of 1715 and 1745 was quite small, and the records, particularly for the latter, are good. David Dobson, who has studied migration from Scotland to America in considerable depth, has compiled a list entitled *Jacobites of the '15* (1993) which includes the names of many known to have been transported. Records of the Jacobites of the '45 are more extensive. Aberdeen

University Press published the *Muster Roll of Prince Charles Edward Stuart's Army 1745-46* (Livingstone et al., 1984). The Scottish Historical Society, in its First Series, issued *A List of Persons Concerned in the Rebellion* (1890) and in its Third Series, volumes 13, 14, and 15, the Society reproduced various documents and provided an alphabetical list of the prisoners of the '45, taken from state papers (Seton & Arnot, 1928-29). The forfeited estates of Jacobite sympathizers were administered by the Exchequer, so these records at the NAS are a valuable resource. In fact, the NAS has available for sale on fiche the *Records of the Annexed Estates 1755-1769* and *Statistics of the Annexed Estates 1755-1769*. The former describes conditions in the Highlands; the latter lists tenants of farms on the annexed estates. All of the above resources are available through the FHL, and they may be in some university libraries. Also available through the FHL and on CD-ROM (*Scotland North*, Ancestry) is the *Jacobite Cess Roll for the County of Aberdeen in 1715* (Taylor, A. & H., 1932).

When searching the records of Scottish courts, it is best to start from reasonably concrete evidence that one of your ancestors was either tried for a crime or ended up in court over a civil matter. Sources for such evidence might include a newspaper report, family papers or tradition, a clue from a death certificate or a parish register, or mention in a volume of local history. You should know that civil cases were dealt with by the Court of Session or (for lesser cases, commonly debt) the Sheriff Courts, and that criminal cases were the responsibility of either the High Court of the Justiciary (major crimes such as murder, arson, robbery with violence, rape, and appeals from the lower courts) or the Sheriff Courts. The Court of Session was convened only in Edinburgh, while for the High Court of the Justiciary the country was divided into four circuits, each with a circuit town.

In Edinburgh the records you require are at West Register House in Charlotte Square. Read the chapters in *Tracing Your Scottish Ancestors* (Sinclair, 1997) and the NAS leaflet on Crime and Criminals. Without such immediate access, you must turn to the published summaries and accounts of legal cases; these should be well represented in the law libraries of the English-speaking world. The published records of the Scottish legal profession are extensive. Discussions with staff at the Priestly Law Library, University of Victoria, B.C., produced the statistic that as many as 80 percent of cases heard at the higher levels would gain some mention in published form.

At the law library, begin by looking for *The Digest: Annotated British Commonwealth and European Cases* (published from 1950 to the present but containing references to many much earlier cases). The older series titled *The English and Empire Digest* (Halsbury & Chitty, 1919-1932) might also be available. The latter volumes, being from an earlier time, are based on fewer cases, and they also contain a greater proportion of Scottish entries, so odds of finding what you want are better. Each edition has a master index by name of those involved in the cases, which refers you to another volume in the set, which in turn encapsulates the case and indicates the publication in which the court report appears. The law library should have the volumes of case reports. Fishing in this reference material for a common surname is not recommended. The steps to follow from the index to locating the report are described on the facing page.

Several series of volumes cover a large proportion of the decisions handed down by judges in cases of the Court of Session. The descriptions make for tedious reading, dealing as they do with judgements and the technicalities of the law; however, these volumes have name indexes. The longest series is the annual volumes of the *Cases Decided in the Court of Session*, beginning in 1821 and running until the present. It would be possible to consult the indexes in these volumes, identify a case, gain some idea of its nature, and, if convinced that it relates to your research, to direct someone in Edinburgh to seek the more detailed proceedings. You can also refer to the minute books (i.e., chronological diaries or summaries) of the Court of Session, which are available as printed volumes or on microfilm at the FHL, 1805-1955, with gaps. Each volume covers roughly twelve months and is indexed. Thus, it is possible to select an entry in the *England and Empire Digest* consolidated indexes, note the year, and locate the summary in the minute books. Refer to the preceding paragraphs for an idea of what may be found in a court report. There is a greater emphasis on the arguments advanced by the judge in reaching a decision than on the testimony of witnesses.

Criminal trials of the nineteenth century have been summarized in the writings of nine court reporters, or, after 1874, incorporated into the annual volumes of *Session Cases*. For a list, see *The Scottish Legal System: An Introduction to the Study of Scots Law* (Walker, 1981). A set of five volumes, *Reports of Cases before the High Court and Circuit Courts of Justiciary in*

Chain of Steps to Locating a Case Report

1. Look up the name or names in one of the two index volumes (A-L or M-Z) of *The English and Empire Digest* (Halsbury & Chitty, 1919-32). The entry will look like this:

   Blair v. Blair (Scot.); 44. Wills. 624, 865.

   (NB: Cases which involve the same name on either side are usually more likely to have genealogical information because they are family disputes of some kind.)

2. The number 44 is the volume in the same set with the brief notation on the case; Wills is its title, and the other numbers are pages.

3. On page 865, actually in a footnote at the bottom, there are a few lines which identify this as a disputed will and which report the decision. The year of the case is given (1849) and two references to reports: 12 Dunl. (Ct. of Sess.) 97 and 21 Sc. Jur. 612.

4. Reference to the list of reports cited and their abbreviations at the front of the volume indicates that Dunlop, *Cases Decided in the Court of Session*...volume 12, p. 97, and *The Scottish Jurist*, volume 21, p. 612, should be checked.

5. The report in the former volume was found. Miss Elizabeth Blair executed a trust-disposition and settlement, by which she conveyed her property to trustees for testamentary purposes. The bulk of the fortune consisted of moveables. ...The principal beneficiaries are named, viz. William Blair of Blair, Miss Rachael M'Cormick, and Miss Helen M'Cormick. Various other members of the family disputed the provisions of the will. (The summary of the will, the positions of those disputing it, and the judge's decision occupy at least a dozen pages.)

Scotland, compiled by the court reporter Alexander Forbes Irvine, covers the years from 1852 to 1867. These volumes are indexed. Some of the crimes dealt with were poaching, fraud, and cattle-stealing, but there were others, such as culpable and reckless driving of a locomotive (which involved speeds of 25 mph!). The latter report included name, residence, occupation, and injury for everyone hurt in the accident. This suggests that you should also consider court records in which your ancestor might be listed a victim or a witness. The forty-five volumes of the *Scottish Jurist* are another significant resource. Further details on these and other secondary sources on criminal cases are included in the bibliography. The procedure is the same as for civil cases. Once you find something, contact a researcher in Edinburgh to find the details of the trial. Also investigate whether a newspaper report exists.

Anyone searching for case records of Scots transported to Australia can find specific instructions at the SCAN website among responses to FAQs. These answers would help others as well. The Knowledge Base section of the same site contains an index to those who went to Australia assisted by the Highlands and Islands Emigration Society, 1852–57; information includes home parish and estate. At West Register House there is a card index to prosecution papers in the Lord Advocates' records for the years 1812 to 1857, helpful in finding cases of those transported.

A good, plain-language description of the essentials of the Scottish legal system is found in the third chapter of *Scottish Local History* (Moody, 1994). If you intend to hire someone in Edinburgh to do more work, it is advisable to read the relevant sections in *Tracing Your Scottish Ancestors* (Sinclair, 1997). The complexity of the records comes through in the description, but comprehension increases as interest grows.

Did someone in your family tree die in a significant disaster? There have been numerous disasters in Scotland resulting in loss of life, sometimes significant; thirty-one Shetland fishing boats foundered all on one day in 1832 and hundreds died when the Tay Bridge collapsed in 1879. Those of the 1800s and 1900s have been described briefly in a series of three booklets by William Cross: *That Dark Inn* (1997), *The Awful Shadow* (1999) and *An Obscure Grave* (2000).

Migrants

First, heed the warnings in chapter 1 about the origins of your immigrant ancestor. A good knowledge of the lives of the first generation or two of newly settled immigrants, and the places where they lived, is important. There is an excellent chance that this knowledge will narrow your search. A line on the paternal side of my family serves as an example. Alexander Campbell, a Loyalist, brought his family to Canada in 1787 and subsequently sought compensation for his losses in America from the British government. He gave his place of settlement as Fort Edward, New York. A study of the settlement of this area, The Argyle Patent, revealed some information about the Campbell origins. The Argyle Patent was settled by descendants of groups of colonists brought from Argyllshire between 1738 and 1740 by Captain Lauchlin Campbell. A dispute with the governor of New York meant that the promised land grants were never made, and the immigrants dispersed. In 1763, redress was sought, and some of the original colonists, along with the descendants of others, were granted 47,500 acres in Washington County.[6] Historical accounts have identified the parts of Argyllshire from whence the settlers came.

The study of the migration of the Scots has attracted the attention of periodical editors, historians, genealogists, and government officials for a very long time. In the middle of the eighteenth century, the *Scots' Magazine* and the *Gentleman's Magazine* both reported from time to time on the numbers leaving for the New World, occasionally naming names. Also in the eighteenth century, the *Virginia Gazette* reported arrivals in all the colonies, not just Virginia. There are numerous books on the subject in general; of interest to those researching immigrants to Canada and the USA are *Emigration to Colonial America* (Dobson, 1994), *The People's Clearance* (Bumstead 1982), and a bibliography of the sources for links between Scotland and America in the eighteenth century, *Scotus Americanus* (Brock, 1982). Not everyone went straight to their final place of residence; *To the Ends of the Earth* (Neil Robinson, 1997) tells the story of Scots who journeyed first to Nova Scotia and then to New Zealand thirty years later.

The British government took an interest in emigration because of such reasons as worries about depopulation and concern for the conditions in the immigrant ships. A number of parliamentary reports were based on information gleaned from officials—customs officers, sheriffs, and local ministers. These shed considerable light on conditions in Scotland in the nineteenth century. *Voyagers to the West* (Bailyn, 1987) analyses in detail the information collected between 1773 and 1776.

The impetus behind an individual's decision to emigrate is not only interesting to know, but is also likely to suggest further study. Was the migration assisted by an emigration scheme? Some of these schemes were very early, some were privately financed, and others came about through the efforts of the Highlands and Islands Emigration Society, or similar groups, in the nineteenth century. Was your ancestor transported, or was he an indentured servant? Was he a member of a Highland regiment that was disbanded in North America? Did he decide to emigrate because of business or trade? There is considerable literature on the tobacco trade, for example. The local history of the area of settlement should reveal this sort of information and may lead you to further documentation which actually lists the earliest residents. In some cases, your research may involve more than one stage. If you have Loyalist ancestors, you need to know something of the history of the Canadian location and of the place of settlement in the United States prior to 1776, before searching for origins in Scotland.

Much effort has been directed to creating lists and databases of Scottish settlers in other parts of the world. Genealogical guides in the country of destination detail immigration records and any lists. There are the usual cautions. Information found in lists and databases needs to be followed to the original source. Many people had the same name so be cautious about jumping to conclusions. Always read and understand the parameters of a particular database so you know the limits of the search. For North America, useful books are *A Dictionary of Scottish Emigrants to Canada Before Confederation* (Donald Whyte, 1986, 1995, 2002) and *A Directory of Scottish Settlers in North America 1625–1825* (David Dobson, 7 vols., 1984–93). Dobson has written a number of small booklets focused on emigrants from different counties of Scotland. An unusual theme is to identify all the passengers carried to Australia in one ship, *Is Yours an SS Great Britain Family?* (Adrian Ball, 1988). Destination countries began to keep information about arriving immigrants in the 1800s; begin a search at the website of the national archives of each country or check the websites at Cyndi's List for passenger and immigration lists, again according to country.

This research into who, where, when, and why paves the way for delving into Scottish records. You hope to begin research in Scotland with a full name and, if it is common, also the names of spouse, and/or parents, children, and siblings, to increase the odds of identifying the right people. If your Scottish ancestors were recent enough emigrants, they or their relations can be found in the indexes to civil registration and your task is therefore not too difficult. Immediately prior to 1855 you may be able to identify families through the 1851 or 1841 census returns if you know the area of origin. Before 1855, however, the most likely starting place is the indexes to church records described in chapter 5. If church records do not exist for the time or area that you want to search, you must assess other surviving records and the circumstances surrounding the decision to emigrate. This is where the research in the records of the place of settlement will be particularly useful. If you find that your ancestor was part of an emigration scheme, or that most of the people of a town came from one part of Scotland, you quite likely can locate enough detail to create a hypothesis to work from. Look through the appropriate *Statistical Account* to check for corroborative reports of emigration before investigating the existence, availability, and location of other records that contain names.

Conclusion

All ancestors are special but those that came in for particular notice of the authorities end up with special records. These can be more difficult to find and to use but the work is never dull. Along the way you collect lots of extra detail about living conditions, justice, politics and economics. You also improve your research skills; this work leads you into new material, new archives, and new libraries.

Notes

1. Lindsay, 1975, 20.
2. Nicholls, 1967, 116.
3. Nicholls, 1967, 114.
4. National Archives of Scotland Kirk Session Records, Fetlar, 1847-55.
5. Hamilton Edwards, 1983, 24.
6. Patten, 1928, 3.

Summary—Records of the Poor

1. Before searching records of poor relief, find out about local conditions for the place and time being researched.

2. The CH 2 repertory at the NAS indicates what kirk session records are there; and/or determine what is held in local archives and libraries. Online resources at the SCAN and SRA websites and direct enquiries will supply the information. Working from a distance, consult the FHLC listing for the parish or burgh and compare against what you have discovered about records in Scotland.

3. For the post-1845 period it will be necessary to discover the whereabouts of the records of the parochial board. Use similar steps as mentioned above.

Summary—Court Records

1. Additional background information can be found in fact sheets from the NAS and in *Scottish Local History* (Moody, 1994). Also, read the appropriate sections in *Tracing Your Scottish Ancestors* (Sinclair, 1997).

2. Consider whether there is enough information to undertake a search; this should include reasonable assurance the ancestor was in court.

3. Visit West Register House if at all possible, but otherwise take time to visit a law library for cases that were heard in the Court of Sessions or the High Court of the Justiciary. Check for the *English and Empire Digest* and volumes of court cases.

4. If you find the case, follow up, if necessary, by requesting an Edinburgh agent to research the proceeding. You can also check the reference when appropriate in the minute books of the Court of Session. These books are obtainable on film in the FHL or through Family History Centers.

Summary—Finding Emigrants

1. Identify the person or persons who left Scotland.

2. Determine the likely date and place of first settlement.

3. Two essential places for finding information are the website of the national archives for the destination country and the material on emigrants at SCAN.

4. If you know the home parish in Scotland, read the information in the *Statistical Accounts of Scotland.* (1790s or 1845).

5. If you do not know the home parish, select the appropriate indexes and finding aids to help you. This will include arrivals lists, special lists such as those of transportees, indexes to emigrants, church record indexes, and census indexes.

6. If there is no result, review the facts of the search, consider name variants, try searching for another member of the family, and check whether a collateral line might be identified in Scotland.

11 • Problem Solving

epend on it: you will get stuck. Ancestors, ancient clerks, and even computer-assisted indexers of today have misled every one of us through outright lies, oversight, fatigue, etc. Not only that, we can mislead ourselves, perhaps by failing to check the base information, or by jumping to hasty conclusions.

Where the problem is a particularly thorny one, develop some sort of process for diagrammatically and verbally presenting it, one that also suggests a means to a solution. The format in figure 11-1 represents one way of doing this. The problem is clearly defined, and segments of charts place it visually in context. There is a reminder about background information. Possible sources to consult are listed, and space has been left to jot down comments or findings. Implicit in this format are the key questions that form the foundation of any new line of enquiry. Once you have identified the quarry and the parameters (of date and area), it is time to review sources by asking the six questions itemized below about each one in turn. Keep these questions handy, and you will always be able to plan a strategy. This approach does not guarantee a solution at the end, but it does provide a common-sense method that will ensure that you have done all you can.

Figure 11-1. A Format for Problem Solving.

Problem: Extend the Pedigree of Mary Rennie

Pedigree Chart Segment

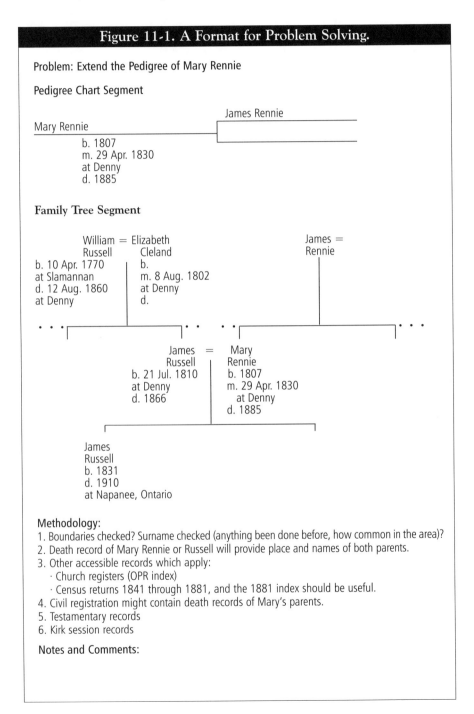

Family Tree Segment

Methodology:
1. Boundaries checked? Surname checked (anything been done before, how common in the area)?
2. Death record of Mary Rennie or Russell will provide place and names of both parents.
3. Other accessible records which apply:
   · Church registers (OPR index)
   · Census returns 1841 through 1881, and the 1881 index should be useful.
4. Civil registration might contain death records of Mary's parents.
5. Testamentary records
6. Kirk session records

Notes and Comments:

1. What time period does the record cover?
2. What geographical area does the record cover?
3. How is the record organized?
4. What information is needed to access the record?
5. What new information will the record supply?
6. Are there computer indexes or finding aids for the record, and where and how can the record be consulted?

Tables 11-1 and 11-2 list roadblocks and solutions. Every genealogical puzzle can be reduced to one or more of these basic generic elements. Once that has been done, you can select possible sources and test their usefulness by applying the questions above.

Problem solving will improve as knowledge and experience grow. Nevertheless, in some instances, only tedious, plodding work offers any hope of producing an answer. Be sure that you have tried all possible short cuts, and that all the facts are gathered and weighed for accuracy. It is sometimes necessary to hypothesize, to assume that one situation was the case and follow through the research on that basis. If it is proven incorrect, the gain is that something has been eliminated, and another theory can be tested.

This is where the concept of reconstruction may come into play. Throughout this book, I have drawn your attention to the importance of the historical and geographical context of the research you are undertaking. Family history is, to some degree, local history; it cannot be studied in isolation from the wider world. If you confine your efforts to the extraction of facts, the results will be deficient, and they may miss the mark. Family history research must incorporate ingenuity and the skillful posing of questions about people, places, and their socio-economic context. Reconstruction of the lives of our ancestors, and of their surroundings, is immensely interesting, satisfying, and potentially rewarding for further research.

> A genealogy is only a skeleton, and the most interesting part of family historical work is to paint in the flesh and to catch the breath of the spirit. . . . Much can be achieved, particularly in the study of ancestors by proxy, as it were. Thus if one's forbear was a weaver living in Glasgow, one can illuminate his existence through a general study of the life of weavers or of Glasgow at that time, even though one has no direct historical references to the ancestor concerned. In this sense, the family his-

torian is also a local historian, able to point to the buildings and institutions in his or her town and to tell a story of the lives and aspirations of
those who built them, lived in them and worked in them.[1]

Meeting the challenge to formulate a research strategy that identifies
the necessary records and recognizes the potential of ancillary historical or
geographical material is one aspect of family history that keeps us interested. Another aspect is the lucky break.

There are lots of wonderful stories about lucky breaks or inspired
guesses and almost spooky visions or impulses which have led researchers
to solutions. For everyone who believes that there is a logical explanation
for everything, a saying of the ancient Persians may have some appeal: *luck
is infatuated with the efficient*. This ties in rather neatly with the idea that
you are the instrument of your own fortune (or misfortune), that you make
your own luck. Put lots of entries in a surname index, browse libraries every
chance you get, talk about your family, follow up on any new leads. People
who do these things create their own lucky breaks.

You can post your problem for hundreds, thousands, or more people
to see. There are club query pages, surname directories, and the Internet.
Personal preference will determine how much you use these vehicles of
exchange. Like me, you may follow the "has it been done before?" routine
mentioned in chapter 1, and then move on to research, or you may chat
by letter, fax, phone, or computer to others, turning up tips and answers. If
you choose the latter, be sure to verify anything for which you have not
received a definite source reference.

There is, ultimately, the matter of proof, or the establishment of the
existence or nonexistence of a fact. When you receive information from
another person, critically examine its validity. Have you been given sources,
and can you verify some of the facts yourself? There is no doubt that many
errors are spread quite innocently and shared through a genuine desire to be
helpful; nonetheless, they are errors. Repetition will not make them true.
There is an excellent discussion of the subject of sources, evidence, and its
analysis in *Evidence! Citation and Analysis for the Family Historian* (Mills,
1997). The author stresses the inseparable link between sound analysis and
correct documentary references.

I want to leave you with one final reminder. You can never know too much about the records you may use in your search. The quest for knowledge of what records exist should be ongoing. Do not confine your inquisitiveness to only the standard genealogical records. Look beyond to what local, economic, political, and social historians have used. Discover where records are kept, where copies may be found, and in what format. Maintain a file or database of possible sources for future use, especially when the inevitable conundrum arises. Extensive knowledge of source material will keep you in the driver's seat, whether you are planning your own activities or directing an agent. In the end, diversity of sources will create a broader picture. Your family history will be more than a flat, two-dimensional chart; it will have an added vitality. You will have put life into history.

Note
1. Moody, 2000, p. 7.

Table 11-1 Roadblocks.

For each roadblock, use the solutions suggested to design your strategy.

1. The basic information you are working from may be inaccurate. (B, C, H, J, K)

2. You may not have gathered enough of or the right kind of information for the record. (H, J, K, L)

3. There may be a gap in the records for the particular time and place. (The records may have been damaged or destroyed, may not have been kept for a time, or may be in private hands.) (A, E, I)

4. No listing has been found in the index or finding aid, although you are certain one must be there (could be due to human error in indexing). (A, F, G, I)

5. A search of a record has produced no result, although many other indicators suggest the anticipated entry should be there (may be due to hurried searching, a forgetful minister at the time, deliberate failure to report an event, tax avoidance). (A, D, E, F, I, N)

6. Your research has turned up several possible solutions. (I, J, K, L, M, N)

7. The scale of the search may be too large (too many years to cover, too large an area, too common a name, or a combination of these). (D, I, L, N)

8. There may be a technical problem involving language, handwriting, or organization (e.g., only chronological, not completely alphabetical, or haphazard geographical arrangement). (D, N, O)

Table 11-2 Solutions.

A. Check the alternate sources that provide similar information.

B. Expand the geographical area of your search, paying close attention to boundaries.

C. Expand the time span of your search.

D. Check that all indexes and finding aids have been identified and checked.

E. Examine another copy of the same source in a different location.

F. Repeat the search.

G. Go directly to the record.

H. Double-check your base information.

I. Carry out the same search for a sibling or other close relative.

J. Try to supplement your base information through additional sources.

K. Improve your historical and geographical background knowledge. Clues found may suggest a different line of enquiry.

L. Create a hypothesis and work through it. You may have to do this more than once.

M. Trace downward from all possible solutions.

N. Check books and periodicals for case studies and talk to other researchers.

O. Hire a professional researcher.

· A ·

INDEXES TO CHURCH OF SCOTLAND BAPTISMS AND MARRIAGES

Two features facilitate access to the records for the established Church of Scotland: they were collected in a central location at an early date, and there is a selection of indexes to marriages and baptisms. The small population of the country is another advantage. There is, however, an unusual pitfall — concluding too soon that the search is finished.

You have seven different ways to access all surviving, recorded baptisms and marriages of the Church of Scotland from the beginning to 1855.

1. Using the GROS computer index at New Register House in Edinburgh and at locations with direct links to this (e.g., the Family Records Centre in London).

2. Using the GROS computer index, found on the Internet at ScotlandsPeople.

3. Using the International Genealogical Index (IGI) online at FamilySearch.

4. Using the IGI on computer (DOS version, keyboard commands only) in the FHL and in Family History Centers.

5. Using the IGI on microfiche in the FHL and in Family History Centers and many libraries and archives.

6. Using Scottish Church Records on computer (DOS version, keyboard commands only) in the FHL and in Family History Centers.

7. Using the OPR Index on microfiche at New Register House, in the FHL and in Family History Centers, and in some other libraries and archives.

This list expands to nine if the two options for using the IGI at the local level are added. The Hugh Wallis Batch Number Index site and Scots Origins parish search make it possible to choose a parish without first figuring out the batch number.

There is also the *British Vital Records Index* (BVRI), which contains approximately 2.5 million baptism/birth and marriage events for Scotland. This is significant; by comparison, the total number in the OPR Index is about 10 million. There is a broader mix of origin in the BVRI — Church of Scotland, secession congregations, other denominations, neglected entries, being several examples. On the other hand, there is a huge imbalance in event type, just 41,080 marriages.

Using the Indexes

There are subtle differences in how you work with each index, which should lead you to consult more than one when results are not forthcoming. Online there are four ways to search the indexes to baptisms and marriages in Church of Scotland registers. Some features are compared in Table A-1 to highlight the necessity of mastering all the possibilities. In each of the four searches these criteria may be influenced by date or geography or some impossible combinations; read the instructions at each site and then experiment. An important caution goes with this: the more information you insert into the search fields the more limited the returns. In other words, by trying to be specific you can prevent the search system from identifying items that contain partially correct information or incomplete information. Some of these entries may be what you need.

Table A-1: A Comparison of Criteria Possibilities in Name Searches Online ▓ =allows criterion	OPR Index at Scotlands-People	IGI at Family-Search	Hugh Wallis IGI Batch Search	Scots Origins IGI Search
A surname alone: (some combinations not possible)	▓	▓	▓	▓
A given name alone:			▓	
A full name:	▓	▓		▓
All entries for one surname by parish or by batch:	▓	▓	▓	▓
All entries for one given name by parish or by batch:			▓	
A search, by parish, for a surname or a full name:	▓	▓		▓
All the entries, all names, by parish or by batch:		▓	▓	▓
A bride and groom together:	▓	▓		▓
The children of couples with specified name combinations:	▓	▓		▓

NOTE: The Hugh Wallis site searches by batch only; all others permit searches across all of Scotland; county searches are possible at FamilySearch and Scots Origins and will soon be possible at ScotlandsPeople (seepage 82).

Search options as well as the data available will definitely change at ScotlandsPeople and at FamilySearch. The most important addition will be the arrival of a burial index for the OPRs at ScotlandsPeople. Now, and with the addition of more data, working in stages is important. If you have specific information and get no results then gradually expand the years of the search and the geographic area. If you are looking generally to start with, add details to the search one at a time and watch the effects of each step on the results. In all cases examine the register entry for all possible matches.

Derivation of the Indexes.

GROS: based on the collection of Old Parochial Registers (OPRs) of the Church of Scotland in its custody; earliest date is 1560 and the most recent is 1855 when civil registration began; includes Neglected Entries; when errors in the index are discovered, corrections are made.

OPR Index: on microfiche, a joint project of the GROS and the Family and Church History Department of The Church of Jesus Christ of Latter-day Saints completed in 1993 from a filming of the OPRs at New Register House; also some from kirk sessions records.

Scottish Church Records on Computer: completed about the same time as the OPR Index and based on a filming of the OPRs; also incorporates some events from kirk session records, some post-1855 entries, and some secession church entries if that church rejoined the Church of Scotland in 1929.

IGI: now maintained on computer (the online version is dated 2002 while the

fiche version is dated 1992 and has an addendum dated 1994); derived from an earlier filming of the OPRs than that used for the OPR Index and may not be as complete or correct as more recently made indexes; includes entries from congregations of other denominations; includes individual submissions by members of the LDS Church; includes the first twenty years of births and marriages from civil records; the majority of recently submitted entries are from individuals.

BVRI: made up of information from birth, christening and marriage records from parishes in the British Isles (England, Ireland, Scotland, Wales, Channel Islands and the Isle of Man); there may be overlap with the IGI; for Scotland there are records from Church of Scotland parishes, other denominations and congregations and from Neglected Entries; number of events for each county varies from a few to half a million.

The given-name-only search feature deserves further discussion because it gives you a different perspective and can help you circumvent potential problems. There are two aspects to consider. First, patronymics were in use in some parts of Scotland. The surname changed with each generation according to the name of the father; thus, the son of James McDougall would be Robert Jamieson. In such circumstances it is easier to use a given-name index. In the other situation, you may not know a woman's maiden name, particularly if she married around the time of emigration. Scottish women retained their birth names, but records elsewhere may not always reveal them. If a woman's surname is not known but the geographic area is, a given-name search, using the IGI online, or the OPR index on microfiche may yield a list of given names for reference as the search for the surname continues.

What the Indexes Tell You

Never forget that these are facts in an index and not information from an original record. An index may provide all the facts that are in the register but you do not know that without looking at a copy of the register entry. Some ministers wrote down the bare minimum, and others added considerable extra detail as the examples in chapter 5 illustrate.

- GROS: the table of results at ScotlandsPeople contains (excluding the numbering on the left) seven columns: year, surname, forename, parent names/frame number, sex, parish, GROS data, image.

- IGI: the information in the IGI can be seen in Figure B-1, a page of the microfiche format: surname, forename, parent(s) or spouse, sex, event, event date, town or parish, three columns of LDS temple information, batch and serial sheet number (source references); information is similar in the computer or online format.

- OPR Index: very similar to the IGI without the temple information; refer to Figure B-2 and you will see there is surname, forename, parent(s), spouse, sex, event, event date, town or parish, miscellaneous notes, batch and serial sheet number.

Figure A-1. IGI Extract—County Angus.

FORRESTER, BESSI — PAGE 6,886

COUNTRY SCOTLAND COUNTY: ANGUS AS OF MAR 1992

NAME	FATHER / MOTHER OR SPOUSE OR RELATIVE (M=MALE F=FEMALE H=HUSBAND W=WIFE)		TYPE	EVENT DATE	TOWN, PARISH	B	E	S	SOURCE BATCH/FILM NO	SOURCE SERIAL/SHEET
FORRESTER, BESSIE										
FOSTER, BESSIE		F	C	09JUL1657	ANGUS, DUNDEE	16MAR1983PV	05APR1983PV	15APR1983PV	C112822	4013
	ALEXR. FOSTER/ELSPETH FOSTER									
FORRESTER, BETSY	ALEXR. JOHNSTON	W	M	05MAR1862	ANGUS, DUNDEE			15JAN1982SL	M112821	6140
FORESTER, BETSY KIDD		F	B	09SEP1861	ANGUS, MONIFIETH	07FEB1980OG	15APR1980OG	04JUN1980OG	C113101	1226
	ROBERT FORESTER/ANN SKIRVING									
FORRESTER, BETSY MCKAY		F	B	29JAN1870	ANGUS, DUNDEE	10MAR1981SL	20MAR1981SL	25MAR1981SL	C112823	10956
	LUNDIE FORRESTER/HELEN KYDD									
FORRESTER, BETTY	WILLIAM ALEXANDER	W	M	01DEC1775	ANGUS, FORFAR			29OCT1981SL	M112882	2714
FORRESTER, BETTY	JOHN FORRESTER/	F	C	21MAY1780	ANGUS, GLAMIS	05JAN1983PV	21JAN1983PV	28JAN1983PV	C112892	5705
FORESTER, BETTY	DANIEL MACPHERSON	W	M	17NOV1786	ANGUS, DUNDEE			14SEP1982OK	M112824	0712
FORRESTER, BETTY	DAVID FORRESTER/ELIZ. LOW	F	C	18JUN1807	ANGUS, KIRRIEMUIR	05MAR1983OG	29MAR1983OG	27APR1983OG	C112992	12040
FORRESTER, BETTY		F	C	11NOV1814	ANGUS, KIRRIEMUIR	08MAR1983OG	29MAR1983OG	28APR1983OG	C112992	13265
	CHARLES FORRESTER/ANN TURNBULL									
FORRESTER, CATHARIN	JOHN FORRESTER/	F	C	02MAY1680	ANGUS, MONTROSE	04JUN1983JR	12JUL1983JR	26JUL1983JR	C113122	6454
FORRESTER, CATHARINE	GEORGE MONRO	W	M	30DEC1854	ANGUS, DUNDEE			22FEB1983PV	M112825	20167
FORRESTER, CATHERINE	ROBERT ANDERSON	W	M	15JAN1763	ANGUS, DUNDEE			08OCT1974AL	7330219	14
FORRESTER, CATHERINE		F	B	29SEP1866	ANGUS, DUNDEE	15JAN1980PV	26MAR1980PV	22APR1980PV	C112821	47809
	JAMES FORRESTER/ALICE GIBB									
FORRESTER, CATHN.	ROBT. ANDERSON	W	M	02FEB1763	ANGUS, DUNDEE			01DEC1982PV	M112822	8975
FORRESTER, CATHREN	DAVID EDGAR	W	M	11JUN1675	ANGUS, DUNDEE			11NOV1982PV	M112822	2918
FORRESTER, CATHREN	THOMAS FORRESTER/	F	C	02DEC1722	ANGUS, LINTRATHEN	07MAY1982OK	17JUN1982OK	24JUN1982OK	C113022	0244
FORRESTER, CHARLES		M	C	13DEC1727	ANGUS, OATHLAW	01APR1982OG	08JUL1982OG	13AUG1982OG	C113152	0189
	ALEXR. FORRESTER/MARGARET HEY									
FORRESTER, CHARLES	WILLM. FORRESTER/	M	C	01JUN1752	ANGUS, GLENISLA	04MAR1982LG	08MAY1982LG	08JUL1982LG	C112902	0766
FORRESTER, CHARLES	ELIZABETH NICOL	H	M	17AUG1754	ANGUS, MONTROSE			04NOV1981SL	M113122	2442
FORRESTER, CHRISTIAN	JOHN FORRESTER/	F	C	10APR1743	ANGUS, GLENISLA	16FEB1982LG	14APR1982LG	11JUN1982LG	C112902	0308
FORRESTER, CHRISTIAN		F	C	13OCT1816	ANGUS, DUNDEE	01FEB1983AZ	15FEB1983AZ	09APR1983AZ	C112827	9644
	ROBT. FORRESTER/ISABELLA GORDON									
FORRESTER, CHRISTIAN	CHARLES URQUHART	W	M	22NOV1847	ANGUS, DUNDEE			10FEB1983PV	M112825	14486
FOSTER, CHRISTIANE		F	C	14MAR1668	ANGUS, DUNDEE	17MAR1983PV	05APR1983PV	15APR1983PV	C112822	7069
	JOHN FOSTER/MARGAT. ALLAN									
FORRESTER, CHRISTINA	CHARLES LAWSON	W	M	19SEP1848	ANGUS, DUNDEE			11FEB1983PV	M112825	14998
FORRESTER, CHRISTINA		F	B	15OCT1870	ANGUS, COUPAR ANGUS	02DEC1980SE	09JAN1981SE	05FEB1981SE	C112793	0290
	JAMES FORRESTER/ANN KENNEDY									
FORRESTER, CHRISTOPHER		M	B	16JUL1856	ANGUS, DUNDEE	11DEC1979PV	21MAR1980PV	04APR1980PV	C112821	5657
	ALEXANDER FORRESTER/JANET BARKER									
FORRESTER, CLEMENTINA	DAVID FORRESTER/	F	C	16OCT1782	ANGUS, GLENISLA	18FEB1982LG	16APR1982LG	16JUN1982LG	C112902	1328
FORRESTER, CLEMENTINA	JOHN KYD	W	M	06JUN1812	ANGUS, KINGOLDRUM			05JAN1982SL	M112952	0442
FORRESTER, DANIEL CAMPBELL		M	B	08JUN1870	ANGUS, DUNDEE	10MAR1981SL	24MAR1981SL	26MAR1981SL	C112823	13567
	JOHN FORRESTER/ELIZABETH CAMPBELL									
FORRESTER, DAUID		M	C	23JAN1672	ANGUS, DUNDEE	15MAR1983PV	30MAR1983PV	08APR1983PV	C112822	8062
	GEORG FORRESTER/MARTHA FORRESTER									
FORRESTER, DAVD.	JAS. FORRESTER/	M	C	APR1776	ANGUS, KIRRIEMUIR	23FLB1983OG	24MAR1983OG	12MAY1983OG	C112992	7578
FOSTER, DAVID	GRISSELL WILLIAMSONE	H	M	12NOV1665	ANGUS, DUNDEE			10NOV1982PV	M112822	2100
FORRESTER, DAVID		M	C	28DEC1690	ANGUS, DUNDEE	18AUG1983JR	17SEP1983JR	04OCT1983JR	C112824	1951
	GEO. FORRESTER/RACHELL YEAMEN									
FORRISTER, DAVID	ALEXR. FORRISTER/	M	C	05NOV1727	ANGUS, KIRRIEMUIR	18FEB1983OG	22MAR1983OG	10MAY1983OG	C112992	1358
FORRESTER, DAVID	HELLEN TALIYER	H	M	24NOV1743	ANGUS, DUNDEE			27NOV1982PV	M112822	7014
FORRESTER, DAVID	HELLEN TAYLOR	H	M	24NOV1743	ANGUS, KINNETTLES			11FEB1982SL	M112972	0136
FORESTER, DAVID	/HELEN FORESTER	M	C	16DEC1744	ANGUS, LINTRATHEN	12MAY1982OK	27AUG1982OK		C113022	1285
FORRESTER, DAVID	DAVID FORRESTER/	M	C	18JAN1745	ANGUS, KINNETTLES	21MAY1982SE	16JUL1982SE	17AUG1982SE	C112972	0801
FORRESTER, DAVID	GRIZEL MILLAR	H	M	29JAN1755	ANGUS, COUPAR ANGUS			10DEC1981IF	M112794	0217
FORESTER, DAVID		M	C	MAR1755	ANGUS, KIRRIEMUIR	19FEB1983OG	23MAR1983OG	11MAY1983OG	C112992	4425
	DAVID FORESTER/MARGT. LAIKIE									
FORRESTER, DAVID		M	C	22JAN1756	ANGUS, COUPAR ANGUS	02JUN1960	06JUL1960LG	22AUG1961SL	C112794	1452
	DAVID FORRESTER/GRIZEL MILLAR									
FORRESTER, DAVID		M	C	08JUN1760	ANGUS, DUNDEE	25SEP1982AZ	26NOV1982AZ	15DEC1982AZ	C112825	2058
	WILLIAM FORRESTER/MARGARET STRACHAN									
FORRESTER, DAVID	ELIZABATH MCLAUCHLAN	H	M	18JUL1778	ANGUS, GLENISLA			19DEC1981SL	M112902	0517
FORESTER, DAVID	ANNE WILL	H	M	04SEP1778	ANGUS, DUNDEE			03DEC1982PV	M112822	11285

Δ= ENTRY ALTERED FROM SOURCE; †,∂,>=RELATIVES NAMED IN SOURCE. SEE "SYMBOLS" IN INSTRUCTIONS.

A = ADULT CHRISTENING B = BIRTH C = CHRISTENING D = DEATH OR BURIAL ALL OTHERS = MISCELLANEOUS
F = BIRTH OR CHRISTENING OF FIRST KNOWN CHILD M = MARRIAGE N= CENSUS W = WILL

- Scottish Church Records: also similar to IGI results: surname, forename, parent(s) or spouse, sex, event, event date, town or parish, additional information, batch and source number.

- BVRI: similar to IGI results: surname, forename, parent(s) or spouse, sex, event, event date, town or parish, additional information, batch and source number.

Benefits of the Indexes

Speed and convenience are the most obvious benefits; a very large group of records can be searched in different ways for different events. The savings in time and the detail of the results permit the use of search tactics not contemplated in the days when all the targeted parish registers had to be read laboriously, one at a time.

The computer indexes open up the greatest number of search opportunities. You can search all of Scotland, looking for births and marriages at the same time or separately; you can choose to be specific right from the first search; or you can gradually add more details and watch how this affects results. The ability to search a broad or limited area is not uniform among the indexes. Computer indexes permit searches for all children of a named couple but in different ways. The IGI and Scottish Church Records have search fields for the full name of the mother as well as the father, although it is recommended that you use only the first name of the mother.

The IGI is the one computer index that permits cross-border searches (i.e., in and out of Scotland). Online at FamilySearch this is limited to specifying the whole of the British Isles. Using the DOS-based IGI you can select the counties you want to search; it is possible to choose all counties of Scotland, all counties of Scotland and England, a select few of Scotland, and even a mix of counties on either side of the border. The DOS-based Scottish Church records permit searches in selected counties of Scotland. This flexibility is most useful when working with common names; keep careful track of the combinations used in any searches.

Scots Origins and the Hugh Wallis site facilitate searches in the IGI at the local level. This is especially important when sorting out families or

Figure A-2. OPR Index Extract—County Angus.

COUNTRY: SCOTLAND COUNTY: ANGUS AS OF MAR 1991 PAGE 2,930

SEX: M MALE/F FEMALE/H HUSBAND/W WIFE/ U UNSTATED

NAME	FATHER/MOTHER OR SPOUSE	SEX	TYPE	EVENT DATE	TOWN, PARISH	MISCELLANEOUS	SOURCE BATCH	SOURCE SERIAL SHEET
FORRESTER, ANN TOSH								
FORRESTER, ANN TOSH	ROBERT FORRESTER/ANN MELDRUM	U	C	09NOV1828	DUNDEE		C112828	7299
FORRESTER, ANN TOSH	ROBERT FORRESTER/ANN MELDRUM	U	C	09NOV1828	DUNDEE		C112828	7328
FORRESTER, BARBARA	JAMES FORRESTER/	F	C	22APR1739	GLAMIS		C112892	3422
FORRESTER, BARBARA	WILM. FORRESTER/MARGT. SWAN	U	C	18MAY1791	DUNDEE		C112826	4330
FORRESTER, BETTY	JOHN FORRESTER/	F	C	21MAY1780	GLAMIS		C112892	5705
FORRESTER, BETTY	DAVID FORRESTER/ELIZ. LOW	U	C	18JUN1807	KIRRIEMUIR		C112992	12040
FORRESTER, BETTY	CHARLES FORRESTER/ANN TURNBULL	U	C	11NOV1814	KIRRIEMUIR		C112992	13265
FORRESTER, CATHARIN	JOHN FORRESTER/	F	C	02MAY1680	MONTROSE		C113122	6454
FORRESTER, CATHREN	THOMAS FORRESTER/	U	C	02DEC1722	LINTRATHEN	FR14	C113022	0244
FORRESTER, CHARLES	ALEXR. FORRESTER/MARGARET HEY	U	C	13DEC1727	OATHLAW	FR93	C113152	0189
FORRESTER, CHARLES	WILLM. FORRESTER/	M	C	01JUN1752	GLENISLA		C112902	0766
FORRESTER, CHRISTIAN	JOHN FORRESTER/	F	C	10APR1743	GLENISLA		C112902	0308
FORRESTER, CHRISTIAN	ROBT. FORRESTER/ISABELLA GORDON	U	C	13OCT1816	DUNDEE		C112827	9644
FORRESTER, CLEMENTINA	DAVID FORRESTER/	F	C	16OCT1782	GLENISLA		C112902	1828
FORRESTER, DAUID	GEORG FORRESTER/MARTHA FORRESTER	M	C	23JAN1672	DUNDEE		C112822	8062
FORRESTER, DAVD.	JAS. FORRESTER	U	C	APR1776	KIRRIEMUIR		C112992	7578
FORRESTER, DAVID	GEO. FORRESTER/RACHELL YEAMEN	U	C	28DEC1690	DUNDEE		C112824	1951
FORRESTER, DAVID	DAVID FORRESTER/	M	C	18JAN1745	KINNETTLES		C112972	0801
FORRESTER, DAVID	DAVID FORRESTER/GRIZEL MILLAR	U	C	22JAN1756	COUPAR ANGUS		C112794	1452
FORRESTER, DAVID	WILLIAM FORRESTER/MARGARET STRACHAN	U	C	08JUN1760	DUNDEE		C112825	2058
FORRESTER, DAVID	JNO. FORRESTER/	U	C	09MAR1779	KIRRIEMUIR		C112992	8023
FORRESTER, DAVID	WILM. FORRESTER/MARGT. SWAN	U	C	16MAY1784	DUNDEE		C112825	12211
FORRESTER, DAVID	JAS. FORRESTER/MARGT. SMITH	M	C	25JAN1789	LINTRATHEN	FR94	C113022	1963
FORRESTER, ELISABETH	WILLM. FORRESTER/MART. STRACHAN	U	C	04NOV1764	DUNDEE		C112825	3391
FORRESTER, ELIZABATH	JOHN FORRESTER/	F	C	26JUL1753	GLENISLA		C112902	0814
FORRESTER, ELIZABETH	DAVID FORRESTER/	F	C	19JUL1680	MONTROSE		C113122	6485
FORRESTER, ELIZABETH	ALEXR. FORRESTER/	U	C	12SEP1707	COUPAR ANGUS		C112792	1297
FORRESTER, ELIZABETH	SYLVESTER FORRESTER/	F	C	18JAN1748	GLENISLA		C112902	0550
FORRESTER, ELSPET	ANDREW FORRESTER/	U	C	23FEB1718	LINTRATHEN	FR8	C113022	0045
FORRESTER, ELSPET	THOMAS FORRESTER/	U	C	12FEB1721	LINTRATHEN	FR11	C113022	0150
FORRESTER, ELSPETH	ALEXANDER FORRESTER/ELSPETH FORRESTER	F	C	16JAN1653	DUNDEE		C112822	2583
FORRESTER, ELSPETH	DAVID FORRESTER/GRISSELL WILLIAMSON	F	C	10MAR1667	DUNDEE		C112822	6792
FORRESTER, ELSPIT	ALEXR. FORRESTER/	F	C	14MAY1727	CORTACHY AND CLOVA		C112782	2529
FORRESTER, EUPHAM	GEORGE FORRESTER/ISABEL PETRIE	U	C	08OCT1754	DUNDEE		C112825	0545
FORRESTER, GEORG	GEORG FORRESTER/MARTHA FORRESTER	M	C	22DEC1664	DUNDEE		C112822	6187
FORRESTER, GEORG	GEORG FORRESTER/MATHILDA FORRESTER	M	C	30NOV1668	DUNDEE		C112822	7257
FORRESTER, GEORGE	DAVID FORRESTER/	M	C	24JUL1755	KINNETTLES		C112972	1031
FORRESTER, GRISSELL	ANDREW FORRESTER/MARJORI WATSONNE	F	C	20OCT1661	DUNDEE		C112822	5317
FORRESTER, HELEN	JAMES FORRESTER/	F	C	19AUG1731	INVERARITY AND METHY		C112922	0757
FORRESTER, ISABELL	JAMES FORRESTER/JEAN ROBERTSON	U	C	28OCT1783	DUNDEE		C112825	11885

B - EVALUATED ENTRY

FR - FRAME NUMBER

A - ADULT CHRISTENING B - BIRTH C - CHRISTENING
M - MARRIAGE ALL OTHERS - MISCELLANEOUS

when verifying whether you have identified every entry for one family in one parish. You have an additional opportunity to catch things hidden by transcription or spelling errors. Scots Origins searches all the batches together and presents a table of results; you then select the batch or batches to look at. The Hugh Wallis site has you select the batch first. I recommend you try them both.

The microfiche indexes have their advantages, besides giving you something to do when all computers in a Family History Center are occupied. The IGI on fiche mixes baptisms and marriages together for each county in a layout that permits quick scanning because all the information is before you. With online or disc versions, the preliminary list is often not enough to pick out items of interest. Using microfiche, it is easy to take a reader/printer "shot" of a frame, and for some names, one or two frames gives you all the entries. The OPR Index on Fiche is comprised predominantly of OPR records; the separate sorts for events, for surnames and for given names allow for a fresh look at the information.

Another advantage, not associated with a single version, is the number of options available. You can search the OPRs using more than one format and based on different mixes of database features. The logic used in name searches is different as are the tools you can manipulate. This is especially useful when you need to be certain the indexes to the OPRs have been searched as thoroughly as possible. It is also important that different people have constructed these indexes. An error in interpretation may happen in one index and not another; an entry may be skipped in one version and not another. In other words, there is some insurance value against human error in having several varieties of indexes to study.

Shortcomings of the Indexes

All these search options generate more work for you. It is not really a shortcoming, but it is something you need to consider. When searches in one of the indexes to Scottish births and marriages fail to produce results, unless you know about the features of the different formats, you will not know whether your work has been thorough. You must be aware of database contents and features.

Indexes contain traps for the unwary. It is a benefit if the county family history society has completed its work for the National Burial Index, and the incorporation of OPR burials into the ScotlandsPeople site will make a difference. You may be able to check whether a "probable" ancestor actually lived long enough to fit all your facts, though not with any real feeling of confidence because so many burial records are missing. There are records for perhaps 65 percent of all burials and the majority of parishes do not have long runs of consecutive years.

The linking of events is always a problem. There is no way to know for certain that a baptism and a marriage using the same name, even in the same parish, are for one and the same person. The IGI is gradually adding some linkage information but it is not supplied by the custodians of the records; it comes from individuals. Where you find connections in any resource, look for the citation of the source used to draw that conclusion.

Sometimes you will get more data than you want and it may be confusing. The search for children of one set of parents is a good example. The ScotlandsPeople search is based upon surnames only, of the father and the mother, and the IGI system recommends the use of the father's full name and the mother's first name. Either way, "strays" can show up because the search system recognizes the combinations asked for and does not know which couple is the correct set of parents. You have to sort this out. Simply having far too many results is another problem. It can happen even when a name appears to be uncommon; it may not be unusual in a particular geographic area. Reading the register is one possible way to resolve the problem, though not always so if entries are short of detail.

Finally, do not disregard your instincts; all this data does not make for foolproof searching. It does not. If you believe that a baptism or marriage should be in a particular place and it is not in the index, read the microfilm of the parish record just to be sure. Construct methodical, gradually shifting searches that fit your base information to some degree. There is all sorts of room for error, and it is your knowledge of databases and records that will get you around the traps.

· B ·

THE
FAMILY HISTORY LIBRARY
CATALOG

The Family History Library Catalog (FHLC) is an invaluable research tool. As with any library catalog it describes the contents of a library, in this case the Family History Library (FHL) of The Church of Jesus Christ of Latter-day Saints in Salt Lake City, Utah. The catalog has been available in computer form for some time and, since the first edition of this book, has appeared on the Web (dated August 2001) and on CD-ROM (second edition dated April 2002). Some Family History Centers will have the computer version as well as Internet access to the Web version; in addition, it is still possible to find the microfiche format of the catalog.

The catalog was created originally with four main sections: Author/Title, Subject, Surname, and Locality so there were four ways to access entries. The Web version offers six search methods and the CD-ROM has eight (see Table A–1). Despite the added flexibility, computer searches do not eliminate the need to understand how the catalog was constructed;

without such knowledge you won't consistently complete thorough catalog searches. In addition, database concepts can be hard to grasp; if you have an opportunity to look at and test the microfiche format it will help. The fiche catalog may remain in drawers in a Family History Center near you; it is in a cabinet on the British floor in the FHL. You will be able to see the original sections and to put a few fiches in a reader. Spend some time with the Locality section; Scotland occupies no more than ten microfiches.

Table B-1: Catalog Searches, CD-ROM, and Web-based Versions.					
Type of search	Avail. on CD-ROM	Avail. on Web	Permits truncated entries	Wildcard symbols available	is case sensitive
Place/ Locality	yes	yes	yes	yes	no
Surname	yes	yes	yes	yes	no
Keyword	yes	no	no, must add a wild card	yes	no
Title	yes	no	yes	yes	no
Author	yes	yes	yes	yes	no
Subject	yes	yes	yes, e.g., "Aber" works	yes	no
Film/Fiche	yes	yes	no	no	no
Call Number (for items on FHL book-shelves)	yes	yes	yes, e.g., "941" works	no	yes

The Searches

Locality Search:

The Locality sort works in descending order (national, county, parish, or town), which can be seen from the progression through listings on the microfiches. For Scotland this means that the top tier contains records created by the national government in Edinburgh, both before and after the union with England in 1707, and records created by the British government, or any other records pertaining to the country as a whole. Figure A-1 shows several consecutive entries at the Scotland level, on microfiche. Next, Scotland is broken down into county divisions based on the names

---

Figure B-1. Family History Library Catalog: National Entries on Fiche.

```
☆☆☆☆☆☆☆☆☆☆☆☆☆☆☆☆☆☆☆☆☆☆☆☆☆☆☆☆☆☆☆☆☆☆☆☆☆☆☆☆☆☆☆☆☆☆☆☆☆☆☆☆☆☆☆☆☆☆☆☆☆☆☆☆☆☆☆☆☆☆☆
SCOTLAND - GENEALOGY
                                                     +-------------+
Eyre-Todd, George, 1862-                             |BRITISH      |
    The highland clans of Scotland : their history and traditions / |FILM AREA  |
    by George Eyre-Todd ; with an introduction by A.M.|0994038     |
    Mackintosh. -- Salt Lake City : Filmed by the Genealogical | item 2 |
    Society of Utah, 1983. -- on 1 microfilm reel : ill., coats +-------------+
    of arms, ports. ; 35 mm.

    Microreprodiction of original published: London : Heath Cranton
        Limited, 1923. 2 v.
    Index in v. 2.

☆☆☆☆☆☆☆☆☆☆☆☆☆☆☆☆☆☆☆☆☆☆☆☆☆☆☆☆☆☆☆☆☆☆☆☆☆☆☆☆☆☆☆☆☆☆☆☆☆☆☆☆☆☆☆☆☆☆☆☆☆☆☆☆☆☆☆☆☆☆☆
SCOTLAND - GENEALOGY
                                                     +-------------+
Eyre-Todd, George, 1862-                             |BRITISH      |
    The highland clans of Scotland : their history and traditions / |BOOK AREA  |
    by George Eyre-Todd ; with an introduction by A.M.|941         |
    Mackintosh. -- Charleston : Garnier, 1969. -- 2 v. in 1 : |H2g  |
    coat of arms                                     +-------------+

    Reprint. Originally published in 1923.
    Includes index.

. ☆☆☆☆☆☆☆☆☆☆☆☆☆☆☆☆☆☆☆☆☆☆☆☆☆☆☆☆☆☆☆☆☆☆☆☆☆☆☆☆☆☆☆☆☆☆☆☆☆☆☆☆☆☆☆☆☆☆☆☆☆☆☆☆☆☆☆☆☆☆
SCOTLAND - GENEALOGY
                                                     +-------------+
Family histories assembled by the Lord Lyon Registry House, |BRITISH |
    Edinburgh, Scotland. -- Salt Lake City : Filmed by the |FILM AREA |
    Genealogical Society of Utah, 1961. -- 1 microfilm reel ; 35 |0277787 |
    mm.                                              +-------------+

    Microreproduction of original. 1 v. (various pagings).

☆☆☆☆☆☆☆☆☆☆☆☆☆☆☆☆☆☆☆☆☆☆☆☆☆☆☆☆☆☆☆☆☆☆☆☆☆☆☆☆☆☆☆☆☆☆☆☆☆☆☆☆☆☆☆☆☆☆☆☆☆☆☆☆☆☆☆☆☆☆☆
SCOTLAND - GENEALOGY
                                                     +-------------+
Fraser, Henry.                                       |BRITISH      |
    Arms drawn with pen and ink for funeral escutcheons, showing |FILM AREA |
    paternal and maternal lines / by Henry Fraser. -- Salt Lake |0277959 |
    City : Filmed by the Genealogical Society of Utah, 1961. -- 1 +-------------+
    microfilm reel ; 35 mm.

    Microreproduction of original.

    Includes index.
```

used between 1897 and 1974, and then into individual parishes and towns. Figure A–2 is a county level entry found using the FHLC at the FamilySearch website. The subject relates to more than one county and can therefore be found in the History category for Angus, Fife, and Perth.

Names of the categories used in all levels of the locality or place search are taken from a standard list. The most commonly encountered category or topic headings appear in table B–2. Sometimes new ones need to be created; there are about one hundred in all.

Remember that different documents or copies in a single class of records may relate to different geographical areas and are therefore listed

Figure B-2. Family History Library Catalog Entry, County Level.

Title	'That important and necessary article' : the Salt industry and its trade in Fife and Tayside, c1570-1850
Stmnt.Resp.	C.A. Whatley
Authors	Whatley, C. A (Main Author)

Notes	"Notes": p. 60-67.

Subjects	Scotland, Fife - History Scotland, Angus - History Scotland, Perth - History

Copies	

Call Number	Location
941.3 H25ab no. 22	FHL BRITISH Book

Format	Books/Monographs
Language	English
Publication	Dundee : Abertay Historical Society, 1984
Physical	68 p. : ill., map.

Subject Class	941.3 H25
Series	Abertay Historical Society publication : no. 22

at different FHLC levels; this means a search of one level is not necessarily a complete search. The record can originate with the parish but a transcription may be included in a book about the whole county or the region, involving several counties. Gravestone inscriptions are a good example; while the graveyard is local, the book probably lists many from different parishes, and perhaps from more than one county. It is therefore necessary to seek out the cemetery inscriptions at the parish, county, and national level in the FHLC. Continuing this example you would therefore look for "Scotland – County name – Parish name – Cemeteries," "Scotland – County name – Cemeteries," and "Scotland – Cemeteries." The quirks of catalogers can also be a factor; you may think a book fits logically at one level while the cataloger saw it another way. Finally, always be alert and think inclusively because there is no guarantee that an item will be listed at every relevant level.

Surname Search:

A surname search finds collection materials that are focused on individuals; a name does not have to be in the main title. It is a fully alpha-

Table B-2 FHLC Subject Headings.	
Archives and Libraries	Maps
Bibliography	Military History
Biography	Military Records
Business and Commerce	Names—Geographic
Cemeteries	Names—Personal
Census	Newspapers
Church Directories	Nobility
Church History	Obituaries
Church Records	Occupations
Civil Registration	Pensions
Court Records	Periodicals
Description and Travel	Politics and Government
Directories	Poor Houses
Emigration and Immigration	Probate Records
Gazetteers	Public Records
Genealogy	Schools
History	Social Life and Customs
Indexes	Taxation
Inventories and Registers	Vital Records
Land and Property	Voting Registers

betical listing and information about geographical location is always in the notes. If there are many books about families with the same surname, they are arranged alphabetically by author. Of course, names may have more than one spelling, and it is possible that items connected to one family will use variations. The CD search tool helps you deal with this; part of a name can be tried, and wild card symbols (! For a single letter and * for several letters) are available.

Author and Title Searches:

Searching according to author is useful in two situations, when looking for a particular book or author and when fishing for resources. Sometimes all you can remember is the name of an author or perhaps only part of the name. Sometimes you find one item by an author (whether person, society or agency) and you go looking for anything else attributed to the same author. You can also use this search to look for all the resources cataloged in the FHLC as being created by a particular agency or record office; it is just another way to get round some of the quirks of catalogers.

A title search can be used in similar fashion; to search for a specific item, whether or not you have the full title, and to play around with words that are likely to be in the title of items you seek.

Subject and Keyword Searches

In the days of card catalogs the subject arrangement was very helpful; now keywords are used more often, particularly with the FHLC. The subject section has a smaller job, and in the fiche catalog is not very big because it excludes anything already listed according to locality or surname. On CD-ROM I sense that this is a better search tool than on the microfiche. It can help you find a range of materials on a variety of subjects like occupations, religious groups and welfare; e.g., input "Scotland history" and there are thirty-seven items (see Table A-3). Remember that this search relates to how items are categorized so it does not find every book on a subject. If you select "Coal-miners – Scotland – History" from the list in the table you get fewer results than a keyword search for "coal Scotland." Experiment with topics that interest you.

After two years of use, at least half of my searches are based upon keyword(s). Results using keyword(s) sometimes surprise me and only after digging deep into the film descriptions is the relevance of an item

Table B-3. Results of a Subject Search
for 'Scotland history' using the CD-ROM Catalog.

Agriculture - Scotland - History

Agriculture - Scotland - History - Maps

Charities - Scotland - History

Church of Scotland - History

Cities and towns - Scotland - History

Clans - Scotland - History

Coal-miners - Scotland - History

Costume - Scotland - Glasgow - History

Dwellings - Scotland - Edinburgh - History

Education - Scotland - History

Elections - Scotland - History

Episcopal Church - Scotland - History

Family - Scotland - History

Famines - Scotland - History - 19th century

Farm tenancy - Scotland - History

Fisheries - Scotland - History

Funeral rites and customs - Scotland - History

Illegitimacy - Scotland - History

Labor and laboring classes - Scotland - History

Marriage - Scotland - History

Medicine - Scotland - History

Millers - Scotland - History

Mineral industries - Scotland - Drongan - History

Occupations - Scotland - History - Sources

Poor - Scotland - History

Poor laws - Scotland - History

Presbyterians - Scotland - History

Public welfare - Scotland - History

Road construction - Scotland - History

Salt industry and trade - Scotland - History

Scotland - Economic conditions - History

Steamboat lines - Scotland - History

Tobacco industry - Scotland - Glasgow - History

Trade-unions - Scotland - History

Transportation - Scotland - History

Weavers - Scotland - History

Whaling - Scotland - history

apparent. This search has retrieved items because it looks further that any other—beyond title, author or subject into all the notes including the detailed descriptions of the contents of every film.

Learning Your Way Around the FHLC

If you own a computer then be sure to buy the CD-ROM format. It will be the best $5 you ever spend on genealogy. For everyone, especially those at some distance from Scotland, the catalog is crucial for identifying records and assessing access.

Begin by reading the Help provided with the CD. Then start experimenting with the searches, being sure to try all eight. One exercise is outlined here—chosen because it illustrates a cataloging problem and the necessity of searching at every level.

1. Begin with a place search and work with the directories category. Try "Scotland – Directories" first. Print out the list of items.

2. Next look at "Scotland – Roxburgh – Directories" and read the details for *The Southern Counties Register and Directory*. Use the menu bar to look at the "copyable" version, and then to print this.

3. Finally, look at "Scotland – Roxburgh – Kelso – Directories."

First, you will notice that the listing for the item in Figure A–3 appears under Roxburgh. The notes tell you it is also cataloged under Selkirk and Berwick; so, the catalog has caught the three county references. The town of Kelso is mentioned as the place of publication for this directory (and may have a section within the book) but it is not in the title. There is no listing for the "Directories" topic when you do a Kelso search.

Another point is that the regional directory entry does not indicate that the item can be found under the "Scotland – Directories" topic. This is odd because at that level there is a listing. Read through the details and you will see that the entry under Scotland is for a microfilm version of the original volume. The item appearing in the Roxburgh, Selkirk, and Berwick county listings is for a modern reprint. Presumably one cataloger

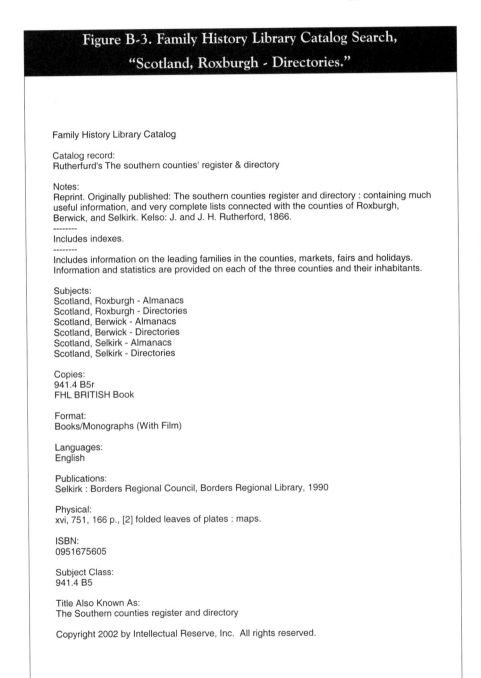

Figure B-3. Family History Library Catalog Search, "Scotland, Roxburgh - Directories."

Family History Library Catalog

Catalog record:
Rutherfurd's The southern counties' register & directory

Notes:
Reprint. Originally published: The southern counties register and directory : containing much useful information, and very complete lists connected with the counties of Roxburgh, Berwick, and Selkirk. Kelso: J. and J. H. Rutherford, 1866.

Includes indexes.

Includes information on the leading families in the counties, markets, fairs and holidays. Information and statistics are provided on each of the three counties and their inhabitants.

Subjects:
Scotland, Roxburgh - Almanacs
Scotland, Roxburgh - Directories
Scotland, Berwick - Almanacs
Scotland, Berwick - Directories
Scotland, Selkirk - Almanacs
Scotland, Selkirk - Directories

Copies:
941.4 B5r
FHL BRITISH Book

Format:
Books/Monographs (With Film)

Languages:
English

Publications:
Selkirk : Borders Regional Council, Borders Regional Library, 1990

Physical:
xvi, 751, 166 p., [2] folded leaves of plates : maps.

ISBN:
0951675605

Subject Class:
941.4 B5

Title Also Known As:
The Southern counties register and directory

Copyright 2002 by Intellectual Reserve, Inc. All rights reserved.

felt that a regional item covering three counties should be under "Scotland" and another, dealing with the reprint, thought it should be listed under each of the three counties.

To finish this exercise, try putting "Roxburgh directory" and "Kelso directory" into the field for a keyword search; both the film of the original volume and the reprint are found. It is apparent that almost identical items are not always categorized the same way and, therefore, any record search, to be thorough, must involve the national, county, and parish levels as well as a check with keywords.

Time spent with the FHLC is never time wasted. Checking the catalog should become routine for every record search. Checking for a record at each level (national, county and parish) and with a keyword search should also be automatic. If you do this and develop an easy familiarity with the CD-ROM version and its eight searches, you will be well on your way to creating useful research strategies for any problem.

Table B-4 Useful Resources Available on Microfiche.

Column one is a list of seven different items; across from each in column two is a fiche number and a brief description.

TITLE	NUMBER AND CONTENT
Records of Births, Marriages and Deaths of Scotland 1855-1875, 1881, 1891, with index 1855-1941	6035516 lists index film numbers and dates, lists of the registers organized as to county and type of event with film numbers
Index to Parishes or Districts in the Census of Scotland for the years 1841-1891	6035795 microfilm numbers for the census arranged by county, then alphabetically by parish; also has lists of street indexes and instructions
Sasines, Service of Heirs and Deeds Register	6054478 parish boundary maps of each county and detailed lists of FHL holdings arranged by county; chart of the levels of Scottish courts
Scottish Testaments	6054479 commissariot maps and detailed descriptions of FHL holdings arranged by commissariot
Key to the Parochial Registers of Scotland	6036348 this is Bloxham and Metcalfe (1979, see bibliography)
Ordnance Gazetteer of Scotland	6020392-0411 F.H. Groome's very useful work (1883-85, see bibliography)
Directory of Gentlemen's Seats, Villages, etc.	6026392 James Findlay's cross-referenced listing of landowners and places (1843, see bibliography)

PARLIAMENTARY PAPERS

Voluminous and interesting as they are, Parliamentary Papers are not often consulted by genealogists; however, technology is improving access and perhaps interest as well. Although there are guides, indexes, and microform copies, the process of identifying, locating, and reading relevant reports has been too difficult for all but the most serious family historians. Now optical character recognition (OCR) and digital technology are making a significant difference. In addition the Internet makes it easy to find out more about Parliamentary Papers and to discover whether collections are nearby.

In the UK, Parliamentary Papers are in all major libraries and repositories, such as the National Library of Scotland and the Guildhall Library; many universities have collections as well as the indexes prepared by Chadwyck-Healey. In Canada, the USA, Australia, New Zealand, and no doubt other countries, the major public and university libraries hold at least partial collections of Papers and indexes. There are some indexes and a limited collection of other volumes in the Family History Library. The efforts of the Irish University Press and the publications issued by Scholarly

Resources about thirty years ago also contributed to the broader distribution of Parliamentary Papers.

You can begin your exploration on the Internet. There is a National Archives information leaflet, *Printed Parliamentary Papers*, and many online guides to content and use prepared by university libraries that hold Parliamentary Papers. Simply type the term into any search engine or try visiting the library web page of a nearby university. The Papers fall into four principal categories: House of Commons Bills, House of Commons Papers, House of Lords Papers, and Command Papers. Some of the common terms likely to turn up in a search are defined here.

- Royal Commission: The members are usually specialists, not Members of Parliament, appointed to investigate a single subject; once the report is submitted, the Commission disbands.
- Select Committee: A committee of Parliament, sometimes meeting for a limited amount of time to hear evidence on a specific topic of focus, sometimes a standing committee meeting regularly over a long period.
- Blue Books: A name for larger Sessional Papers, usually presented to Parliament inside a blue paper cover.
- White Papers: A name for smaller Sessional Papers, usually presented to Parliament without a cover.
- Sessional Papers: The more formal name for any papers presented to Parliament, originated by an order of the House.
- Command Papers: Those prepared at the Command of the Crown; sometimes, but not always, include the reports of Royal Commissions.
- Parliamentary Papers: The umbrella term for all papers and reports, bills, accounts, and records of debates.

Parliamentary Papers may reveal the minute details of an occupation or industry (as in figure C-1) or provide statistical information (as in Figure C-2). There are reports on prisons, poorhouses, schools, conditions in factories, and the plight of the handloom weavers, to name just a few. Two books that give further information on the uses of these reports are *Scottish Family History* (Moody, 2000) and *Sources for English Local History* (Stephens, 1994). One of the published guides is devoted to Scottish sub-

Figure C-1. *Sessional Papers of the 18th Century*, vol. 131, 53.

In the End of October a vast Collection of Boats, with Fishermen, Nets, and Fishing Materials, repair to Burntisland, not only from all the Ports and Creeks in the Vicinity, but from the North Shore, as far as the Coast of Caithness, from the South Shore, as far as Berwick upon Tweed, and from the West Coasts through the Canal. When all those Bye Boats are assembled, they may amount to from 8 to 900, which when joined by the Boats attached to upwards of 360 Sail of Shipping upon the Fishery, it is a modest Computation to say, that at the throngest Time of the Fishing in some Seasons, the Number of Boats employed at one Time have exceeded 1,200.

The Herrings being caught and landed fresh, as above mentioned, are commonly gutted, but often are not. The gutting, when thought necessary, being performed by Women and Girls. In either Case, they are taken and roused with Salt in a wooden Vessel, called a Rousing Tub, that is, a Parcel of Fresh Herrings are put into the Tub, and a sufficient Quantity of Salt is sprinkled among the Herrings by the Hand from a Platter, and they are stirred about in the Tub, so as every herring may partake of an equal Portion of the Salt; this also keeps the Herrings asunder when packing as they would otherwise stick together when packed, and would not cure properly; about Half of bushel of Salt is usually expended in rousing.

This is an example of the material to be found in the testimony of witnesses before investigating committees. The questioning of James Strachan, of the Customs at Burntisland, reveals quite a bit about the herring fishery.

jects, *Scottish Economic History in the 19ᵗʰ Century: an analytical bibliography of material relating to Scotland in Parliamentary Papers 1800–1900* (Haythornthwaite, 1993). For information on using the Papers with reference to a particular family, see "British Parliamentary Papers" in the *Utah Genealogical Journal* (J. Wight, 1994).

The reports are a rich resource for information that is either directly connected to a family or filled with detailed information about living conditions. The example quoted here indicates that you will come across vivid explanations of occupations and may even discover that your own ancestors were interviewed. If your genealogy has led you deeper into historical research and if you enjoy a challenge, then Parliamentary Papers should be part of your strategy.

Figure C-2. A Table from *The Comparative Account of the Population of Great Britain 1801, 1811, 1821, 1831*

Shire of Lanark.

PARISHES, TOWNSHIPS, &c.	Annual Value of the Real Property, as assessed April 1815.	POPULATION 1801.	1811.	1821.	1831.	Aggregate POPULATION of Connected Places (1831.)
	£.					
Avendale - - - - - - - Parish	16,287	3,623	4,353	5,030	5,761	
Biggar - - - - - - - Parish	4,017	1,216	1,376	1,727	1,915	
Blantyre - - - - - - - Parish	4,438	1,751	2,092	2,630	3,000	
Bothwell - - - - - - - Parish	16,053	3,017	3,745	4,844	5,545	
Cadder - - - - - - - Parish	14,439	2,120	2,487	2,798	3,048	
Cambuslang - - - - - - Parish	8,578	1,558	2,035	2,301	2,697	
Cambusnetham - - - - - Parish	9,271	1,972	2,591	3,086	3,824	
Carluke - - - - - - - Parish	8,553	1,756	2,311	2,925	3,288	
Carmichael - - - - - - Parish	4,236	832	926	963	956	
Carmunnock - - - - - - Parish	6,002	700	670	637	692	
Carstairs - - - - - - Parish	4,022	899	875	937	981	
Carnwath - - - - - - - Parish	10,384	2,680	3,789	2,888	3,505	
Cathcart (part of) - (*) - Parish	2,827	- -	55	171	200	
Covington - - - - - - Parish	1,720	456	438	526	521	
Crawford - - - - - - - Parish	16,016	1,671	1,773	1,914	1,850	
Crawfordjohn - - - - - Parish	5,014	712	858	971	991	
Culter - - - - - - - Parish	2,769	369	415	467	497	
Dalserf - - - - - - - Parish	5,355	- -	1,660	2,054	2,680	
Dalzell - - - - - - - Parish	2,751	611	758	955	1,180	
Dolphinton - - - - - - Parish	1,301	231	268	236	302	
Douglas - - - - - - - Parish	7,538	1,730	1,873	2,195	2,542	
Dunsyre - - - - - - - Parish	2,006	352	345	290	335	
Glasford - - - - - - - Parish	5,627	953	1,213	1,504	1,730	
GLASGOW City:						
East, or Outer High - - - Parish		5,253	6,159	7,198	9,137	
Enoch, St. - - - - - - Parish		6,440	7,715	7,038	7,921	
James, St. - - - - - - Parish		- -	- -	7,263	8,217	
John, St. - - - - - - Parish		- -	- -	7,965	11,746	
Middle, or St. Andrew's - - Parish		4,338	5,250	5,731	5,923	
North, or St. Mungoes - - Parish	234,216	8,089	11,159	8,823	10,295	
North-West, or Ramshorn, now St. David's - - - Parish		7,401	9,940	6,013	6,268	202,426
South, or Blackfriars - - - Parish		4,901	5,758	6,266	7,569	
South-West, or St. Mary's - Parish		6,594	8,163	6,865	7,529	
West, or St. George's - - - Parish		3,799	4,190	9,603	15,242	
Suburbs:						
Barony - - - - - Parish	110,696	26,710	37,216	51,919	77,385	
Gorbals - - - - - Parish	31,035	3,896	5,199	29,359	35,194	
Govan (part of) - - (ᵇ) - Parish	14,086	6,701	11,581	3,775	4,967	
Hamilton - - - - - Par. & Town	18,863	5,908	6,453	7,613	9,513	
Kilbride - - - - - Par. & Town	16,363	2,330	2,906	3,485	3,789	
Lamington and Wandell - - - Parish	3,335	375	356	359	382	
LANARK - - - - - { Burgh & Parish	3,194 / 6,521	4,692	5,667	7,085	7,672	
Lesmahagow - - - - - Parish	17,481	3,070	4,464	5,592	6,409	
Liberton - - - - - Parish	3,790	706	749	785	773	
Monkland, New - - - - Parish	13,903	4,613	5,529	7,362	9,867	
Monkland, Old - - - - Parish	19,806	4,006	5,469	6,983	9,580	
Pettinairn - - - - - Parish	2,082	430	401	409	461	
RUTHERGLEN - - - - { Burgh & Parish	5,263 / 4,508	2,437	3,529	4,091 / 549	4,741 / 762	5,503
Shotts - - - - - - Parish	9,012	2,127	2,933	3,297	3,820	
Stonehouse - - - - Town & Parish	5,289	1,259	1,655	2,038	2,359	
Symington - - - - - Parish	1,984	308	364	472	489	
Walston - - - - - - Parish	1,730	383	377	392	429	
Wiston and Roberton - - - Parish	4,162	757	836	927	940	
SHIRE of LANARK - - - - -	686,531	146,699	191,752	244,387	316,800	

Increase of POPULATION *in three periods* - - 31 ⅌ Cent. - 27 ⅌ Cent. - 30 ⅌ Cent.

(ᵃ) Cathcart Parish is mostly in Renfrewshire, and is wholly entered there in 1801; the entire Parish contains 2,383 Inhabitants.

(ᵇ) Govan Parish is partly in Renfrewshire; the entire Parish in 1801 and 1811, it now contains 19,170; the difference of these numbers being added to Gorbals in 1821 and 1831, as a Suburb of Glasgow.

It is interesting to note the population figures for each county and parish in each census year. What was the rate of population growth or decline in the parishes of your ancestors? Why?

Figure C-2 cont'd. Published in London by Order of the House of Commons, 1831.

SCOTLAND.

COUNTIES OF	1801.	Increase ⅌ Cent.	1811.	Increase ⅌ Cent.	1821.	Increase ⅌ Cent.	1831.
ABERDEEN	123,082	10	135,075	15	155,387	14	177,651
ARGYLE	71,859	19	85,585	14	97,316	4	101,425
AYR	84,306	23	103,954	22	127,299	14	145,055
BANFF	35,807	2	36,668	19	43,561	12	48,604
BERWICK	30,621	1	30,779	8	33,385	2	34,048
BUTE	11,791	2	12,033	15	13,797	3	14,151
CAITHNESS	22,609	4	23,419	29	30,238	14	34,529
CLACKMANNAN	10,858	11	12,010	10	13,263	11	14,729
DUMBARTON	20,710	17	24,189	13	27,317	22	33,211
DUMFRIES	54,597	15	62,960	13	70,878	4	73,770
EDINBURGH	122,954	21	148,607	29	191,514	15	219,592
ELGIN	26,705	5	28,108	11	31,162	10	34,231
FIFE	93,743	8	101,272	13	114,556	12	128,839
FORFAR	99,127	8	107,264	6	113,430	23	139,606
HADDINGTON	29,986	4	31,164	13	35,127	3	36,145
INVERNESS	74,292	5	78,336	15	90,157	5	94,797
KINCARDINE	26,349	4	27,439	6	29,118	8	31,431
KINROSS	6,725	8	7,245	7	7,762	17	9,072
KIRKCUDBRIGHT	29,211	15	33,684	15	38,903	4	40,590
LANARK	146,699	31	191,752	27	244,387	30	316,819
LINLITHGOW	17,844	9	19,451	17	22,685	3	23,291
NAIRN	8,257	—	8,251	9	9,006	4	9,354
ORKNEY AND SHETLAND	46,824	—	46,153	15	53,124	10	58,239
PEEBLES	8,735	14	9,935	1	10,046	5	10,578
PERTH	126,366	7	135,093	3	139,050	3	142,894
RENFREW	78,056	19	92,596	21	112,175	19	133,443
ROSS AND CROMARTY	55,343	10	68,853	13	68,828	9	74,820
ROXBURGH	33,682	11	37,230	10	40,892	7	43,663
SELKIRK	5,070	16	5,889	13	6,637	2	6,833
STIRLING	50,825	14	58,174	12	65,376	11	72,621
SUTHERLAND	23,117	2	23,629	—	23,840	7	25,518
WIGTOWN	22,918	17	26,891	23	33,240	9	36,258
	1,599,068	14	1,805,688	16	2,093,456	13	2,365,807

SUMMARY OF GREAT BRITAIN.

	1801.	Increase ⅌ Cent.	1811.	Increase ⅌ Cent.	1821.	Increase ⅌ Cent.	1831.
ENGLAND	8,331,434	14 ½	9,551,888	17 ⅞	11,261,437	16	13,089,338
WALES	541,546	13	611,788	17	717,438	12	805,236
SCOTLAND	1,599,068	14	1,805,688	16	2,093,456	13	2,365,807
ARMY, NAVY, &c.	470,598	—	640,500	—	319,300	—	277,017
	10,942,646	15 ¼	12,609,864	14	14,391,631	15	16,537,398

THE Rate of Increase of the Population of Great Britain has not varied much during the last Thirty Years, even when the Increase or Diminution of the Army, Navy, &c. is thus taken into the Calculation; but a more accurate knowledge of the Increase of Population may be obtained by adverting to the Increase of the Female Sex exclusively; thereby virtually omitting throughout the Calculation such of the Army, Navy, and Merchant Seamen as were not domiciled in Great Britain.

1801. Females.	Increase ⅌ Cent.	1811. Females.	Increase ⅌ Cent.	1821. Females.	Increase ⅌ Cent.	1831. Females.
5,492,354	14.15	6,269,650	15.71	7,254,613	15.45	8,375,780

Bibliography

Chadwyck-Healey Index to the House of Commons Parliamentary Papers. CD-ROM. Cambridge: Chadwyck-Healey, 1998.

Chaloner, W.H., ed. *Six Reports From the Select Committee on Artisans and Machinery 1824*. London: Cass, 1968.

Comparative Account of the Population of Great Britain in the Years 1801, 1811, 1821, 1831. By Order of the House of Commons, 1831.

Ford, P., and G. Ford, eds. *Hansard's Catalogue and Breviate of Parliamentary Papers 1696-1834*. Shannon: Irish University Press, 1968.

Ford, P., and G. Ford. *A Guide to Parliamentary Papers: What they are, How to find them, How to use them*. Shannon: Irish University Press, 1972.

Ford, P., and G. Ford. *Select List of British Parliamentary Papers 1833-1899*. Rev. ed. Shannon: Irish University Press, 1969.

General Index to the Reports of Select Committees 1801-1852. Printed by Order of the House of Commons. Index #2. Reprint. Shannon: Irish University Press, 1968.

Haythornthwaite, J. A. *Scottish Economic History in the 19th Century: an analytical bibliography of material relating to Scotland in Parliamentary Papers 1800-1900*. Wilmington, Delaware: Scholarly Resources, 1993.

Lambert, Sheila, ed. *House of Commons Sessional Papers of the 18th Century. Volume 131, George III, Food Supply, Fisheries, 1799-1800*. Wilmington, Delaware: Scholarly Resources, 1975.

Lambert, Sheila, ed. *House of Commons Sessional Papers of the 18th Century. Volume 2, George I, Scotland, 1717-1725*. Wilmington, Delaware: Scholarly Resources, 1975. Contains references to the management of the forfeited estates of Jacobites.

Moody, David. *Scottish Family History*. London: B.T. Batsford, 1988. Reprint. Baltimore: Genealogical Publishing Co., 2000.

Powell, W.R. *Local History from Blue Books: A Select List of the Sessional Papers of the House of Commons.* London: Historical Association and Routledge and Kegan Paul, 1962.

Stephens, W.B. *Sources for English Local History.* Chichester: Phillimore, 1994.

Wight, Judith E. "British Parliamentary Papers—A Source for Family History," *Genealogical Journal* 21, nos. 3-4 (1993): 144-155. Utah Genealogical Association. Describes the arrangement of the Papers, particularly interesting reports, and the author's own study of a Hebrides family.

· D ·

LIST OF USEFUL ADDRESSES AND WEBSITES

Local government in Scotland was reorganized in 1996. The changes have resulted in new regional names (and the restoration of some old ones) as well as the relocation of materials, collections, and archives. To help overcome the difficulties this can create, the names of all pre-1974 counties of Scotland appear in this list. If there is not an address associated with that name then a note directs you to look at the appropriate listing. Using these geographic divisions parallels the way Scottish information is structured at the Genuki website and within the locality/place search of the Family History Library Catalog.

Several family history societies are included here but not all; consult the Scottish Association of Family History Societies website, the Genuki website, or the *Family and Local History Handbook* if your area does not appear to have a society listed.

Websites are included here where possible. In addition, at the end of the list there is a commentary on using the Web for Scottish research along with many other URLs that are not associated with a physical address.

**Aberdeen & North East Scotland
Family History Society**
164 King Street
Aberdeen, AB24 5BD, Scotland
Produces an excellent journal and has an
extensive publications list.

Aberdeen Central Library
Local Studies Department
Rosemount Viaduct
Aberdeen, AB25 1GW, Scotland
Aberdeen City Archives
Town House
Aberdeen, AB10 1AQ, Scotland
www.aberdeencity.gov.uk

Access to Archives
www.a2a.pro.gov.uk
The English strand of the UK archives
network; similar to SCAN; offers access to
over 250 archives catalogs; many search
options; use this URL or enter through
the National Archives gateway website.

Angus Archives
Montrose Public Library
214 High Street
Montrose, DD10 8PH, Scotland
www.angus.gov.uk/history/history.htm

Archives of Australia
Queen Victoria Terrace
PO Box 7425
Canberra, ACT, 2610
www.naa.gov.au

Argyll and Bute District Archives
Manse Brae, Lochgilphead, PA31 8QU,
Scotland

**Association of Professional
Genealogists**
P.O. Box 350998
Westminster, CO 80035-0998
www.apgen.org
Offers an online directory of members.

**Association of Scottish Genealogists
and Record Agents**
51/3 Mortonhall Road
Edinburgh, EH9 2HN, Scotland
www.asgra.co.uk
Offers an online directory of members.

Ayrshire Archives Centre
Craigie Estate
Ayr, KA8 0SS, Scotland
www.south-ayrshire.gov.uk/archives/

Banff
See Aberdeen and Moray entries

Berwickshire
See Scottish Borders

The British Library
Newspaper Library
Colindale Avenue
London, NW9 5HE, England
www.bl.uk/collections/newspapers.html

Business Records Centre
13 Thurso Street
Glasgow, G11 6PE, Scotland

Bute
See Argyll and Bute

Canada: National Archives of Canada
395 Wellington Street
Ottawa, ON, K1A 0N3, Canada
www.archives.ca

Caithness
See North Highlands Archive, Wick

Clackmannanshire Archives
Alloa Library
26/28 Drysdale Street
Alloa FK10 1JL Scotland
www.clacksweb.org.uk/dyna/archives

Companies House (Scotland)
100-102 George Street
Edinburgh EH2 3DJ Scotland
Maintains lists of registered companies.

Dumbarton Public Library
Strathleven Place
Dunbarton, G82 1BB, Scotland

Dumfries and Galloway Archives
Archive Centre
33 Burns Street
Dumfries, DG1 2PS, Scotland
www.dumgal.gov.uk
The website gives free access to several
local databases.

Dundee Central Library
The Wellgate
Dundee, DD1 1DB, Scotland
www.dundeecity.gov.uk/

Dundee City Archives
21 City Square
Dundee, DD1 3BY, Scotland
Formerly the Dundee District Archive
and Record Centre. This repository will
continue to hold core records of the
Tayside region; address initial enquiries
here.

**East Dunbartonshire Local Record
Offices**
William Patrick Library
2 West High Street
Kirkintilloch, G66 1AD, Scotland
www.eastdunbarton.gov.uk

East Lothian Libraries
Local History Centre
Haddington Branch Library
Newton Port
Haddington, EH41 3NA, Scotland
www.eastlothian.gov.uk/libraries/loch.html

Edinburgh City Archives
Department of Administration
City Chambers
High Street
Edinburgh, EH1 1YJ, Scotland

**Falkirk Museum History Research
Centre**
Callendar House, Callendar Park
Falkirk, FK1 1YR, Scotland
www.falkirkmuseums.demon.co.uk

The Family History Library
35 West North Temple Street
Salt Lake City, UT 84150 USA

The Family History Department
50 East North Temple Street
Salt Lake City, UT 84150 USA

Family Records Centre
1 Middleton Street
London, EC1R 1UW, England
www.familyrecords.gov.uk

Federation of Family History Societies
P.O. Box 2425
Coventry, CV5 6YX England
www.ffhs.org
www.ffhs.co.uk (publications)
An umbrella organization for societies in
the UK and elsewhere with a primary
interest in British research.

Fife Council Archive Centre
Carleton House
Balgonie Road, Markinch, Glenrothes,
KY6 7AH, Scotland

Fife Family History Society
Glenmoriston, Durie Street
Leven, KY8 4HF, Scotland
www.fifefhs.pwp.blueyonder.co.uk/

General Register Office (Scotland)
New Register House
Princes Street
Edinburgh, EH1 3YT, Scotland
www.gro-scotland.gov.uk/
Indexes to vital records and census
returns, along with a growing collection
of digital images, can be accessed
through <www.scotlandspeople.com>.

Glasgow City Archives
Mitchell Library
201 North Street
Glasgow, G3 7DN, Scotland

**Glasgow and West of Scotland Family
History Society**
Unit 5
22 Mansfield Street
Glasgow, G11 5QP, Scotland
www.gwsfhs.org.uk
Publishes some very useful aids for west
of Scotland research.

Glasgow University Archives Service
13 Thurso Street
Glasgow, G11 6PE, Scotland
www.archives.glas.ac.uk

Highland Council Genealogy Centre
Inverness Public Library
Farraline Park
Inverness, IV1 1NH, Scotland

Historical Manuscripts Commission
www.hmc.gov.uk
In April 2003 joining with the Public
Record Office to form the National
Archives. It reports on and maintains
information about record collections
throughout the UK.

India Office Library
British Library
96 Euston Road,
London, NW1 2DB, England

www.bl.uk/collections/orientalandindian.
html
This website includes a section of advice
for family historians.

Isle of Lewis
Stornoway Record Office
Townhall
2 Cromwell Street
Stornoway, HS1 2BD, Scotland

Kilmarnock—East Ayrshire Libraries
Dick Institute
Elmbank Avenue
Kilmarnock, KA1 3BU, Scotland

Kinross
See Perth and Kinross

Kircudbright
The Stewartry Museum
St. Mary Street
Kirkcudbright, DG6 4JG, Scotland
Also, see Dumfries

Kirkcaldy District Libraries
Reference and Local Studies Department
Central Library
War Memorial Gardens
Kirkcaldy, KY1 1YG, Scotland

Lanark Library
Lindsay Institute
16 Hope Street
Lanark, ML11 7LZ, Scotland
www.southlanarkshire.gov.uk

Lyon Office Library
Court of the Lord Lyon
HM New Register House
Edinburgh, EH1 3YT, Scotland

The Mariners' Museum Library
100 Museum Drive
Newport News, VA 23606-3759 USA

Maritime History Archive
Memorial University of Newfoundland
St. John's, NF A1C 5S7, Canada

McLaughlin Library
University of Guelph
Guelph, ON N1G 2W1, Canada

Midlothian Archives and Local Studies Centre
Library Headquarters
2 Clerk Street
Loanhead, Midlothian, EH20 9DR, Scotland

Moray Local Heritage Centre
Grant Lodge, Cooper Park,
Elgin, IV30 1HS
www.moray.org/heritage/roots.html

Nairn
See Moray

National Archives
Ruskin Avenue
Kew, Richmond
Surrey TW9 4DU England
www.nationalarchives.gov.uk
This is the new name of the now combined resources of the Public Record Office and the Historical Manuscripts Commission. Further information on future plans can be found at the website.

National Archives of Scotland
HM General Register House
Edinburgh, EH1 3YY, Scotland
www.nas.gov.uk/

National Army Museum
Royal Hospital Road
London, SW3 4HT, England
www.national-army-museum.ac.uk

National Library of Scotland
George IV Bridge
Edinburgh, EH1 1EW, Scotland
www.nls.uk

National Library of Scotland
Map Library
Causewayside Building
33 Salisbury Place
Edinburgh, EH9 1SL, Scotland

National Maritime Museum
Manuscript Section
Greenwich
London, SE10 9NF, England
www.nmm.ac.uk

National Register of Archives (Scotland)
See National Archives of Scotland
Operates as a clearinghouse of information about collections in private hands in Scotland, providing advice on whereabouts of papers relating to the enquirer's subject.

National War Museum of Scotland
Edinburgh Castle
Edinburgh, EH1 2NG, Scotland
www.nms.ac.uk/services

New Zealand Archives
10 Mulgrave Street
Thorndon,
PO Box 12 - 050
Wellington
New Zealand
www.archives.govt.nz

North Aryshire Libraries
39 Princes Street
Ardrossan, KA22 8BT, Scotland
www.north-ayrshire.gov.uk

North Highland Archive
Wick Library
Sinclair Terrace
Wick, KW1 5AB, Scotland
www.highland.gov.uk/

Orkney Library and Archives
Laing Street
Kirkwall, KW15 1NW, Scotland

Office for National Statistics
Postal Applications
Smedley Hydro
Southport
Merseyside, PR8 2HH, England
www.statistics.gov.uk/registration/
default.asp
This is where to obtain forms for ordering certificates of birth, marriage and
death in England and Wales that
occurred after July 1, 1837.

Peebles
See Scottish Borders

Perth and Kinross Council Archive
A. K. Bell Library
2 - 8 York Place
Perth, PH2 8EP, Scotland
www.pkc.gov.uk/archive/library.htm

Public Record Office
www.pro.gov.uk
In April 2003 joining with the Historical
Manuscripts Commission to form the
National Archives . It is the repository of
the national records of the United
Kingdom.

Renfrewshire Archives
Central Library
High Street
Paisley, PA1 2BB, Scotland

Ross and Cromarty
*See Highland Council Archives and Isle of
Lewis*

Roxburgh
See Scottish Borders

**Royal College of Physicians and
Surgeons**
234 St. Vincent Street
Glasgow G2 5RJ Scotland
Royal College of Physicians of Edinburgh
9 Queen Street
Edinburgh EH2 1JQ Scotland

Royal Museum of Scotland
Chambers Street
Edinburgh, EH1 1JF, Scotland
www.nms.ac.uk

Salt Lake Distribution Center
1999 West 1700 South
Salt Lake City UT 84104-4233 USA
Write to this address to obtain LDS publications, including fiche.

Scottish Archive Network
Thomas Thomson House
99 Bankhead Crossway North
Edinburgh, EH11 4DX
www.scan.org.uk/
The website is a must; all sorts of excellent background information such as a
glossary, and some useful databases
including a list of transportees to
Australian and a direct link to the testamentary index.

**The Scottish Association of Family
History Societies**
c/o Aberdeen & NE Scotland FHS
164 King Street
Aberdeen AB2 3BD Scotland
www.safhs.org.uk
Contact this organization for details of all

family history societies in Scotland; publishes several useful guides.

Scottish Borders Archive & Local History Centre
Regional Library HQ
St. Mary's Mill
Selkirk TD7 5EW Scotland
www.scotborders.gov.uk/libraries

Scottish Catholic Archives
Columba House
16 Drummond Place
Edinburgh EH3 6PL Scotland

Scottish Genealogy Society
15 Victoria Terrace
Edinburgh EH1 2JL Scotland
www.scotsgenealogy.com
Library and office; publishes the volumes of MIs; quarterly journal.

Department of Scottish History Edinburgh University
17 Buccleuch Place
Edinburgh, EH8 9LN
Founded in 1886; the leading publisher of manuscript sources relating to the history of Scotland.

Scottish Maritime Museum
Laird Forge
Gottries Road
Irvine KA12 8QE Scotland

Scottish Mining Museum
Lady Victoria Colliery
Newtongrange EH22 4QN Scotland
www.scottishminingmuseum.com

Scottish Record Society
Dept. of Scottish History
University of Glasgow
Glasgow G12 8QQ Scotland
Created in 1897; publishes an annual volume of records.

The Scottish Records Association
HM General Register House
Princes Street
Edinburgh EH1 3YY Scotland
www.scottishrecordsassociaton.org/
Concerned with the preservation and use of public and private records; a partner in the Scottish Archives Network; home of *Summaries of Archival Holdings*

Selkirk Library
Ettrick Terrace
Selkirk, TD7 4LE, Scotland
Also, see Scottish Borders

Shetland Archives
44 King Harald Street
Lerwick
ZE1 0EQ, Scotland

Shire Publications Limited
Cromwell House
Church Street
Princes Risborough
Bucks HP27 9AA England
www.shirebooks.co.uk

Society of Genealogists
14 Charterhouse Buildings
Goswell Road
London, EC1 , England
www.sog.org.uk
Holds many Scottish resources and publishes a guide to them.

South Ayrshire Libraries
Local Collection
Carnegie Library
12 Main Street
Ayr KA8 8ED Scotland

Stirling Central Library
Corn Exchange Road
Stirling FK8 2HX Scotland

Summerlee Heritage Trust
Heritage Way
Coatbridge, Lanarkshire, ML5 1QD,
Scotland

Sutherland
See North Highland Archive, Wick

Tay Valley Family History Society
FH Research Centre
179 Princes Street
Dundee DD4 6DQ Scotland
www.tayvalleyfhs.org.uk

Tuckwell Press
The Mill House, Phantassie
East Linton
East Lothian, EH40 3DG, Scotland
www.tuckwellpress.co.uk

West Lothian Council Archives
7 Rutherford Square
Bracefield, Livingston
West Lothian EH54 9BU Scotland

Wigtownshire
Stranraer Museum
35 George Street
Stranraer, DG9 7JP, Scotland

Scotland on the World Wide Web

There are many books on using the Internet, some designed specifi-cally for genealogists. It is also easy to find published lists of website addresses. The fat ones make good doorstops.

Learning to use the Web is up to you and depends on your objectives, the way you work, and the way you like to find information. I recommend you spend less time reading what others have to say and more time under-standing your browser, selecting a couple of favorite search engines and creating your own directory of sites for Scottish genealogy.

For those of you who want help getting started or some information to give you new direction, here are a few ideas.

1. Begin with a visit to <www.infopeople.org/search/> and <www. searchenginewatch.com>. These sites offer infor-mation about search engines and how they work. It is important to identify one or two that you truly understand because search engines are not all the same and they refer-ence different sites.

2. Peter Christian has written a short guide, *Finding Genealogy on the Internet,* and the entire text of the latest edition (2002)

can be found online at <www.spub.coluk/fgi/index.htm>. The author writes a regular column for the PRO magazine *Ancestors*.

3. Bookmark your favorite sites and organize them in folders in your browser. No list of favorites should be so long it disappears off the bottom of your screen.

4. Explore sites, new ones and old favorites. Chances are you have never adequately read the background material or the 'help' sections. It is amazing what you can discover by doing this.

5. Finally, go on a tour of the Web arranged around the categories of sites listed on the following pages. They are divided into sections: finding broken links, general information, history, geography, guidance for sources, and databases. In every case, there is nearly always something else to discover by concluding your tour with a visit to the appropriate sections of Genuki <www.genuki.org.uk/big/sct/> and Cyndi's List, where I recommend you bookmark one of the simpler formats, e.g., *Text Only Category Index*, <www.cyndislist. com/textonly.htm>.

Finding Broken Links

The addresses in this appendix and others you come across are bound to contain entries that have changed no matter how accurate the list is at time of printing. When you find a link does not work, try one or more of the following steps.

1. Truncate the URL; in other words cut back to the core address, usually recognizable because it is where the first forward slash appears.

2. Use ARCHON (Archives Online), the locator service of the Historical Manuscripts Commission for finding archives, Familia to find libraries <www.familia.org.uk/libraries. html#scotland> and the Scottish Association of Family History Societies <www.safhs.org.uk> for societies.

3. Use Genuki – Scotland to check the list of archives and libraries for that particular place; or, alternatively, Cyndi's List for Scotland (*see* above).

4. Put the name of the archive, library, agency, or society into a search engine (e.g., <www.google.com> or <www. alltheweb.com>).

5. Look at the current edition of *The Family and Local History Handbook* (Blatchford, published annually).

6. For websites that are not societies, archives, or libraries, truncation is the first step, followed by using steps 3 and 4.

General Information about Scotland

There are almost too many of these sites. Two that I have used are <www.rampantscotland.com> and <www.onlinescotland.com>. The Rampant Scotland homepage has links to dozens of related topics and you can sign up for a newsy and interesting weekly letter. For travel information I go to the official British Tourist Authority site and select the appropriate region and topic <www.visitbritain.com>.

History of Scotland

Start with Rampant Scotland where you will find a timeline and links to many history sites. Take a look at the BBC History site as well <www.bbc.co.uk/history>; it has a section devoted to Scottish history. Don't forget that the first and second *Statistical Accounts* can also be found on the Web <http://stat-acc-scot.edina.ac.uk/stat-acc-scot/stat-acc-scot. asp>.

If your interest is in a particular place or topic, use the gateway sites and search for links at the websites of local archives, libraries, and societies. A very good example of a local history site that can be invaluable to genealogists is found at Tayside, A Maritime History <www.tamh.org>.

The Internet Library of Early Journals <www.bodley.ox.ac.uk/ilej/> includes Blackwood's Magazine, the Gentleman's Magazine and the Annual Register. There are at least twenty years of each at the site; all can be browsed and some can be searched. This is very interesting, either to look for a specific person or event or to read for a significant year of an ancestor's life.

Geography and Maps of Scotland

The National Library of Scotland has over 800 maps in the online digital collection. This can be found at <www.nls.uk/digitallibrary/map/early>. Modern maps are found at the Ordnance Survey, Britain's national mapping agency, www.ordnancesurvey.com. For local maps, check the individual county and parish pages through Genuki.

For gazetteers and information about places in Scotland visit The Gazetteer of Scotland, <www.geo.ed.ac.uk/scotgaz>, a joint project of the University of Edinburgh and the Royal Scottish Geographical Society. Also, check out the place name references and linked maps at <www.old-maps.co.uk/gazetteer.htm>. The detail in the place name list at Scots Origins, www.scotsorigins.com, is excellent; it is based on the addesses used in the 1881 census.

Help with Sources

Fact sheets and information leaflets are available at several locations on the Internet, notably at the websites of the National Archives of Scotland <www.nas.gov.uk> and the Scottish Archives Network (Knowledge Base) <www.scan.org.uk>. These should definitely be among your bookmarked locations; add the National Archives at Kew as well <www.nationalarchives.gov.uk> if you have an interest in the military or other British national records. For background and source information related to vital records, explore inside the site of the General Register Office (Scotland) <www.gro-scotland.gov.uk>; select "Family History" at the home page to get started. This is where to find the Detailed List of the Old Parish Registers of Scotland, a list of registration districts, the facts about surviving irregular marriages, an article on the DIGROS project, etc.

Articles that I have written on Scottish topics for *Ancestry Daily News* can be found at www.ancestry.com; they are part of the free information found in the "Library." Other resources can be found using the record type topics at Genuki and Cyndi's List.

Some classes of records seem to generate more support information. Military records are a good example. The National Army Museum <www.national-army-museum.ac.uk> is one source and the site *Land Forces of Britain, the Empire and Commonwealth* gives lots of information on the regimental system including lists of all regiments at key times in history <www.regiments.org>.

On the topic of the poor, there is a very informative and well-designed site on workhouses in Britain at <www.workhouses.org.uk>. It includes a section that lists and gives details about workhouses in Scotland.

Databases

There are many databases, large and small, paid access and free. Several have been discussed in the text because they are so important for record access: <www.ancestry.com>, <www.familysearch.org>, <www.scan.org.uk>, <www.scottishdocuments.com>, and <www.scotlandspeople.com>. New databases are likely to appear, both at these sites and at new locations. Genuki and Cyndi's List can keep you informed, as can print or electronic newsletters and discussion groups.

These are the biggest and better-known sites; however, small databases lurk inside the websites of local repositories, societies, universities, and individuals. They may or may not turn up using a search engine. I suggest you try three things: thoroughly explore the appropriate geographical area using Genuki and Cyndi's List; use the search engine at Genuki which searches all sites that are part of that system; and then try the engine at Origin Search (there is presently a small user fee) <www.originsearch.com>, designed specifically to find and scan genealogical lists.

Browsing for Books

The major societies have an extensive stock of books, CDs, maps, etc., for sale. Try the Scottish Genealogical Society, Aberdeen and North East Scotland Family History Society, Glasgow and West of Scotland Family History Society, Fife Family History Society, Tay Valley Family History Society, and the Federation of Family History Societies (England). A less extensive list of titles, but a useful one, can be found at the Scottish Association for Family History Societies. Among publishers, take a look at Tuckwell Press and Shire Publications.

• Bibliography •

The bibliography that follows is an extensive though not exhaustive list of books; annotations are included as much as possible. Many titles are no longer in print but the arrival of online book sales has made it much easier to find older books. In particular, the cooperative listings of hundreds of used bookshops through <www.abebooks.com> make a difference. For titles specifically related to your area of interest, whether a region or a record class, consult the area family history society or the major retailers of genealogy books on Scotland.

Section A—Reference Books

This is a list of how-to books, guides to contents of record offices, encyclopedias, dictionaries, gazetteers, atlases, and related materials. They will be useful throughout your research. Those items preceded by an asterisk (*) are referred to again in individual chapter sections. As the second reference is just a reference, the asterisk will help you identify the full-length description.

*Bevan, Amanda ed. *Tracing Your Ancestors in the Public Record Office*. Kew: PRO Publications, 6th edition, 2002. An essential guide for anyone interested in records of the British government.

Bigwood, Rosemary. *Tracing Scottish Ancestors*. Edinburgh: HarperCollins, 1999. A pocket- size guide written by an acknowledged expert.

Blatchford, Robert. *The Family and Local History Handbook*. Dunkinfield, Yks: Genealogical Services Directory, 2002. Issued early every year; contains articles, address, and website information; informative and a good value.

Burness, Lawrence R. *A Scottish Historian's Glossary*. Aberdeen: Aberdeen and North- east Scotland Family History Society, 1997. There are glossaries in other books, but this is more extensive.

*Campbell, Sheila. *Sources in Kirkcaldy Central Library*. Kirkcaldy District Council, 1994. A good example of a local guide, it shows the extent of library holdings.

Collins, Ewan K. *Beginners' Guide to Scottish Genealogy*. Dundee: Tay Valley Family History Society, 1992. This little book is of great value, mixing mainly nineteenth-century source information for each of the Scottish regions with remarks on basic records; includes suggested exercises for beginners.

*Cox, Michael. *Exploring Scottish History*. Hamilton: Scottish Library Association, Scottish Local History Forum, and Scottish Records Association, 2nd ed., 1999. A directory of resource centers. Collections described are in libraries, archives, universities, galleries, and museums.

Diack, H. Leslie. *North East Roots: A Guide to Sources*. 3rd ed. Aberdeen: Aberdeen and North East Scotland Family History Society, 1996. Another helpful guide to regional sources.

Family History Department. *Scotland Research Outline*. Salt Lake City: The Church of Jesus Christ of Latter-day Saints, 1997. Helpful for basic research techniques; includes outlines of various types of records in the Family History Library, but be sure to read more than this work alone.

*Findlay, James. *Directory To Gentlemen's Seats, Villages, Etc. in Scotland*. Edinburgh: Kennedy, 1843. The subtitle to this adds, "giving the counties in which they are situated—the post-towns to which each is attached—and the name of the resident," so it is a wonderful tool for locating obscure place names;

it was reissued in 1852 and 1857, then continued as the *County Directory of Scotland* 1862, 1868, 1872, 1875, 1878, 1882, 1886, 1894, 1902, and 1912 (this last issue included farms).

Fowler, Simon. *Tracing Scottish Ancestors, A Pocket Guide.* Kew: PRO, 2001.

*Groome, Francis H. *Ordnance Gazetteer of Scotland: A Survey of Scottish Topography, Statistical, Biographical and Historical.* 6 vols. Edinburgh: T.C. Jack, 1883-85. CD-ROM (ed. Mike Spathaky, Genfair, 2001).This may be in the permanent collection (on fiche) of many LDS family history centers; always look up the description of a place in it. The supplementary information is useful, too, including brief descriptions of all the religious denominations in Scotland.

*Hamilton-Edwards, Gerald. *In Search of Scottish Ancestry.* 2nd ed. Chichester, England: Phillimore, 1983. This remains useful because of the detailed examples for some records, notably the Registry of Deeds and Sasines.

*Humphery-Smith, Cecil. *Atlas and Index of Parish Registers.* 2nd ed. Chichester, England: Phillimore, 1995. This edition includes Scotland, showing parish and commissariot boundaries.

Index to British and Irish Biographies, 1840-1940. Cambridge: Chadwyck-Healey, 1990. A finding aid of more than 6,000 fiche, located at the Family History Library, which incorporates many useful lists of people.

*Keay, John, and Julia Keay, eds. *Collins Encyclopaedia of Scotland.* London: Harper Collins, 1994. A wonderful source of enlightenment, very readable, sometimes humorous; over 4,000 entries.

Kalopulu, Karen and Rosemary Deane. *Researching Family History in the Collections of Auckland City Libraries.* Auckland: Auckland City Libraries, 1997.

Little, William, H.W. Fowler, and J. Coulson. *The Shorter Oxford English Dictionary on Historical Principles.* 3rd ed. Oxford: Clarendon Press, 1973. One can never have too many dictionaries, and this one, showing historical change in usage, is fascinating.

*Miller, Susan. *Strathclyde Sources: A Guide for Family Historians.* 2nd ed. Glasgow: Glasgow and West of Scotland Family History Society, 1995. The introductory essay on research is useful; covers Glasgow, Argyll and Bute, Ayrshire, Dunbartonshire, Lanarkshire, Renfrewshire, and part of Stirlingshire.

*Moody, David. *Scottish Family History.* London: B.T. Batsford, 1988. Reprint. Baltimore: Genealogical Publishing Co., 2000. Not really a handbook but an essay on the importance of incorporating social history into genealogical research; as in his other book, Moody makes you think; essential reading.

*Moody, David. *Scottish Local History.* London: B.T. Batsford, 1986. Reprint. Baltimore: Genealogical Publishing Co., 1994. This is one of my favorites; the source suggestions are endless, and the perspective on local history is very helpful when it comes to considering new approaches to research; extensive bibliography.

Moore, Marjorie. *Sources for Scottish Genealogy in the Library of the Society of Genealogists.* London: Society of Genealogists, 1996.

National Inventory of Documentary Sources in the United Kingdom. Cambridge: Chadwyck-Healey, various dates, mainly 1980s. This contains summaries of holdings of many repositories in the UK. Usually individual pieces are found in the appropriate part of the Locality section of the FHLC.

New Statistical Account of Scotland. Edinburgh: W. Blackwood, 1845. Undertaken by a committee of the Society for the Benefit of the Sons and Daughters of the Clergy forty-five years after Sinclair's first survey, this series of volumes gives a picture of the parishes of Scotland following a period of considerable change. Also found on the Web, see page 216 in appendix D.

*Scottish Records Association. *Data Sheet No. 6, Summaries of Archival Holdings.* Edinburgh, 1994. Until recently this was issued as a series of leaflets by the Association; now the information appears in the newsletter and at the website; see *Summaries of Archival Holdings* on page 23 in chapter 2.

Sinclair, Cecil. *Tracing Scottish Local History.* Edinburgh: HMSO, 1994. This is the local historians' version of Sinclair's book on Scottish ancestors; you will find the same wording occasionally in both, but this altered perspective is often helpful.

*Sinclair, Cecil. *Tracing Your Scottish Ancestors in the Scottish Record Office.* 2nd ed. Edinburgh: Stationery Office, 1997. Take time to read this book; although the exact instructions of what to do in the NAS are a little tedious at times (you will be glad of them if you make a trip), the source descriptions are invaluable.

*Sinclair, Sir John, Bt. *Analysis of the Statistical Account of Scotland. With an analysis of the history of that country and discussions on some important branches of political economy, in particular a discussion on the various classes into which the inhabitants of Scotland may be divided, e.g., productive, useful and useless.* London: John Murray, 1826. Those far-from-politically-correct terms are actually used in the book; Sinclair's own reflections on the reports from the parishes make very interesting reading.

*Sinclair, Sir John, Bt. *The Statistical Account of Scotland.* 1791-99. Reprint, edited by Donald J. Withrington and I. R. Grant. Wakefield: E.P. Publishing, 1979. Volumes referred to in the text are II, III, IV, and VI. *Always* look up a parish in this; this was followed in the 1830s and 1840s by the *New (or Second) Statistical Account of Scotland* (see above) and in this century by the *Third Statistical Account of Scotland*; interesting comparisons arise when more than one account of a parish is examined. Also found on the Web, see page 216 in appendix D.

*Steel, Don. *National Index of Parish Registers. Scotland. Vol. XII.* London: Society of Genealogists, 1970. Do not be deceived by the title or the date. This remains an interesting and useful book that does much more than discuss parish registers.

*Timperley, Loretta R., ed. *A Directory of Land Ownership in Scotland circa 1770,* n.s., vol. 51. Edinburgh: Scottish Record Society, 1976. The usefulness of this volume is fully explained in the text; if you are interested in other volumes published by this society, check university libraries, and use the author part of the FHLC, treating Scottish Record Society as an author—there are about 100 entries.

Torrance, D. Richard. *Scottish Personal Names and Place Names—a bibliography.* Edinburgh: Scottish Genealogy Society, 1992. This should provide lots of ideas of other titles to watch for or to try to obtain by interlibrary loan.

Vine Hall, Nick. *Tracing Your Family History in Australia.* 2 vols. The Author, 3rd ed., 2002.

*Whitaker's Almanac. London: J. Whitaker and Sons, published annually since 1868. A good reference resource for finding names and addresses of societies, schools, and associations.

Section B—References by Chapter

Books in this section are arranged according to the chapters in the text. Where a book has already received a full description in section A or an earlier chapter, the reader is asked to refer back to the first entry, which is preceded by an asterisk (*).

Chapters 1 and 2

Anderson, William. *The Scottish Nation: or the surnames, families, literature, honours and biographical history of the people of Scotland.* 3 vols. 1866-77. This covers a wide mix of material and includes lots of interesting people.

Banks, Noel. *Six Inner Hebrides.* Newton Abbot, England: David and Charles, 1977. One of a series of books on islands, this one is about Eigg, Rum, Cann, Coll, Muck, and Tiree; Scottish islands covered in other volumes include Shetland, Orkney, Mull, Bute, Harris, and Lewis.

Black, George F. *The Surnames of Scotland.* New York: New York Public Library, 1999. First printing: 1946. Do more than simply look up a name in this; read the introduction, not only to understand the nature of the study, but for the interesting detail about name origins and use of nicknames in villages where there were only a few surnames between several hundred inhabitants.

Bulloch, John, ed. *Scottish Notes and Queries.* 2nd ser. Aberdeen: Rosemount Press, 1906-07. If you can find any of these, take time to dip into them. The articles may relate to what you are researching, and the queries and answers are often genealogical; long before the age of computers, people seemed to delight in sharing obscure information.

Castleden, Rodney. *Harrap's Book of British Dates.* Bromley, Kent: Harrap, 1991. A chronological dictionary from prehistoric times, arranged by year and category, each with a distinct symbol.

Cox, M. See section A.

Donaldson, Gordon, and Robert S. Morpeth. *A Dictionary of Scottish History.* Edinburgh: John Donald, 1977; rep. 1994.

*Donnachie, Ian, and George Hewitt. *A Companion to Scottish History: From the Reformation to the Present*. New York: Facts on File, 1989. In dictionary form, this book describes or defines significant people, events, and topics, some not found in other works of reference. There is a list of royal burghs with dates of foundation, and county populations through many censuses.

Dorward, David. *Scottish Surnames*. Glasgow: Harper Collins, 1995. Describes over 1000 names with meanings and origins.

Dunbar, John T. *The Costume of Scotland*. London: B.T. Batsford, 1981. Describes the dress of your ancestors and explains the origins of the kilt; illustrated.

Edward, Mary. *Who Belongs to Glasgow: 200 Years of Migration*. Glasgow: Glasgow City Libraries, 1993.

Ferguson, Joan P.S., comp. *Scottish Family Histories held in Scottish Libraries*. Edinburgh: Scottish Central Library, 1968. This is useful when surveying what has been done by others.

Findlay, J. See section A.

Fraser, George Macdonald. *The Steel Bonnets*. London: Barrie and Jenkins, 1971. Still in print in soft cover, this is essential reading for anyone with ancestors in the border counties.

Gillespie, J.D. "Gregorian Calendar." *The Scottish Genealogist* 35, no. 1 (March 1988): 24. Edinburgh: Scottish Genealogical Society.

Graham-Campbell, David. *Portrait of Argyll and the Southern Hebrides*. London: Robert Hale, 1978. A good example of the many books of history, geography, and local history that may be found in used bookshops.

Grant, Sir Francis J., ed. *Index to Genealogies, Birthbriefs and Funeral Escutcheons Recorded in the Lyon Office*. Edinburgh: J. Skinner, 1908.

Groome, F. H. See section A.

*Hinchliff, Helen. "William Edward, Part 1, Identifying an Eighteenth-Century Miller." *Aberdeen and North East Scotland Family History Society Journal* 53 (November 1994): 6-11. An example of reconstruction of family and community with some excellent examples of how resources outside your time frame can help.

Humphery-Smith, C. See section A.

Johnson, Keith A., and Malcom R. Sainty. *Genealogical Research Directory*. Melbourne: published by the editors, 2002 (issued annually). Contains listing of subscribers' research interests, and names and addresses; useful for checking who might be researching similar lines.

Keay, J., and J. Keay. See section A.

Lang, Theo, ed. *The Border Counties*. London: Hodder and Stoughton, 1957. Volume IV of *The Queen's Scotland*, a descriptive series in eight volumes, organized alphabetically by place name.

Lewis, Samuel. *A Topographical Dictionary of Scotland*. Two volumes. London: S. Lewis, 1851. Reprint. Baltimore: Genealogical Publishing Co., 2002. Another informative source of nineteenth-century descriptive detail.

Macdonald, Angus. *The Highlands and Islands of Scotland*. London: Weidenfeld and Nicolson, 1991. Well-illustrated and interesting mix of history, geography, and natural history.

MacLean, Fitzroy. *A Concise History of Scotland*. London: Thames and Hudson, 1973. A readable overview, well-illustrated.

Macleod, John. *Highlanders: A History of the Gaels*. London: Sceptre Paperback, 1997.

Millman, R.N. *The Making of the Scottish Landscape*. London: B.T. Batsford, 1975. Contains an extensive bibliography of works on the changing face of the Scottish landscape, many on individual parishes; also maps of patterns of growth of Scottish cities.

Ordnance Survey Maps. The government mapping agency began in the late eighteenth century under the authority of the Army Board of Ordnance (which ultimately supplied the army with all its needs, including maps), hence the name. For Scotland, there are reprints of the 1890 series of one-inch-to-one-mile plans, various nineteenth-century town plans, and the modern series. Some of these can be consulted in the FHL; many public libraries hold O/S modern series and they can be purchased through map dealers, genealogy book vendors and some societies.

Powell, Bob. *Scottish Agricultural Implements*. Princes Risborough, England: Shire, 1988. An interesting survey of machinery from the rudimentary to the complex.

Robinson, Mairi. *The Concise Scots Dictionary*. Oxford: University of Aberdeen Press, 1985.

Rosie, Alison. *Scottish Handwriting 1500-1700: A Self-Help Pack*. Edinburgh: NAS and the Scottish Records Association. This can be purchased from the NAS.

Rhys, Ernest. *A Dictionary of Dates*. Everyman's Library Edition. London: Dent, 1940. A small treasure of information; alphabetical by topic.

Sinclair, Cecil. *Jock Tamson's Bairns: A History of the Records of the General Register Office for Scotland*. Edinburgh: GRO (Scotland), 2000.

Sinclair, Sir John, Bt. *Analysis*. See section A.

Sinclair, Sir John, Bt. *Statistical Accounts*. See section A.

Smout, Thomas C. *Century of the Scottish People 1830-1950*. London: Fontana, 1987.

Smout, Thomas C. *A History of the Scottish People 1580-1830*. London: Fontana, 1985. Lots of social history and good bibliographies.

Stevenson, David, and Wendy B. Stevenson. *Scottish Texts and Calendars: An Analytic Guide to Serial Publications.* Edinburgh and London: Scottish History Society and Royal Historical Society, 1987. Concentrates on providing notations on the contents of the volumes of private historical societies, but includes some works issued by official bodies. It serves as an update to and partial replacement for *A catalogue of the publications of Scottish Historical and Kindred Clubs and Societies, and of the volumes relevant to Scottish history issued by His Majesty's Stationery Office 1780-1908* (C.S. Terry, 1909) and the follow-up of the same title for the years 1908-1927 (C. Matheson, 1928).

Strawhorn, John. *Ayrshire: The Story of a County.* Ayr: Ayrshire Archaeological and Natural History Society, 1975. A very good example of a county history, it covers all aspects of social, economic, and political history, with insights into change, growth, and controversial issues.

Stuart, Margaret. *Scottish Family History: A Guide to Works of Reference on the History and Genealogy of Scottish Families.* Oliver and Boyd, 1930. Reprint. Baltimore: Genealogical Publishing Co., 1994.

Summaries of Archival Holdings. Edinburgh: Scottish Records Association, 2002. This replaces the series of leaflets in *Datasheet #6* and describes in summary form the holdings of Scottish record offices; it is printed in the Newsletter and uploaded to the Association website.

Thoyts, E.E. *How to Read Old Documents.* Chichester, England: Phillimore, 1980. Although written at the turn of the century, this remains a useful work on the handwriting, contractions, etc., found in British records.

Timperley, L.R. See section A.

Torrance, D. R. See section A.

Way, George, and P. Squire. *Collins Scottish Clan and Family Encyclopaedia.* Glasgow: Harper Collins, 1994. Another recently published, well-illustrated, and informative reference work.

West, T.W. *Discovering Scottish Architecture.* Princes Risborough, England: Shire, 1985. An introductory guide to the built heritage of Scotland.

Wilkes, Margaret. *The Scot and His Maps.* Scottish Library Association, 1991. Written by the Keeper of the Map Library of the National Library, this is an enjoyable read which will be useful background for any genealogist.

Williamson, Elizabeth, Anne Riches, and Malcolm Higgs. *The Buildings of Scotland.* London: Penguin, in association with the National Trust for Scotland, 1980. Selects the buildings that represent the architectural heritage; one of a series.

Wilson, Rev. John. *The Gazetteer of Scotland.* 1882. Reprint. Lovettsville, Va.: Willow Bend Books, 2002. Less extensive than Groome, but mentions every town and village and gives some description.

Chapter 3

Bloxham, V. Ben, and D.K. Metcalfe. *Key to the Parochial Registers of Scotland.* See chapter 4.

Collins, E.K. See section A.

Miller, Susan. See section A.

*Spiers, S.M., ed. *Parishes, Registers and Registrars of Scotland.* Scottish Association of Family History Societies, 1993. Contains county maps showing parish boundaries, the addresses for local registrars, and the parish numbers for each parish.

Chapter 4

1881 British Census and National Index, CD-ROM. Salt Lake City: Intellectual Reserve and The Church of Jesus Christ of Latter-day Saints, 1999.

Abstract of the Answers and Returns Made Pursuant to an Act, Passed in the 41st Year of His Majesty King George III: an act for taking an account of the population of Great Britain and the increase and diminution thereof. London, 1801.

Adam, Sir Charles E., ed. *A View of the Political State of Scotland in the last century: A confidential report on the . . . 2662 County Voters about 1788.* Edinburgh, 1887. Volumes with similar titles appeared again in 1790 (A. Mackenzie, ed.) and 1812 (James Bridges, ed.).

Bigwood, A. Rosemary. "Pre-1855 Communion Rolls and Other Listings in Kirk Sessions Records." *The Scottish Genealogist* 35, no. 2 (June 1988): 73-85. Edinburgh: Scottish Genealogical Society.

*Bloxham, V. Ben, and D.K. Metcalfe. *Key to the Parochial Registers of Scotland.* 2nd ed. Provo, UT: Stevenson Genealogical Supply, 1979. Based on the *Detailed List of the Old Parochial Registers of Scotland* (see below). Each listing includes the parish number and the dates of surviving records; note that the film numbers are from an earlier filming, still available. The second filming is better, but some entries in the earlier filming are not found in the later one (which has numbers of 900,000 or higher).

Campbell, Sheila. See section A.

Celtic Monthly. A Magazine for Highlanders. First published in October of 1892 by the Glasgow Celtic Press. Some volumes are on film in the FHL.

Chapman, Colin. *An Introduction to Using Newspapers and Periodicals.* Birmingham, England: Federation of Family History Societies, 1993.

Chapman, Colin. *Pre-1841 Censuses and Population Listings in the British Isles.* 4th ed. Dursley, England: Lochin Publishing, 1994. Could be more extensive on the subject of Scottish listings, but useful nonetheless.

Collins, Audrey. *Basic Facts About Using Colindale and Other Newspaper Libraries.* Birmingham: Federation of Family History Societies, 2001.

Cox, Michael. See section A.

Ferguson, J.S.P. *Scottish Newspapers Held in Scottish Libraries.* Edinburgh: National Library of Scotland, 1984.

Family History Department. *1881 British Census Indexes Research Outline.* Salt Lake City: Church of Jesus Christ of Latter-day Saints, 1996.

Gibson, J.S.W. *Poll Books, c. 1695-1872: A Directory to Holdings in Great Britain.* 3rd ed. Bury, Lancs., England: Federation of Family History Societies, 1994. Scottish entries in Gibson guides are brief but they are useful.

Gibson, J.S.W., and Elizabeth Hampson. *Marriage and Census Indexes for Family Historians.* 8th ed. Bury, Lancs.: Federation of Family History Societies, 2000.

*Gibson, J.S.W. and Elizabeth Hampson. *Specialist Indexes for Family Historians.* Bury, Lancs.: Federation of Family History Societies, 2nd ed., 2000.

Gibson, J.S.W. and Elizabeth Hampson. *Census Returns 1841 – 1891 in Microform: A Directory ot Local Holdings in Great Britain; Channel Islands; Isle of Man.* 6th ed. Bury, Lancs.: Federation of Family History Societies, 2001.

Gibson, Jeremy, and Mervyn Medlycott. *Local Census Listings 1522-1930.* 3rd ed. Bury, Lancs.: Federation of Family History Societies, 1997. A particularly useful guide.

Gibson, J.S.W., and C. Rogers. *Electoral Registers Since 1832 and Burgess Rolls.* Bury, Lancs., England: Federation of Family History Societies, 1989.

Gilhooley, J., comp. *A Directory of Edinburgh in 1752.* Edinburgh: Edinburgh University Press, 1988.

Hamilton-Edwards, G. See section A.

*Hinchliff, Helen. "William Edward, Part 1, Identifying an Eighteenth-Century Miller." See r section A.

Johnson, Gordon. *Census Records for Scottish Families at Home and Abroad.* 3rd ed. Aberdeen: Aberdeen and North East Scotland Family History Society, 1997. Packed with useful information about nominal censuses 1841-91 and earlier listings. Also includes a discussion of the value of statistical evidence.

Lumas, Susan B. *Making Use of the Census.* 2nd ed. Kew: PRO Publications, 2002. Interesting background to the census, plus useful tips.

McLaughlin, Eve. *Family History from Newspapers.* Aylesbury, England: McLaughlin, 1993. Informative, with a lighthearted touch.

Miller, Susan. *A Guide to Glasgow Addresses, Part 1, 1700 – 1825.* Glasgow and West of Scotland Family History Society, 2001. For the old city center before the use of street numbers.

*Miller, Susan. A. *A Guide to Glasgow Addresses, Part 2, 1826 – 1950*. Glasgow and West of Scotland Family History Society, 2nd ed., 2001. Details of changes to Glasgow street names as the city grew.

Murray, Peter R. *Scottish Census Indexes 1841-1871*. 2nd ed. Aberdeen: Scottish Association of Family History Societies, 1998. Lists indexes available for these census returns and their locations.

North, John S. *The Waterloo Directory of Scottish Newspapers and Periodicals 1800-1900*. Vol. I. Waterloo: North Waterloo Academic Press, 1989. All you need to know about old Scottish newspapers.

Spiers, S.M., ed. *Parishes, Registers and Registrars of Scotland*. See chapter 3.

Scots Magazine. First published in 1739, now issued monthly from D. and C. Thompson, Dundee. It contains articles of local history, new books about Scotland, and sometimes genealogical items or letters.

Stirling Journal and Advertiser: a local index. Volume 1, 1820-1869. Stirling: University of Stirling, n.d.

The 1881 Census Indexes of Scotland. Salt Lake City: The Church of Jesus Christ of Latter-day Saints, 1994. Guide to the use of these indexes on fiche.

Willings Press Guide. London: James Willing, published annually.

Chapters 5 and 6

Baird, Douglas J. "Scottish Marriages." *The Scottish Genealogist* 26, no. 4 (December 1979). Edinburgh: Scottish Genealogical Society.

Baptie, Diane. *Registers of the Secession Churches in Scotland*. Aberdeen: Scottish Association of Family History Societies. 2000.

Bayne, Gillian. "St. Andrew's Database," *Newsletter* (Spring 1992). Glasgow: Glasgow and West of Scotland Family History Society.

Bigwood, A. Rosemary. "Dissenting Congregations in Pre-Disruption Ayrshire and Their Importance to the Genealogist." *The Scottish Genealogist* 34, no. 2 (June 1987): 238-239. Edinburgh: Scottish Genealogical Society. Proves that a statistical angle on research can be informative.

Bigwood, A. Rosemary. "Pre-1855 Communion Rolls and Other Listings in Kirk Sessions Records." See under chapter 4.

British Isles Vital Records Index: England, Ireland, Scotland and Wales, CD-ROM. Salt Lake City: Intellectual Reserve and The Church of Jesus Christ of Latter-day Saints, 2nd ed., 2001.

Burleigh, J.H.S. *A Church History of Scotland*. Edinburgh, 1960. The book where the flow chart of Scottish church history first appeared.

The Catholic Directory for Scotland. Edinburgh and Dundee, 1831-35. This continues to be published; the Mitchell library holds volumes from 1836, complete
from 1861; some are in the FHL.

Couper, W.J. *The Reformed Presbyterian Church in Scotland, Its Congregations,
Ministers and Students 1743 – 1876.* Edinburgh, 1925.

Detailed List of the Old Parochial Registers of Scotland. Edinburgh: Murray and Gibb,
1872. List of parishes with their numbers, including the different 1851 numbers.

Fleming, Stuart. *A List of Published and Unpublished Monumental Inscriptions Held
by the Scottish Genealogy Society.* Edinburgh: Scottish Genealogy Society, rev.
ed., 2002.

Gandy, Michael, ed. *Catholic Parishes in England, Wales and Scotland, an Atlas.*
London: Gandy, 1993.

Gordon, Anne. *Candie for the Foundling.* Edinburgh: Pentland Press, 1992. A history of kirk sessions and how they influenced the lives of our ancestors.

Groome, F.H. See section A.

Humphery-Smith, Cecil. See section A.

Lindsay, Jean. *The Scottish Poor Law: Its Operation in the North East, 1745-1845.*
Ilfracombe, England: Stockwell, 1975. An absolutely fascinating study, with
many interesting examples; well-written.

Mitchell, Alison, ed. *Pre-1855 Gravestone Inscriptions in Angus.* 4 vols. Edinburgh:
Scottish Genealogical Society, 1979-1984. Part of a series published by the society.

National Burial Index For England and Wales, CD-ROM. Bury, Lancs: Federation of
Family History Societies, 2001.

New Statistical Account of Scotland, Volume VI, Lanark. See under section A; this
volume includes Rutherglen.

Old Parochial Registers (OPR) Index for Scotland. Salt Lake City: The Church of
Jesus Christ of Latter-day Saints, 1994. One of their helpful research guides.

Orr, Brian J. *As God Is My Witness: The Presbyterian Kirk, the Covenanters and the
Ulster Scots.* Heritage Books, 2002. Interesting history and includes a list of
Covenanters.

Records of the Church of Scotland and Other Presbyterian Churches. Edinburgh:
National Archives of Scotland, 1994. Similar information to what is in this set
of microfiche can be found in a series of lists within the General Register Office
(Scotland) website.

Retours of Services of Heirs 1544–1699, CD-ROM. Edinburgh: Scottish Genealogy
Society, 1999.

Scottish Parish Records: Scotland (General), CD-ROM. Provo, UT: Ancestry.com,
2001.

Scottish Parish Records: Scotland (North), CD-ROM. Provo, UT: Ancestry.com, 2001.

Scottish Parish Records: Scotland (South), CD-ROM. Provo, UT: Ancestry.com, 2001.

Scottish Parish Records: Scotland (West Lothian, Midlothian), CD-ROM. Provo, UT: Ancestry.com, 2001.

Services of Heirs in Scotland 1700–1859, CD-ROM. Edinburgh: Scottish Genealogy Society, 1999.

Richardson, Ruth. *Death, Dissection and the Destitute*. London: Penguin, 1989. A gruesome topic, but this study of the trade in bodies for the anatomists of the late eighteenth and early nineteenth centuries makes interesting reading and tells much about values and superstitions of the day.

Pre-1855 Fife Deaths Index. Fife Family History Society, CD-ROM, 2000. Contains roughly 250,000 names and comes with explanatory booklet.

Sinclair, Sir John, Bt. *Analysis*. See section A.

Sinclair, Sir John, Bt. *The Statistical Account of Scotland*. (Full details in section A.) Note in particular Vol. III: *The Eastern Borders*, which includes reference to Lamberton Toll, and Vol. IV: *Dumfriesshire*, which includes a comment on clandestine marriages at Graitney (informing everyone that the fellow who performs them is without manners or morals and usually drunk).

Steel, Don. See section A.

The Scots Magazine. See chapter 4.

Willing, June A., and J. Scott Fairie. *Burial Grounds in Glasgow*. Glasgow: Glasgow and West of Scotland Family History Society, 1986. A guide to burial grounds with date of earliest burial and surviving registers.

Willsher, Betty. *Understanding Scottish Graveyards*. Reprint. Edinburgh: Council for Scottish Archaeology, 1995. Historical background, types of monuments and inscriptions, how to record graveyards.

Chapter 7

Calendar of Confirmations and Inventories Granted and Given Up in the Several Commissariots of Scotland in the Year 1876. Edinburgh: Neil and Co. for HMSO, 1877. This is the first volume of the series.

Donnachie, Ian, and George Hewitt. See under chapters 1 and 2.

Gibson, J.S.W. *Guide to Probate Jurisdictions*. 5th ed. Birmingham, England: Federation of Family History Societies, 2002.

Gouldesborough, P., ed. *Formulary of Old Scots Documents*. Edinburgh: The Stair Society, 1985. Texts of old Scots documents with translations.

Hamilton-Edwards, G. See section A.

MacLeod, John, ed. *Services of Heirs, Roxburghshire, 1636-1847.* Edinburgh: Scottish Record Society, 1934.

Sinclair, C. *Tracing Your Scottish Ancestors.* See section A.

Steel, Don. See section A.

"The Campbells of Strachur." *The Scottish Historical Review* 4 (1907): 234. Glasgow: James Maclehose.

Chapter 8

Adam, Frank. *The Clans, Septs and Regiments of the Scottish Highlands.* 6th ed. Revised by Sir Thomas Innes of Learney. Edinburgh: Johnston and Bacon, 1960.

Addison, W.I. *Roll of Graduates, University of Glasgow, 1727-1897.* Glasgow, 1898. Includes short biographical notes.

Addison, W.I. *The Matriculation Albums of the University of Glasgow, 1728-1858.* Glasgow, 1913.

Anderson, James R., ed. *The Burgesses and Guild Brethren of Glasgow, 1573-1750.* Edinburgh: Scottish Record Society, 1925.

Anderson, James R., ed. *The Burgesses and Guild Brethren of Glasgow, 1751-1846.* Edinburgh: Scottish Record Society, 1935.

Army List. London, annually since 1754.

Barriskill, D. *A Guide to Lloyd's Marine Collection at Guildhall Library and Related Marine Sources.* London: Guildhall Library, n.d.

Baxter, I.A. *India Office Library and Records: A Brief Guide to Biographical Sources.* 2nd ed. London: British Library, 1990.

Bevan, A. See section A.

Campbell, Sheila. See section A.

Clabburn, Pamela. *Shawls.* Rev. ed. Princes Risborough, England: Shire, 2000. The weaving and printing of shawls was a major industry in Paisley in the nineteenth century; this book features the designs, patterns, and fabrics.

Cook, Frank, and Andrea Cook. *The Casualty Roll for the Crimea: the casualty rolls for the siege of Sebastopol and other major actions during the Crimean War, 1854-1856.* London: Hayward, 1976. Indexed.

Cox, Michael. See section A.

Crowder, Norman K. *British Army Pensioners Abroad, 1772-1899.* Baltimore: Genealogical Publishing Co., 1995. Especially useful for those who retired from the British Army after serving in Canada or the Caribbean.

Customs and Excise Records as Sources for Biography and Family History. Richmond, England: Public Record Office, 1986. Clear summary of the various record groups for these categories.

Dalton, Charles. *English Army Lists and Commission Registers, 1661-1714.* Reprint. London: Francis Edwards, 1960. Many Scottish officers were serving in these regiments.

Dalton, Charles. *The Waterloo Roll Call: with biographical notes and anecdotes.* London: William Clowes, 1890.

Dobson, David. *Scottish Seafarers of the Seventeenth Century.* Aberdeen: Scottish Association of Family History Societies, 1992. One of a series of small booklets listing seafarers and emigrants; David Dobson has also issued a series of booklets on the mariners of several regions of Scotland. A list and prices are available from the Scottish Genealogy Society or the Aberdeen and North East Scotland Family History Society.

Donohoe, James Hugh. *Remote Garrison: The British Army in Australia 1788 – 1870.* Kangaroo Press, 1986. Includes a list of personnel.

Durie, Alastair J. *The Scottish Linen Industry in the Eighteenth Century.* Edinburgh: John Donald, 1979.

Dwelly, E. *A Muster Roll of the British non-commissioned officers and men present at the Battle of Waterloo.* Edinburgh, 1934.

Edwards, Cliff. *Railway Records.* Kew: PRO Publications, 2001. A guide to the collections at Kew up to 1948.

Ewing, William. *Annals of the Free Church of Scotland 1843-1900.* 2 vols. Edinburgh, 1914.

Fasti Academiae Mariscallanae Aberdonensis, 1593-1860. 3 vols. Spalding Club, 1889-98. Selections from the records of the Marischal College and University.

Farrington, Anthony. *Guide to the Records of the India Office Military Department.* London: India Office Library, 1982.

Fitzhugh, T.V.H. "East India Company Ancestry," *Genealogists' Magazine* 21, no. 5 (March 1984): 150-154.

Fowler, Simon, and William Spencer. *Army Records for Family Historians.* 2nd ed. Kew: PRO Publications, 1998. Outlines the records of the army in a number of categories such as officers, enlisted men, special branches, corps, and militia.

Frederick, J.B.M. *Lineage Book of British Land Forces.* Wakefield, England: YKS, 1984. A genealogy of British army units, including history and mergers.

Gibson, J.S.W. and Elizabeth Hampson. *Specialist Indexes.* See chapter 4.

Gibson, J. S. W., and M. Medlycott. *Militia Lists and Musters, 1757-1876.* 4th ed. Bury, Lancs, England: Federation of Family History Societies, 2000.

Gibson, J.S.W., Mervyn Medlycott and Dennis Mills. *Land and Window Tax Assessments*. Bury, Lancs, England: Federation of Family History Societies, 2nd ed., 1998.

Gilchrist, Alex. "The Use of School Admission Registers for Genealogical Research," *The Scottish Genealogist* 34, no. 4 (December 1987): 402-403.

Graham, E.J. *A Maritime History of Scotland, 1650-1790*. Edinburgh: Tuckwell Press, 2001.

Grant, Sir Francis J., ed. *The Faculty of Advocates, 1532-1943*. Edinburgh: Scottish Record Society, 1943.

Grierson, Lt. Gen. Sir James Moncrieff. *Records of the Scottish Volunteer Force, 1859-1908*. London: Frederick Muller, 1972 (facsimile of the 1909 original).

Harrison, John, ed. *Stirling Burgesses, 1600-1699*. Stirling: Central Scotland Family History Society, 1991.

Hawkings, David T. *Railway Ancestors*. Sutton: Stroud, Glos., 1992. A very comprehensive account of surviving records of British railways.

History of the Society of Writers to H.M. Signet . . . with List of Members . . . 1594-1890. Edinburgh, 1890.

Hoskins, W.G. *History from the Farm*. London: Faber and Faber, 1968. Probably not widely available, this book describes eighteen farms in England and Scotland in detail (three are in Scotland); very informative on history, farming methods, etc.

Kitzmiller, John M. *In Search of the Forlorn Hope: a comprehensive guide to locating British regiments and their records 1640 to World War I*. Salt Lake City: Manuscript Publishing Foundation, 1987. A book of considerable detail that can help you narrow a search in army records.

Lindsay, Alastair, and Joan Kennedy. *The Burgesses and Guild Brethren of Ayr, 1647-1846*. Ayr: Ayrshire Federation of Historical Societies, 2003.

List of the Colonels, Lieutenant Colonels, Majors, Captains, Lieutenants and Ensigns of His Majesty's Forces. London, 1740. Reprint. Society for Army Historical Research, 1931. This provides name, rank, regiment, date of appointment to present rank, and date of first commission.

Livingstone Alastair, C.W.H. Aikman and B.S. Hart. *No Quarter Given: The Muster Roll of Prince Charles Edward Stuart's Army, 1745-46*. Glasgow: Neil Wilson Pub., 2001.

Lloyd's Captains' Registers, 1869-1948. Compiled from the records of Lloyd's Underwriters; at the Guildhall Library, London, with copies also at the National Archives of Canada.

Lloyd's Register of Shipping. London: Lloyd's Registry. Published annually since 1760. Includes ships of British registry to 1889 and ships of the world since 1890.

Mackelvie, William. *Annals and Statistics of the United Presbyterian Church*. Edinburgh: Oliphant and Elliot, 1873.

Matthias, Peter, and A.W.H. Pearshall, eds. *Shipping: A Survey of Historical Records*. Newton Abbot, England: David and Charles, 1971.

*McDougall, Ian. *A Catalogue of Some Labour Records in Scotland and Some Scots Records Outside Scotland*. Scottish Labour History Society, 1978.

Medical Directory. 94 vols. London: J. and A. Churchill, 1846-1940. These are available at the Family History Library on fiche within the British and Irish Biographies series issued by Chadwyck-Healey, Cambridge, 1990. Each volume has a separate index for Scotland (and other parts of Britain).

Muniments of the University. Maitland Club, 1854. Graduates, Glasgow down to 1727.

Navy List. London: HMSO, quarterly since 1814.

Officers and Graduates of University and King's College, 1495-1860. Aberdeen: Spalding Club, 1893.

Pappalardo Bruce. *Tracing Your Naval Ancestors*. Kew: PRO Publications, 2003.

Payne, Peter L. *Studies in Scottish Business History*. London: Frank Cass and Co., 1967.

Probert, Eric. D. *Company and Business Records for Family Historians*. Birmingham, England: Federation of Family History Societies, 1994. Informative guide to companies and their records.

Raymond, Stuart. *Occupational Sources for Genealogists*. Birmingham, England: Federation of Family History Societies, 1992. A useful bibliography.

Richards, T. *Was Your Grandfather a Railwayman?* 2nd ed. Birmingham, England: Federation of Family History Societies, 1995. How to find railway records.

Ritchie, L.A. *Modern British Shipbuilding: A Guide to Historical Records*. Greenwich, England: National Maritime Museum, Maritime Monographs and Reports No. 48, 1980.

Rodger, N.A.M. *Naval Records for Genealogists*. 2nd ed. Kew: PRO Publications, 1998. Provides extensive detail on the records of the Royal Navy.

School, University and College Registers and Histories in the Library of the Society of Genealogists. 2nd ed. London: Society of Genealogists, 1996. It is worthwhile knowing what is in this collection.

Scott, Hew. *Fasti Ecclesiae Scoticanae: the succession of ministers in the parish churches of Scotland from 1560*. New ed., rev. by W.S. Crockett and Sir Francis J. Grant. 9 vols. 1915-1961.

Scottish Records Association. See under section A.

Sinclair, C. *Tracing Scottish Local History*. See section A. Contains more extensive information about burgh records than his other book.

Sinclair, C. *Tracing Your Scottish Ancestors*. See section A.

Sinclair, Sir John, Bt. *Statistical Accounts*. See section A.

Smith, K and C. Watts. *Records of Merchant Shipping and Seamen*. Kew: PRO, 1998.

Small, Robert. *History of the Congregations of the United Presbyterian Church 1733-1900*. 2 vols. Edinburgh: D.M. Small, 1904.

Spencer, William. *Records of the Militia and Volunteer Forces 1757-1945*. 2nd ed. Kew: PRO Publications, 1997. Discusses records of militia, volunteers, yeomanry, and the Territorial Army.

Stewart, Charles H. *The Service of British Regiments in Canada and North America*. Ottawa, 1962. Not easy to find, but a useful outline of when and where various regiments served.

Swinson, Arthur, ed. *A Register of the Regiments and Corps of the British Army: the ancestry of every regiment with battle honours*. London: Archive Press, 1972.

Torrance, D. R. *Scottish Trades, Professions, Vital Records and Directories*. Aberdeen: Scottish Association of Family History Societies, 1998.

Warden, Alex. J. *The Linen Trade Ancient and Modern*. London, 1864.

Wareham, Heather, and Roberta Thomas. *A Guide to the Holdings of the Maritime History Archive*. St. John's: Memorial University of Newfoundland, 1991.

Watson, C.B. Boog, ed. *Roll of Edinburgh Burgesses and Guild Brethren 1701-1760*. Edinburgh: Scottish Record Society, 1930.

Watson, C.B. Boog, ed. *Roll of Edinburgh Burgesses and Guild Brethren 1761-1841*. Edinburgh: Scottish Record Society, 1933.

Watts, C.T. and M.J. *My Ancestor Was a Merchant Seaman*. London: Society of Genealogists, 2nd ed., 2002.

Watts, C.T., and M.J. Watts. *My Ancestor Was in the British Army: How can I find out more about him?* London: Society of Genealogists, 1992 (reprint with addendum 1995).

Webster, David W. *The Naming and Numbering of Scottish Regiments of Foot, Cavalry and Militia*. Edinburgh: Scottish Genealogy Society, 2002.

Whitaker's Almanac. See section A.

Wise, Terence. *A Guide to Military Museums and Other Places of Military Interest*. 7th ed. Knighton, Wales: Imperial Press, 1992.

Wood, Margaret. *Register of Edinburgh Apprentices 1756-1800*. Edinburgh: Scottish Record Society, 1963.

Chapter 9

Findlay, James. See section A.

Gibson, J.S.W. *The Hearth Tax, other later Stuart Tax Lists and the Association Oath Rolls*. 2nd ed. Birmingham, England: Federation of Family History Societies, 1996.

Groome, F. H. See section A.

Miller, Susan. A Guide to Glasgow Addresses 1826 – 1950. See the entry in chapter 4.

Moody, David. *Scottish Family History.* See section A.

Moody, David. *Scottish Local History.* See section A.

Pollable Persons within the Shire of Aberdeen, 1696. 2 vols. Aberdeen: Spalding Club, 1844. Everyone in the county over the age of sixteen, except for the poor. Now reissued in a series of booklets by the Aberdeen and North East Scotland Family History Society.

Return of Owners of Lands and Heritages (Scotland) 1872-1873. Edinburgh: HMSO, 1874.

Scottish Genealogy Society. *Scottish Poll Tax.* Edinburgh, 1991. (Leaflet # 11.)

Semple, David. *The Poll Tax Rolls of the Parishes in Renfrewshire for the Year 1695.* Edinburgh, 1864. The further extension of the title is, "containing the names of the persons in the county with their calling and residence, and the names of their wives, children, and servants."

Sinclair, C. *Tracing Your Scottish Ancestors.* See section A.

Steel, Don. See section A.

Timperley, L.R. See section A.

*Taylor, Alistair, and Henrietta Taylor, eds. *The Jacobite Cess Roll for the County of Aberdeen in 1715.* Aberdeen: Spalding Club, 1932. This list of those paying tax includes details of ownership back to 1696, occupations, and some genealogical details.

Whiteford, J.L., ed. *Stirling Burgesses, 1790-1799.* Stirling: Central Scotland Family History Society, 1992.

Whiteford, J.L., ed. *Stirling Burgesses, 1800-1902.* Stirling: Central Scotland Family History Society, 1992.

Wood, Margaret, ed. *Edinburgh Poll Tax Returns, 1694.* Edinburgh: Scottish Record Society, 1951.

Chapter 10

Bailyn, Bernard. *Voyagers to the West.* New York: Alfred A. Knopf, 1987. The analysis of people departing for the new world 1773-1776—their social station, occupations, points of origin, and ports of departure—makes for fascinating reading; the ports mentioned are Dumfries, Stranraer, Greenock, Kirkwall, Leith, Gigha, Dunstaffnage Bay, Fort William, Lochbroom, Stornoway, Lerwick, Lochindale, Water of Fleet, Kirkcaldy, Kirkcudbright, Wigtown, Campbelltown, Glasgow, and Ayr.

Ball, Adrian. *Is Yours an SS Great Britain Family?* Emsworth, Hants: Kenneth Mason, 1988.

Brock, W. R. *Scotus Americanus—a survey of the sources for links between Scotland and America in the 18th century.* Edinburgh University Press, 1982. Obviously a tedious job putting this together, but wonderful that it was done—an amazing array of sources.

Bumstead, J.M. *The People's Clearance—Highland Emigration to British North America, 1770-1815.* Edinburgh University Press, 1982. Still a recognized authoritative account, with over sixty pages of ships' passenger lists.

Campbell, A.J. *Fife Convict Transportees 1752 - 1867.* Fife Family History Society, 1998. One example of the numerous small lists and databases on fiche, CD, or in booklet form that can be found offered for sale by county family history societies – check their websites.

Cases Decided in the Court of Session, Teind Court, and Court of Exchequer. Vol. XII. Edinburgh: T. and T. Clark, 1850. This series of volumes began appearing in 1821. The recorders and editors changed at intervals, and after 1907 they were issued by the Faculty of Advocates.

Cox, Michael. See under section A.

Dickson, J.W., W.H. Dunbar, and J. Rymer, eds. *The Scottish Jurist.* Vol. 2. Edinburgh: M.A. Anderson, 1829. (Editors and publishers changed from time to time over the years.) The subtitle explains the contents—containing reports of cases decided in the House of Lords, Court of Session, Teinds, Exchequer, and the Jury and Justiciary Courts.

Dobson, David. *Directory of Scots Banished to the American Plantations, 1650-1775.* Baltimore: Genealogical Publishing Co., 1983.

Dobson, David. *Directory of Scottish Settlers in North America, 1625-1825.* 7 vols. Baltimore: Genealogical Publishing Co., 1984-1993.

Dobson, David. *Jacobites of the '15.* Aberdeen: Scottish Association of Family History Societies, 1993. A partial list taken from official records.

Dobson, David. Scots in Australasia, 1788-1900. 3 Vols., D. Dobson, 2000.?

Dobson, David. *Scots in the West Indies, 1707-1857.* D. Dobson, 1998.

Dobson, David. *Scottish American Heirs.* Baltimore: Genealogical Publishing Co., 1990.

Dobson, David. *Scottish Emigration to Colonial America.* Athens: University of Georgia Press, 1994. Lots to learn from this one, and it focuses on the earlier periods.

Donnachie, Ian, and George Hewitt. See under chapters 1 and 2. If your ancestors left Scotland because of the Highland Clearances, you will want to read the brief summary of that unhappy period, and the explanation of the role of tacksmen.

European Immigration into Scotland. Glasgow and West of Scotland Family History Society, 1993. Four papers presented at the fourth conference of the Scottish Association of Family History Societies, including one on Irish immigration and one on Glasgow poor law records.

Filby, P. William, with Mary K. Meyer. *Passenger and Immigration Lists Index: a guide to published arrival records of about 500,000 passengers who came to the United States and Canada in the 17th, 18th and 19th centuries.* Detroit: Gale Research, 1981. There have been a number of supplements.

Filby, P. William. *Passenger and Immigration Lists Bibliography, 1538-1900: being a guide to published lists of arrivals in the United States and Canada.* Detroit: Gale Research, 1981.

Ford, Percy, and Grace Ford. *Select List of British Parliamentary Papers, 1833-1899.* Blackwell, 1953.

Gentleman's Magazine. Published from 1731 to 1908, it contained birth, marriage, and death notices to 1861, and some obituaries. Some parts have been indexed.

Graham, Ian C.C. *Colonists from Scotland: Emigration to North America, 1707-1783.* Kennikat Press, 1956.

Halsbury, The Rt. Hon. Earl of, and Sir Thomas W. Chitty, eds. *The English and Empire Digest.* London, 1919-1932. Indexes and abstracts to cases heard in British courts.

Hamilton-Edwards. See under section A.

Harper, Marjory. *Emigration from North-East Scotland.* 2 vols. Aberdeen: Aberdeen University Press, 1988.

Haythornthwaite, J. *Scottish Economic History in the 19th Century: an analytical bibliography of material relating to Scotland in Parliamentary Papers 1800-1900.* Scholarly Press, 1993. The key to identifying the most useful Parliamentary Papers.

Hunter, James. *A Dance Called America.* Edinburgh: Mainstream, 1994. The author tells the story of emigration from the Highlands and describes the places of settlement today.

Irvine, Alexander Forbes. *Reports of Cases Before the High Court and Circuit Courts of Justiciary in Scotland.* Vol. 1. T. and T. Clark, 1855.

Lawson, James. *The Emigrant Scots.* Aberdeen: Aberdeen and North East Scotland Family History Society, 1990. Describes records of Scottish immigrants in the National Archives of Canada.

Lindsay, Jean. *The Scottish Poor Law.* See under Chapters 5 & 6.

List and Index Society. *Scottish Record Office Court of Session Productions, 1760-1840.* Vol. 23, special series. London: HMSO, 1987. This volume summarizes evidence in actions before the Court of Sessions, giving details of those involved and of the cases, along with reference numbers. Publications of the List and Index Society are in collections of some reference and university libraries.

Livingstone, Alastair, et al. See under chapter 8.

Logan, Roger. *An Introduction to Friendly Society Records.* Bury, Lancs: Federation of Family History Societies, 2000.

MacDougall, Ian. See under chapter 8.

MacLean, J.P. *An History of the Settlements of Scotch Highlanders in America Prior to the Peace of 1783.* 1900. Reprint. Baltimore: Genealogical Publishing Co., 1968.

MacQueen, Malcolm A. *Skye Pioneers and the Island.* Stovell Co., 1929. Details, including many genealogies of families who went to Prince Edward Island.

Moody, David. *Scottish Local History.* See under section A.

Nicholls, Sir George. *A History of the Scotch Poor Law.* London: Murray, 1856. Reprint. New York: Augustus M. Kelley, 1967. Includes much interesting information from two early nineteenth-century surveys of the poor.

Patten, Jennie M. *The Argyle Patent and Accompanying Documents.* Published as part of the History of the Somonauk Presbyterian Church, 1928. Reprint. Clearfield Company, 1991. An account of this settlement near Fort Edward, New York, including a map with settlers' names.

Robinson, Neil. *To the Ends of the Earth.* Auckland: Harper Collins, 1997. The story of emigrants from Scotland to Nova Scotia to New Zealand.

Seton, Sir Bruce Gordon, Bt., and Jean Gordon Arnot, eds. *The Prisoners of the '45.* Vols. 13-15, 3rd series. Edinburgh: Scottish Historical Society, 1928-29.

Sinclair, C. *Tracing Your Scottish Ancestors.* See under section A.

Sinclair, Sir John, Bt. *Statistical Accounts.* See under section A.

Taylor, Alistair, and Henrietta Taylor, eds. *The Jacobite Cess Roll for the County of Aberdeen in 1715.* See under chapter 9.

The Digest: Annotated British Commonwealth and European Cases. London: Butterworths, 1994. There is also a user's guide issued by the same publisher, no author given.

Virginia Gazette. Published weekly at Williamsburg, 1736-1780. This was filmed by the Institute of Early American History and Culture in 1950, and is available on microfilm.

Watson, Fiona. *In Sickness and in Health.* Aberdeen and North East Scotland Family History Society, 1988.

Walker, David M. *The Scottish Legal System—An Introduction to the Study of Scots Law.* 5th ed. Green, 1981. Try to get a look at this if you are going to dig into court cases, as it is filled with details of Scots law, the published court cases, and the repositories of legal documents.

Whyte, Donald. *A Dictionary of Scottish Emigrants to Canada Before Confederation.* Toronto: Ontario Genealogical Society, 1986 (Part I) and 2002 (Part III).

Whyte, Donald. *A Dictionary of Scottish Emigrants to the USA.* 2 vols. Baltimore: Magna Carta Books, 1972 (Part I) and 1995 (Part II).

Whyte, Donald. *The Scots Overseas: A Select Bibliography.* 2nd ed. Aberdeen: Scottish Association of Family History Societies, 1995. Does not include any family histories; greatest emphasis on Canada.

Young, George, H.L. Tennant, P. Fraser, and W.H. Murray. *Cases Decided in the Court of Session, Teind Court, and Court of Exchequer, Nov. 1849 to July 1850.* Edinburgh: T. and T. Clark, 1850.

Chapter 11

Hinchliff, Helen. "William Edward, Part 1, Identifying an Eighteenth-Century Miller." See under chapters 1 and 2.

Mills, Elizabeth Shown. *Evidence! Citation and Analysis for the Family Historian.* Baltimore: Genealogical Publishing Co., 1997 (Revised edition due Autumn 2003).

• Index •

• About the Author •

 Sherry Irvine has been researching her roots for thirty years and writing about British and Irish family history for fifteen. The first edition of this book received the National Genealogical Society Award of Merit - Methods and Sources - in 1998. Sherry's articles appear in both print and online publications, including *Ancestry Daily News*. She teaches Scottish and English research methods at the Institute for Genealogy and Historical Research at Samford Univeristy and leads their study tours to the UK. She has lectured across North America and in New Zealand and Australia.